T0145318

Knowledge-Based Explorable Extended Reality Environments

Jakub Flotyński

Knowledge-Based Explorable Extended Reality Environments

 Springer

Jakub Flotyński
Department of Information Technology
Poznań University of Economics and Business
Poznań, Poland

ISBN 978-3-030-59967-6   ISBN 978-3-030-59965-2   (eBook)
https://doi.org/10.1007/978-3-030-59965-2

This Springer imprint is published by the registered company Springer Nature Switzerland AG.
The registered company address is: Gewerbestrasse 11, 6330 Cham, Switzerland

To Dominika, for her understanding, patience, and support.

Preface

Extended reality (XR) is a term coined based on virtual reality (VR) and augmented reality (AR). While VR is a view of a world consisting only of virtual objects, which may be interactive, AR is a view of the real world with superimposed virtual objects. XR covers different forms of combined real and virtual environments, which range between these two complementary technologies in the virtuality-reality continuum (J. P. Gownder, C. Voce, M. Mai, D. Lynch 2016). Real and virtual objects in XR environments may also have combined properties, which can be borrowed from real objects, inspired yet different from real, or entirely virtual.

Elements that are inherent to virtually every XR environment are users and interactive three-dimensional (3D) content. XR users and 3D content objects typically have behavior, which encompasses autonomous actions and interactions of users and objects. Users' and objects' behavior influences the XR environment, including creation, modification, and destruction of objects in 3D scenes. Modeling and tracking users' and objects' behavior in XR is fostered by the available systems for motion and eye tracking, controllers, and haptic devices.

This book is devoted to *explorable XR environments*—their concept, architectures as well as methods and tools for spatial–temporal composition based on domain knowledge, including geometrical, presentational, structural, and behavioral elements. Explorable environments' features and behavior, covering past, current, and potential states, can be subject to knowledge exploration with automated reasoning and queries constructed by XR users and external services. It enables monitoring, analyzing, comprehending, examining, and controlling XR environments as well as users' skills, experience, interests, and preferences, and XR objects' features.

The approach we propose in this book relies on two main pillars. The first are knowledge representation technologies, such as logic programming, description logics, and Semantic Web standards, which permit reasoning and queries. The second are imperative programming languages, which are a prevalent solution for building XR environments. We combine both within widely used integrated development environments. XR exploration can be especially useful when the acquired knowledge is represented using domain terminology, which is intelligible to specialists who are the primary users of the environments. Potential applications of our approach can be indicated for a variety of domains, e.g., education, training, medicine, design, tourism, marketing, merchandising, engineering, and entertainment.

Explorable XR environments are an emerging field of research and applications on the intersection of extended reality, artificial intelligence, software design and development, modular and service-oriented architectures as well as programming, data engineering, and data modeling. In recent years, we observe the intensive development of new IT solutions in all of these disciplines as well as the growing interest of researchers, practitioners, students, and users. Nonetheless, the connection of these disciplines is still very new and hardly addressed by the available literature and solutions. The book is a guide to novel approaches and tools for building explorable XR environments.

The key benefit for the book's readers is understanding the emerging domain of knowledge-based explorable XR environments—its concept, motivations, applications, and system development. We pay attention to an in-depth discussion of the field with taxonomy and classification of the available related solutions. We analyze relationships between behavior-rich XR and knowledge representation, which are supported by numerous examples of modeling, reasoning, and querying temporal objects. We also provide examples and design patterns of knowledge-based composition and exploration of XR behavior. Last but not least, we have extensively evaluated and analyzed the proposed approaches.

The problems and solutions addressed by the book are relevant to the international community. The book's target audience encompasses industrial, training, and educational institutions, including IT enterprises, universities, and colleges. The book can be useful for IT researchers, practitioners, freelancers, undergraduate and graduate students as well as a wide range of creators and users of IT systems in the domains mentioned earlier.

The book leads readers step by step from the basic ideas to advanced concepts of XR systems, knowledge representation, and programming. In the vast majority of cases, we address the foundations and provide illustrative examples to make users acquainted with the topic or at least to suggest knowledge sources that readers could consult on their own. The most important prerequisite courses helpful to understand the book are virtual and augmented reality, object-oriented programming, and logic programming. In addition, the book could be adopted as a supplementary textbook for knowledge representation and logic programming.

We address scientists', lecturers', teachers', instructors', and trainers' needs by starting the book with a general introduction to XR systems, 3D modeling tools, and game engines. Then, we go into more advanced aspects of XR composition and sophisticated cases of knowledge engineering, which we thoroughly discuss. We intend to stimulate intuitive understanding of the presented concepts to enable next its formal and precise understanding. Hence, the book can help scientists who conduct research in these areas as well as lecturers and students who search for clearly presented information supported by use cases.

For XR and game developers as well as graphic designers, the book can be a valuable source of knowledge and examples in XR development and composition. Moreover, it may show a completely new approach to the development and use of XR, opening yet undiscovered opportunities related to XR-based knowledge exploration. Due to the presentation of modeling behavior by composing independent XR components, this work may also interest graphic designers who are keen to get familiar with the augmentation of 3D models and scenes by activities designed in a reusable service-oriented fashion.

Programmers, data engineers and modelers, and database and web developers can find the book interesting as the proposed ideas are illustrated by various examples demonstrating design patterns and development guidelines in object-oriented, procedural, and declarative programming. Multiple discussed examples are related to semantic knowledge-based representation of temporal data, including objects, properties, and relations, which change over time. In this regard, the book can be an exciting proposition for programmers, data engineers, and data modelers who want to extend knowledge and skills about more complex solutions. In addition, the book may gain web developers' interest by connecting XR and web-based systems, which mostly benefit from semantic technologies. On the one hand, these target groups may realize what possible alternatives to widely used programming languages and approaches to data modeling are. On the other hand, they can learn how to apply the best practices of knowledge representation to describing dynamic, temporal domains, such as virtual worlds.

Although we guide readers through details of creating and using explorable XR environments, the more general introductory sections can also interest non-professionals who would like to get acquainted with the related disciplines of computer science.

Poznań, Poland

Jakub Flotyński

Acknowledgments

I would like to thank Professor Wojciech Cellary and Professor Krzysztof Walczak for their support and valuable remarks on this book.

I would also like to thank the members of the Department of Information Technology and the students at the Poznań University of Economics and Business: Anna Englert, Marcin Krzyszkowski, Mikołaj Maik, Adrian Nowak, and Paweł Sobociński for the collaboration on implementing XR environments presented in this book.

Contents

Chapter 1
Introduction

In recent years, we observe the rapid development of new IT technologies, including virtual reality (VR) and augmented reality (AR), mobile devices and applications, wireless networks, and artificial intelligence. They are widely considered the top emerging and most influential technologies that will change people's lives within the next decade (Bernard Marr 2019; Ashley Watters 2020). While VR is a view of a world consisting only of interactive virtual objects, AR is a view of the real world with superimposed virtual objects. VR and AR enable realistic presentation and interaction with complex data and objects in virtual and combined—real and virtual—environments in multiple application domains, such as education, training, medicine, design, prototyping, marketing, merchandising, and engineering.

The growth of VR and AR is stimulated by the expanding range of available devices employing increasingly efficient CPUs and GPUs as well as growing memory size, which is accompanied by falling prices. With worldwide spending $18.8 billion on VR and AR in 2020, the market is foreseen to exceed $117 billion by 2024 (IDC 2019; MarketWatch 2020), reflecting its enormous potential and interest of users. One of the significant factors contributing to the evolution of VR and AR is new types of mobile devices, especially smartphones and tablets equipped with high-resolution screens that have sufficient refresh rate. They have allowed for building head-mounted displays (HMDs), which have become widely used, affordable VR and AR platforms for a number of applications, e.g., Oculus Rift (Facebook Technologies 2020), HTC Vive (HTC Corporation 2020), and Samsung Gear VR (Samsung 2020). In addition, the development of high-speed 5G networks with low latency and reduced energy consumption will enable new applications and services in VR and AR, including collaboration on massive photorealistic 3D scenes and objects on mobile devices in real time. The mobile market is expected to significantly grow from $106.27 billion in 2018 to $407.31 billion by 2026 (Allied Market Research 2019), which will probably further foster the expansion of VR and AR. Last but not least, VR and AR will also benefit from the advent of new artificial intelligence software and services. Intelligent environments based

© The Author(s), under exclusive license to Springer Nature Switzerland AG 2020
J. Flotyński, *Knowledge-Based Explorable Extended Reality Environments*,
https://doi.org/10.1007/978-3-030-59965-2_1

on machine learning and knowledge representation will analyze and adapt to users' needs, preferences, and interests as well as the context of use. Like for the other technologies, the expected spread of the market in this domain is vast and can achieve $126.0 billion by 2025 from $10.1 billion in 2018 (Informa 2020).

The specificity of VR and AR allows us to use both technologies in different cases. For instance, whereas a VR guide is appropriate for marketing purposes to encourage potential customers to buy new products, an AR service guide can instruct users on how to repair a real machine by presenting contextual animated guidelines for the current view of the appliance. The amount of reality and virtuality may vary in different systems, leading to the emergence of the term *mixed reality* (MR) (Milgram, Takemura, Utsumi, & Kishino 1995), which encompasses solutions with fuzzy borders in the middle of the continuum. In MR environments, also real and virtual objects' properties may interlace. It can result in real objects with virtual properties, e.g., a room presented with virtual wallpaper, as well as virtual objects with properties inspired by the reality, e.g., new furniture with texture a bit smoother than the texture of the real furniture in the room. Virtual objects and properties can be the result of the designer's imagination, e.g., designed virtual pipes in a bathroom, or counterparts of real objects and properties, e.g., virtual pipes equivalent to real pipes hidden in a wall.

Despite various possible structures of mixed reality scenes, a lot of common technologies for immersive presentation of and interaction with VR, AR, and MR have been developed, such as HMDs, controllers, haptic devices, and motion tracking systems. Therefore, capturing the whole bunch of such technologies under a single, more general term—extended reality (XR)—has been justified. XR covers different forms of combined real and virtual environments, ranging between two complementary technologies—VR and AR—in the virtuality–reality continuum (J. P. Gownder, C. Voce, M. Mai, D. Lynch 2016).

Nevertheless, along with devices, other inherent elements of virtually every XR environment are users and interactive three-dimensional (3D) content. Users and 3D content in XR are typically characterized by behavior, which may be regarded as autonomous actions (e.g., running avatar and flying aircraft) and interactions between them (e.g., a ball going into the goal, a serviceman repairing a device, and a salesman showing products to customers). Such behavior can be expressed by various changes in the XR environment state, in particular, 3D animations and modification of its attributes, which encompass creation, manipulation, and destruction of objects in scenes.

The diversity of available systems for motion and gesture capture, eye tracking as well as trackable HMDs and interactive controllers offer high potential for modeling realistic behavior and tracking users' and objects' actions and interactions in XR environments. This potential is additionally strengthened by the increasing dissemination of behavior-rich XR environments in multiple application domains. Such environments are created based on *knowledge* expressed by domain experts, which is encoded by developers and graphic designers. Knowledge is *understanding or information about a subject gained by experience or study, either known by one person or by people generally* (Cambridge University 2020). A more technical definition, related to information systems, emphasizes possibilities of practical usage of knowledge, which is *the awareness and understanding of a set of information and the ways that information can be made useful to support a specific task or reach a decision* (Stair & Reynolds 2017).

The availability of knowledge—expressed by domain authors and collected while using XR environments—opens new opportunities and challenges for *knowledge exploration* in XR. *Knowledge exploration* is a process in which new knowledge is acquired, providing new resources to an organization (Liu 2006). In this book, knowledge exploration is defined as acquiring new knowledge about users' and objects' behavior in XR with *automated reasoning* and *queries*. Automated reasoning permits the inference of implicit (tacit) knowledge from explicitly asserted knowledge, which enables drawing new conclusions (Russell & Norvig 2009). In turn, queries enable acquisition of knowledge about environments' interesting features while also filtering out the other knowledge that is irrelevant to the query conditions.

The acquired knowledge can serve to monitor, analyze, comprehend, examine, and control XR environments as well as users' skills, experience, interests, and preferences, and XR objects' characteristics. Behavior exploration can be especially useful when the acquired knowledge is represented using domain terminology, which is intelligible to specialists who are the primary users of the XR environments. For example, information collected during surgery can be used to consider diverse possible situations and teach students. Information collected during a design process can enable analysis of the project at its different stages, including the contribution of particular designers and the consistency with the original requirements. Collected information about customers' activities in virtual stores can help discover their interests and preferences for marketing and merchandising purposes. It may facilitate the arrangement of real stores and the preparation of personalized offers. Collected information about the states and behavior of appliances can serve to analyze how they work and to identify possible faults. Collected information about virtual guided tours can be used to join the most interesting ones and address customers' interests in a tourist program.

The cases mentioned above show high potential for behavior exploration in XR environments. These opportunities can be fully exploited in case of covering past, current as well as possible future users' and objects' behavior with its necessary conditions and potential effects. However, the available technologies for XR development, including 3D formats, e.g., VRML (Web3D Consortium 1995) and X3D (Web3D Consortium 2020b), programming languages, e.g., C# and Java, and libraries, e.g., OpenGL (Khronos Group 2020a) and WebGL (Khronos Group 2020b), as well as 3D modeling tools, e.g., Blender (Blender Foundation 2020) and 3ds Max (Autodesk 2020a), animation modeling tools, e.g., Motion Builder (Autodesk 2020b) and Cinema 4D (Maxon 2020), and game engines, e.g., Unity (Unity Technologies 2020a) and Unreal (Epic Games 2020), have not been intended to achieve the aforementioned goals. The existing solutions have been designed for 3D representation, modeling, and programming, but not for knowledge representation and modeling, which are essential to exploring users' and objects' behavior. Furthermore, although several artificial intelligence technologies enable knowledge representation, modeling, and exploration, including logic programming, description logics, and the Semantic Web, in arbitrary application domains, only their basic functions have been employed in XR. The available approaches to knowledge-based XR focus on modeling static (time-independent) 3D content using Semantic Web technologies. The solutions do not enable development of XR environments with explorable behavior described using domain-specific terminology and knowledge.

This book aims to develop an approach to *creation of explorable XR environments*, called E-XR. The concept of the approach is depicted in Fig. 1.1. An *explorable XR environment* is an XR application in which users' and 3D objects' behavior, including actions and interactions, is represented using temporal domain knowledge and visual descriptors. Such behavior can be subject to exploration with reasoning and queries constructed by XR users and external services.

On the one hand, behavior exploration covers past, current, and possible future environment states. Past and current environment behavior is logged (registered) during sessions of using the environment, which allows users to analyze occurred actions and interactions. Potential behavior, which may occur, is represented due to the knowledge-based composition of the environment from independent, reusable behavioral XR components. The composition is based on queries, which specify desirable workflow in the target XR environment in a declarative way, using knowledge specific to a particular domain of use. Since the functions of behavioral XR components are described using domain knowledge, the potential behavior of the composed environment can be inferred. Like exploration, the composition is performed on demand based on queries constructed by users or services responsible for XR creation. As the used terminology is common to past, current, and possible future behavior, both XR development and usage are attainable to domain experts.

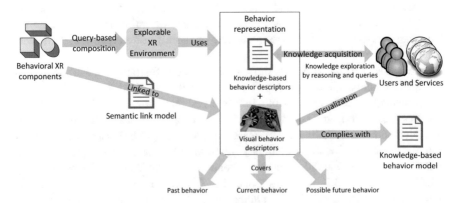

Fig. 1.1 The concept of E-XR approach to creation of explorable XR environments

On the other hand, behavior exploration covers knowledge acquisition about environment states at different moments and intervals in time as well as visualization of the states, with regard to created, modified, and destructed objects in 3D scenes.

Hence, it allows for the comprehension of the environment, including users' skills, experience, interests and preferences, and 3D objects' features, in formal and visual terms. The representation of users' and objects' behavior can be perceived as four-dimensional (4D) in contrast to the representation of time-independent (3D) properties.

The approach is built upon knowledge representation technologies and imperative programming languages (e.g., C#) to extend available integrated development environments (e.g., MS Visual Studio and Unity). For knowledge representation, we use first-order logic and description logics implemented by the Prolog logic programming language (Clocksin & Mellish 1984) as well as the Semantic Web standards—the Resource Description Framework (RDF) (W3C 2014a), the Resource Description Framework Schema (RDFS) (W3C 2014b), and the Web Ontology Language (OWL) (W3C 2012). Prolog is a declarative rule-based programming language capable of representing potential environments' behavior. The Semantic Web technologies are prevalent solutions for knowledge representation on the Web, with well-investigated computational profiles (W3C 2012b), sufficient to represent registered environment behavior.

The E-XR approach consists of the following four interrelated elements:

1. The *visual knowledge-based behavior model*, which enables composition of the required behavior of an XR environment and specification of logging behavior demonstrated by the environment while it is running. Behavior representation encompasses users' and 3D objects' autonomous actions and interactions. Required behavior, which is declaratively specified during the composition, covers actions and interactions that may potentially occur in the environment. In turn, while the composed environment is running, selected occurred actions and interactions are registered in the form of visual descriptors and behavior logs that are compatible with the behavior model. Hence, the specification of required behavior as well as generated logs can be subject to knowledge-based exploration, while logged behavior can also be visualized.

2. The *semantic link model*, which enables connection of imperative implementation of XR components, consisting of classes and methods, with knowledge-based behavior representation compliant with the behavior model. Thereby, the model links imperative and declarative representations of environment behavior. The linked knowledge-based representation enables query-based composition of environment behavior from class methods, which implement users' and objects' actions and interactions. Furthermore, while the composed environment is used, linked class methods generate visual descriptors and behavior logs, which can be presented and explored.

3. The *development pipeline of explorable environments*, which uses the aforementioned data models. The pipeline consists of several steps completed by users with different knowledge and skills in 3D modeling and knowledge modeling. The focus is on reusing behavioral XR components prepared by developers and enabling domain experts to compose and explore various XR environments in their field of specialty. The created XR environments can be subject to

exploration of behavior that may potentially happen as well as behavior that happened while using an environment.

4. The *exploration methods for XR environments*, which enable visual and knowledge-based exploration of XR environments developed using the pipeline. Exploration is based on reasoning and queries and includes users' and objects' features and behavior regarding their past, current, and potential future activities.

The thesis of this book is formulated as follows:

The E-XR approach enables efficient creation and use of explorable XR environments based on domain knowledge.

The remainder of this book is structured as follows. Chapter 2 provides an overview of the main groups of methods and tools for XR development: programming languages and libraries, 3D content formats, and visual 3D and animation modeling tools, including game engines. The solutions are presented with the focus on behavior representation and modeling, which is relevant to the main contribution of this book. In this chapter, we also outline the main human–system interfaces for XR, including presentation and interaction devices, such as motion and eye tracking systems, controllers, and displays. We can observe considerable progress in the functionality and performance of such systems in the last years, which enable the realistic presentation of and interaction with 3D objects in XR. It attracts new people to use XR in various application domains.

Chapter 3 is devoted to the main approaches to knowledge representation, which have been derived from mathematical methods and applied to artificial intelligence systems in various domains, such as robotics, expert systems, and the Web, a long time ago. They cover first-order logic and declarative languages for logic programming, description logics, and the Semantic Web. We also discuss the relationships between them. The technologies are analyzed with regard to the possibilities of representing temporal data. It is crucial to XR environments, whose users and 3D objects are characterized by behavior, which determines environment changes over time. We also explain the idea of reasoning and queries illustrated by examples specific to XR. Reasoning is the process of inferring implicit (tacit) knowledge, which has not been explicitly specified in a knowledge base, from explicitly specified knowledge. Both explicit and implicit knowledge can be subject to queries, which extract desirable information while filtering out information irrelevant to a particular use case.

In Chap. 4, we present the main approaches to ontology-based creation of XR, which form the primary group of knowledge-based solutions for XR development, mostly focused on 3D content. The approaches are based on the Semantic Web technologies. We propose a taxonomy and classify the solutions in terms of the goal, level of specificity of 3D content, represented content elements, Semantic Web technologies used, and the way of encoding the semantics of 3D content. Along with available solutions, we describe their main application domains and show illustrative examples.

In Chap. 5, we discuss the main problems with the creation of XR environments and modeling XR behavior. These include limited possibilities of using domain terminology in XR development, focus on technical steps rather than domain-specific goals as well as the lack of tools for on-demand composition of XR behavior and exploration of past, current, and possible future behavior. Further, we specify functional and non-functional requirements for a new approach to creating XR environments that is intended to overcome the limitations. Finally, we introduce the *E-XR approach to the creation of explorable XR environments*, which is the main contribution of this book. Explorable environments are XR applications in which the behavior of users and 3D objects, including their autonomous actions and interactions, can be subject to exploration with reasoning and queries. In E-XR, environment behavior is represented by temporal knowledge bases, which conform to the terminology specified in ontologies and rule sets. Explorable environments are composed of users and services on demand—in response to semantic queries that express desirable environment behavior. Due to the use of knowledge representation in behavior composition, potential actions and interactions, which may happen in the environment, can be explored prior to using the environment. In addition, while using explorable environments, behavior logs are generated, which enable exploration of actions and interactions that occurred.

In Chap. 6, we describe the *E-XR knowledge-based behavior model*, which represents actions and interaction of XR users and objects in an explorable form. The possibilities of exploration cover the processing of knowledge interrelated with visualization of behavior, which can be presented to users. The model is capable of representing potential behavior, which may occur in an environment, as well as past and current behavior, which occurred and occurs while using the environment. Hence, it consists of two parts. The first part—the *ontology-based component*—is based on the Semantic Web standards, which offer expressivity sufficient to represent demonstrated behavior of XR environments. The second part—the *rule-based component*—is based on logic programming. It offers high expressivity suitable to represent application logic with its workflow and dataflow. The model falls into well-defined decidability and computational complexity classes due to the use of the Semantic Web and logic programming, making computation more predictable than in the case of using arbitrary logical formulas.

In Chap. 7, we describe the *E-XR semantic link model*, which connects imperative—object-oriented or procedural—implementation of XR environments based on classes and methods to their knowledge-based representation built upon the behavior model. While the former representation is necessary to execute the environments, the latter representation is vital to explore them. The model semantically describes imperative code elements in the aspect-oriented fashion, links the execution of class methods to events and states, and provides a mapping between classes and events in both imperative and knowledge-based representations of explorable environments. Finally, we present imperative code templates used to compose explorable environments.

In Chap. 8, we present the *E-XR development pipeline of explorable environments*. The pipeline uses the visual knowledge-based behavior model—to enable behavior representation, and the semantic link model—to enable query-based composition of explorable XR environments. The pipeline consists of several stages, which are accomplished by users with different skills, including developers and domain experts. The stages performed by developers provide libraries of reusable XR components, which are further used by domain experts composing various explorable XR environments. The pipeline can be used in two ways. It enables development of explorable XR environments from scratch and transformation of existing environments into their explorable counterparts.

In Chap. 9, we present methods of exploring XR environments created using the development pipeline. Two types of exploration are distinguished. The first type—simulation and forward exploration—enables specification of potential users' and objects' behavior that can occur in an environment. Such behavior can be queried about different states concerning the made assumptions. The second type— backward exploration—is query-based analysis and visualization of occurred users' and objects' behavior represented by visual semantic behavior logs. In the chapter, the necessary algorithms are presented in line with the exploration methods.

In Chap. 10, we describe E-XR development tools, which implement the development pipeline as well as the behavior and semantic link models used in the pipeline. The tools support the pipeline at its consecutive steps. The tools are plug-ins to MS Visual Studio, which is integrated with the Unity game engine. Thereby, our tools are built into an extensive, well-established XR development toolkit. The developed tools support coding attributes in VS by providing contextual suggestions as well as visual design of users' and objects' activities describing behavior. In addition, the tools enable mapping of environment classes to ontology classes. We also explain how explorable environments are composed and compiled using the developed toolkit. The final XR implementations generated by the compiler use a log library, which generates visual semantic behavior logs.

In Chap. 11, we exemplify E-XR with two explorable XR environments developed using the approach and the toolkit. The first environment—the explorable immersive car showroom—permits watching and configuring virtual cars, and logging users' actions and interactions with the cars, e.g., watching from around, getting in, and selecting colors. On the one hand, the immersive presentation and interaction with 3D objects can be attractive to potential customers of real car showrooms. On the other hand, it allows car producers and distributors to improve their products based on fast feedback about customers' interests and preferences. The other environment—the explorable immersive service guide for home appliances—enables training technicians in servicing and testing induction hobs. It has been developed for Amica S.A., one of the leading manufacturers of home appliances in Poland. Logging interactions between technicians and home appliances in the environment allows for their further visualization and knowledge exploration, which can be helpful for beginners. The environments are based on head-mounted displays and hand tracking devices. We explain the systems' architectures and functionality as well as an example of a behavior log used for reasoning and queries about customers' behavior.

In Chap. 12, evaluation results are described. We have analyzed the approach in terms of the users' effort in behavior composition compared to another representative tool for creating XR. We have also tested the performance of the elaborated development tools regarding different steps of the pipeline: environment composition, activity compilation, logging behavior, and the rendering performance of generated environments. Moreover, the tests have encompassed the complexity and size of data structures created according to the data models and used in the pipeline: activity representation, code injected to XR environments, mapping knowledge bases, and behavior logs. Last but not least, the approach is discussed, including the evaluation results, possible alternative implementations, requirements for knowledge and skills necessary to use the approach, properties of the applied logical systems, and alternative probabilistic approaches to knowledge representation.

Finally, in Chap. 13 the book concludes, the main contributions and achievements are summarized, and possible directions for future research and development activities are indicated.

Chapter 2
Extended Reality Environments

2.1 Relationships Between Users, Content, and Interfaces

The main elements of XR environments are users, content, and human–system interfaces. With the development of the Web and high-speed networks, increasing attention is paid to multi-user and collaborative environments in a variety of application domains, such as entertainment, training, education, e-commerce, and tourism. Users immersed in XR environments perceive the content of the environments and interact with the content. The vast majority of environments are built upon synthetic behavior-rich 3D content. Such content is characterized by various elements, including geometry, structure, space, appearance, and animations. 3D content is specific to a particular XR environment and corresponds to the environment goal, use cases, and the specialty of users. For instance, different 3D content represents virtual stores and hospitals. The main approaches—domain-specific and domain-independent—to creating 3D content are described in Sect. 2.2.

In addition to users and 3D content, an indispensable element of XR environments are human–system interfaces. They enable users' immersion into the environments, including presentation of and interaction with the content. The interfaces for content presentation stimulate different human senses, typically sight and touch. The interfaces for interaction with content rely on various characteristics of users' behavior, including whole body movements, hand movements and gestures, touch gestures, eye movements, and manipulation of controllers. In comparison to 3D content, human–system interfaces are less specific to an individual environment, i.e., particular interfaces can be successfully reused in different environments. For instance, the same head-mounted displays and gloves can be used for shopping in virtual stores and surgery in virtual hospitals. We present the main types of interfaces in Sect. 2.3. Such interfaces can provide a lot of raw data about users' activities, including autonomous actions and interactions. In turn, the collected data can potentially be transformed into valuable domain knowledge linking the users'

© The Author(s), under exclusive license to Springer Nature Switzerland AG 2020
J. Flotyński, *Knowledge-Based Explorable Extended Reality Environments*,
https://doi.org/10.1007/978-3-030-59965-2_2

behavior with environment objects. We explain this aspect in more detail in the following chapters.

2.2   Creation of XR Environments

In this section, we present the main approaches to creation of XR environments with the focus on creation and representation of interactive 3D content. The solutions are categorized into three main groups: 3D content formats, approaches to programming XR environments, and visual tools for XR modeling.

2.2.1   Programming XR Environments

Programming is the primary approach to creating XR environments, which can address all elements of XR, including interactive content with all its components and properties, interaction between users and the content as well as presentation of content to users. A number of languages and libraries have been devised to enable programming of XR environments. The solutions cover languages and libraries for imperative—procedural and object-oriented—programming. Imperative programming of 3D content focuses on steps that must be performed to achieve the desirable presentational effects. Besides, we also discuss aspect-oriented programming, which is a declarative extension to object-oriented programming facilitating development of applications in which certain aspects are related to different classes and methods. Programming XR environments typically employs 3D formats to represent particular 3D models in 3D scenes, which we outline in Sect. 2.2.2. Programming is enabled by multiple visual 3D modeling tools, which we review in Sect. 2.2.3.

Procedural and Object-Oriented Programming

Several approaches have been devised to enable imperative programming of 3D content. The Open Graphics Library (OpenGL) (Khronos Group 2020a) is the primary cross-platform and open-source API designed for procedural programming of 3D content. OpenGL has been used in multiple projects—computer games, simulations, and visualizations—as well as multiple frameworks and libraries designed for 3D content creation. OpenGL-based applications may be launched on various operating systems—Windows, Linux, Mac OS, and Android—on desktop as well as mobile devices. Another API frequently used for procedural programming of 3D content and the main competitor of OpenGL is Direct3D (Microsoft 2020). Unlike OpenGL, Direct3D is not open source and it is available under a proprietary license. Both libraries offer a diversity of functions for 3D modeling and rendering.

There are several widely used imperative languages for creating 3D content embedded in web pages, which use OpenGL and Direct3D as well as other libraries based on them. Several libraries have been developed for JavaScript. The primary one is WebGL (Khronos Group 2020b), which is based on OpenGL. The use of the specific low-level API of WebGL may be time consuming in large projects. Therefore, other libraries have been developed based on WebGL—three.js (Three.js 2020), AwayJS (Away3D 2020), and Unity (Unity Technologies 2020a), which simplify programming of 3D content in comparison to directly using WebGL. 3D content based on WebGL may be presented in most web browsers without installing any additional plug-ins.

Object-oriented programming extends procedural programming with classes and objects, which are instances of classes. For different object-oriented programming languages, such as Java, Python, and C#, various 3D graphics libraries have been developed. Java3D (Oracle 2020) is a 3D graphics library for Java, which takes advantage of such low-level libraries as OpenGL and Direct3D. Windows Presentation Foundation (Microsoft 2020) is a library that enables declarative specification of 3D content using an XML-based language. Scenes and objects encoded in such a way can also be accessed using .NET languages, such as C#.

Aspect-Oriented Programming

Aspect-oriented programming extends object-oriented programming by *aspects*, which cut across different software modules, classes, and methods (Kiczales et al. 1997). Clear definitions related to recent implementations of aspect-oriented programming can be found in Spring Framework (2020). An *aspect* is a set of functions (referred to as *advices*), which implement new behavior of an application that should be executed in different places in the code, including different methods of different classes and different points within the methods. A place in the environment code where an invocation of an advice is injected is called a *join point*. Code annotations and attributes are typically used to indicate advices and join points. Aspect-oriented programming is available for Java in the Spring library (Spring Framework 2020) and C# in the PostSharp library (SharpCrafters 2020).

An example aspect may contain new functions that can be added to an application to log transactions. In such a case, advices are functions responsible for logging the source and destination accounts, their balance, and the status of the transaction. In turn, join points are the beginnings, exits, and throw-exception clauses in the relevant methods in the application code. In such an application, once a join point is reached in an annotated method, the appropriate advice is invoked.

Aspect-oriented programming can be especially useful when a new function should be added to multiple classes of an existing application with minimal effort and changes in the available code. Moreover, it is suitable when the classes are of a different kind, so as it is challenging to implement common superclasses for inheriting functions.

2.2.2 3D Content Formats

A number of formats enable declarative specification of 3D content. It would not be possible to outline all available 3D formats in this section. Therefore, we mostly focus on formats used in web-based environments, which become increasingly popular in multiple application domains.

The Virtual Reality Modeling Language (VRML) (Web3D Consortium 1995) is an open, textual language devised by the Web3D Consortium to describe static and animated 3D content. A VRML scene is a graph comprising nodes reflecting different 3D content elements—geometry, structure, space, appearance, animation, and behavior. VRML also supports linking external multimedia resources—image, audio, and video. In addition to the use of specific behavioral VRML nodes (e.g., sensors and interpolators), 3D objects' behavior may be described by embedded imperative ECMAScript code. ECMAScript is an object-oriented programming language, a dialect of JavaScript standardized for web-based applications (ECMA International 2020). Several VRML browsers are available, e.g., Cortona3D Viewer (Cortona3D 2018), BS Contact (Bitmanagement 2020), FreeWRL (Lukka, Stewart, et al. 2009), and Instant Reality (Fraunhofer IGD 2020a).

The Extensible 3D (X3D) (Web3D Consortium 2020b) is the successor to VRML. X3D introduces several functional extensions to VRML such as Humanoid Animation, NURBS, and CAD geometry. Furthermore, it supports additional binary and XML-based encoding formats as well as metadata descriptions. Depending on the desirable complexity of 3D content, different X3D profiles may be selected—interchange, interactive, immersive, and full. Like VRML scenes, X3D scenes can be accessed by ECMAScript code using a scene access interface. Several X3D browsers are available, e.g., BS Contact, FreeWRL, and InstantReality.

VRML and X3D enable the standardized representation of 3D content on the Web, which is attainable with additional plug-ins to web browsers. X3DOM (Fraunhofer IGD 2020b) has been designed to enable seamless integration of X3D content with web pages. It is an open-source framework intended as a potential extension to HTML5. 3D content encoded using X3DOM can be presented without additional plug-ins in the majority of the available web browsers (supporting WebGL (Khronos Group 2020b)), in Instant Reality and using Flash plug-ins—in other browsers. Like X3D, X3DOM supports animation nodes and attributes, such as sensors and interpolators.

XML3D (XML.org 2020) is another solution designed for seamless integration of 3D content with web pages. XML3D enables declarative representation of such 3D content components as groups of objects, meshes, light sources, and textures. XML3D supports animations based on keyframes. Furthermore, XML3D scenes can be manipulated by JavaScript code. XML3D content may be presented in web browsers supporting WebGL, without installing additional plug-ins.

COLLADA (Sony Computer Entertainment, Khronos Group 2008) has been intended as a language for exchange of 3D content between different tools. The language permits representation of geometry, shaders, physics, animations, and kinematics. Currently, numerous projects use COLLADA not for content exchange but for content publication, e.g., Unreal Engine (Epic Games 2020) and Unity (Unity Technologies 2020a).

PDF3D is another approach to publishing 3D content. It utilizes the U3D (ECMA International 2007) file format for encoding 3D objects, and a proprietary JavaScript API for programming behavior of objects (Adobe Systems 2015). A PDF document with 3D content may be directly embedded in a web page and presented with the Adobe Reader plug-in.

The formats outlined in this section are supported by different programming libraries and visual 3D modeling tools. Plenty of proprietary 3D formats have also been developed for particular 3D modeling tools, such as Blender and 3ds Max. However, their discussion is out of the scope of this book.

2.2.3 Visual Modeling of XR Environments

Numerous tools have been developed for visual modeling of 3D content, an essential element of XR environments. Advanced tools intended for professional users, such as Blender (Blender Foundation 2020) and 3ds Max (Autodesk 2020a), offer rich functions of modeling various content elements—geometry, structure, appearance, and animations. The tools enable implementation of complex logic and behavior of 3D content by using imperative programming languages, which are Python in Blender and MAXScript in 3ds Max. The tools can be extended with plug-ins developed using appropriate APIs. The available plug-ins support multiple 3D formats, including VRML and X3D. In contrast to 3ds Max, Blender is open source.

User-friendly tools for modeling 3D content typically offer more limited capabilities than advanced tools. However, they are more intuitive and enable relatively quick and efficient modeling without requiring users' high technical skills. SketchUp (Trimble 2020) enables creation and manipulation of 3D objects, e.g., texturing, rotating, and translating objects. Furthermore, it provides a rich web repository of 3D objects that can be assembled into complex 3D scenes. 3DVIA (Dassault Systémes 2020) is another user-friendly tool for 3D content creation. It permits modeling geometry, appearance, structure, and animations of 3D objects.

Several user-friendly tools have been developed for modeling 3D content in specific domains, e.g., medicine, interior design, and engineering. Ghost Productions (Ghost Productions 2020) permits modeling of interactive 3D medical animations, e.g., surgical e-learning content. Sweet Home 3D (eTeks 2020) permits modeling of interiors by drawing and editing rooms, walls, doors, windows, and furniture. AutoCAD Civil 3D (AutoCAD Civil 3D 2020) permits creation of building information models (BIMs) and modeling diverse civil constructions, such as bridges, railway tracks, and pipe networks.

If an XR environment has to include objects that are equivalents of real objects, the real objects are typically captured using 3D scanners. For instance, the handheld Artec Eva scanner (Artec Europe 2020) moved around an object takes multiple images per second and uses software to automatically calibrate them, build a 3D mesh, and cover it with textures derived from the images (Fig. 2.1). Such a process can be extended with the post-processing of the captured geometry and textures to improve their visual quality.

Fig. 2.1 Artec Eva handheld 3D scanner (Artec Europe 2020). ©Jakub Flotyński 2020, all rights reserved

Another group of environments for 3D content creation are game engines. In comparison to 3D modeling tools, game engines offer extensive functions ranging from assembly of 3D objects, creating animations and programming interactions, behavior, networking, multi-user access, physical effects, sounds, memory management, and multithreading. Unity (Unity Technologies 2020a) and Unreal Engine (Epic Games 2020) are widely used powerful game engines that combine visual design of 3D content with imperative programming (with C# and JavaScript in Unity and C++ in Unreal Engine). Animations can be created using state diagrams and keyframes with interpolation of objects' properties, e.g., geometry, position, orientation, and colors. XR environments developed with the engines may be presented in web browsers.

2.3 Human–System Interfaces for Extended Reality

In this chapter, we outline the most common human–system interfaces for XR, such as motion and eye tracking systems, controllers, and displays. An extensive presentation of this topic can be found in numerous publications, e.g., Dix, Finlay, Abowd, & Beale (2003). Hence, we focus on how such interfaces are relevant to explorable XR environments by the information they provide. Interfaces that are common to various classes of IT systems, in particular, widely disseminated aural and voice interfaces, are out of the scope of this book. Although they are an important element of multiple XR environments, they have been intensively addressed by the available literature, e.g., Cohen, Giangola, & Balogh (2004), Harris (2004), Pearl (2016).

2.3.1   Motion Tracking

Motion tracking systems capture the movements of objects, including their position and orientation in the space. It makes such systems suitable for creating XR environments, particularly animations, and interaction with XR objects triggered by users. Several types of motion tracking systems are distinguished depending on the technology used: optical systems, mechanical systems, inertial systems, and magnetic systems.

Optical Motion Tracking

Optical motion tracking systems use cameras to track objects. We distinguish *systems with markers* and *markerless systems*. In systems with markers, passive or active markers are attached to the objects being tracked. Passive markers are reflective elements that differ significantly from the tracked objects and from the background in the images captured by the cameras. Active markers are electronic elements emitting some form of radiation. The elements typically sequentially emit light, which makes them distinguishable by the cameras. Powering the elements makes the systems with active markers more complex and error prone than the systems with passive markers.

The preparation of an optical system for work requires to calibrate it using an object with markers attached at known positions. *Calibration* provides information about such cameras' properties as focal length, skew, distortion, position, and orientation. Cameras of an optical system track every marker with three degrees of freedom (DoF)—the positions along every axis. Information about the orientation of the tracked object is inferred from the relative positions of the markers. If at least two cameras see a marker, its position in the 3D space can be determined.

In contrast to optical systems with markers, software used in markerless systems determines characteristic points of the tracked objects on its own, without markers attached to the objects. In the case of tracking humans, the actors do not have to wear costumes with markers. It is especially appreciated when using the system by larger groups of people in terms of the time spent and hygienic reasons. However, the lack of markers typically decreases the precision of tracking, which may be, however, improved by post-processing.

Motion tracking systems are widely used for *motion capture*, which is recording of animations of moving objects by sampling their positions and orientations. Typically, the scanned objects are humans, who have markers attached close to the joints in systems with markers, or their joints are the characteristic points recognized by markerless systems. In such a case, the system's software analyzes the recognized shape and extracts the model of the human's skeleton with its bones and joints. It permits further application of arbitrary 3D models of avatars, which thereby get animated likewise the skeleton is. In Fig. 2.2, tracking a skeleton and applying an avatar in the Organic Motion OpenStage 2 markerless system (Tracklab

2020) is presented. This function has intensely populated motion capture in film-making, military, and entertainment, including computer games. Motion tracking can also be applied to such body parts as face or hands. It opens opportunities for recognizing users' facial expressions and gestures. In turn, it enables inference of such features as emotions, gender, and age and building advanced human–system interfaces. A popular markerless optical system for tracking skeleton was Microsoft Kinect released with the XBox console (Microsoft 2020). Another frequently used markerless optical system is Leap Motion (Ultraleap 2020), which permits hand gestures tracking. Motion capture enables better quality and more natural effects of animations compared to animation modeling with keyframes. Motion capture is also more efficient, which is critical to producing long clips. However, as opposed to 3D modeling, motion capture is confined by the captured area and physically possible movements.

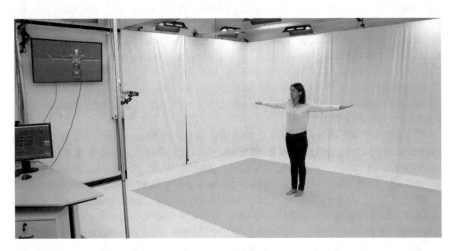

Fig. 2.2 Markerless motion capture system Organic Motion OpenStage 2 (Tracklab 2020) tracking a skeleton and applying a 3D avatar. Source: http://labvr.pl/. ©Krzysztof Walczak 2016, reprinted with permission

Mechanical Motion Tracking

Mechanical motion tracking systems, also referred to as exoskeletons, are structures of rods with sensors, e.g., potentiometers, that measure joint deflation. Therefore, they are mostly used to track humans' motion. Exoskeletons have relatively high tracking precision. Exoskeletons can be used only for tracking the user's motion or be a part of larger mechanical systems that extend possible user's movements, e.g., treadmills for running and robot arms for flying and jumping. The former are portable and can be used in large as well as small areas due to the lack of cameras.

Mechanical systems may be limited to tracking selected body parts. For instance, gloves can be used for hand tracking. In XR environments, gloves are an alternative to optical hand tracking systems. The use of gloves may be especially beneficial if hand gestures are difficult to be tracked by a single camera, e.g., due to covering some fingers by the hands. Besides, gloves may provide haptic feedback, which enables interaction with the users triggered by XR objects, e.g., Bebop haptic gloves (Bebop Sensors 2020) (Fig. 2.8).

Inertial Motion Tracking

Inertial motion tracking systems use *inertial measurement units* (IMUs), which combine accelerometers, gyroscopes, and magnetometers. Like optical systems with markers, inertial systems require to attach elements to the tracked objects. An IMU has 6 DoF—for the positions and orientations relative to every axis. IMUs are typically wirelessly connected to a workstation, which processes the collected data. The lack of cameras makes inertial motion tracking systems more portable and usable in large or small spaces in which it would be difficult to set up optical systems. The availability of IMUs in the majority of smartphones opens opportunities for motion tracking in widely accessible XR environments. An example of an inertial system is Yost Labs 3-Space Sensors (Yost Labs 2020), which includes several IMUs, which can be attached to object.

Magnetic Motion Tracking

Magnetic motion tracking systems use transmitters of the magnetic field and magnetic sensors (receivers) attached to the tracked objects, e.g., Polhemus (2020). The position and orientation of a sensor are determined with 6 DoF based on the intensity of the voltage or current measured on the coils of the sensor and transmitter. The area covered by magnetic systems is significantly smaller than the area covered by optical systems, restricting their usage.

2.3.2 Eye Tracking

Eye tracking systems, also referred to as *eye trackers*, measure eye position and movement, including eye translation (changing position) and eye rotation (changing orientation). Two types of eye trackers may be distinguished: in terms of the reference point and the tracking method used. In terms of the first criteria, we distinguish trackers that measure eye movement relative to the head or relative to the point of regard (also called the point of gaze) on which the eyes are focused. According to the second classification criteria, we distinguish methods based on scleral contact lens/search coil, electrooculography, photo- and videooculography, and video-based pupil and corneal reflection. The methods have been discussed in detail in Duchowski (2003).

Scleral Contact Lens/Search Coil

This method tracks mechanical or optical reference objects that are worn directly on the eyes. The reference objects are typically coils or diagrams attached to lenses, tracked using electromagnetic field meters or cameras. The objects are tracked relative to the head. It is the most intrusive of the discussed methods as the lenses may cause inconvenience.

Electrooculography

The method based on electrooculography measures differences in potential in different points of the area around the eyes. The potential is measured by electrodes attached to the face via wearable goggles (Bulling, Roggen, & Tröster 2009; Aminifar, Sopic, Atienza Alonso, & Zanetti 2019). The potential changes as the eyes move, enabling to track the eyes position relative to the head. The method does not depend on light conditions and can be used in darkness and when the eyes are closed. Thus, it is useful to treat sleeping patients.

Photo- and Videooculography

Photo- and videooculography methods track eyes based on their distinguishable visual properties, such as the limbus position, pupil shape, and corneal reflections from a close light source. These methods typically track eyes relative to the head. Furthermore, they require more computational power than electrooculography.

Video-Based Pupil and Corneal Reflection

Video-based combined pupil and corneal reflection enables tracking eyes by measuring the position of corneal reflections relative to the pupil center. Usually, an infrared light source is used to generate reflections. The images of the eyes are captured by a camera and processed by the system. Corneal reflections, also called Purkinje reflections (Crane 1994), are light reflections from different structures of the eye: from the outer and inner surface of the cornea as well as from the outer and inner surface of the lens. The last reflection is the inverted image. The position of Purkinje reflections relative to the pupil enables the system to differentiate eye translation (head movement) from eye rotation. The relative position does not significantly change with the movements of the head, and it changes with the movements of the eyes. Like photo- and videooculography, this method requires more computational power than electrooculography.

Such systems are non-intrusive and inexpensive. Depending on the system's location, it can track the eyes relative to the head (e.g., headset) or relative to the point of regard (e.g., system on a table). The method is the most widely used in XR environments, especially based on HMDs (cf. Sect. 2.3.4).

Applications and Relationships to Motion Capture

Eye tracking plays a significant role in multiple application domains, marketing, merchandising, and psychology. In particular, it can be used to control and interact with XR environments and collect information about the main points of users' interests. In marketing, eye tracking permits creation of heat maps, which visually present the most exciting parts of advertisements, posters, and products. It can also accelerate rendering by increasing the quality of the watched elements of the scene in comparison to other scene elements.

The discussed eye tracking methods can also be compared to the motion tracking methods, as explained in Duchowski (2003). The method based on scleral contact lens/search coil and electrooculography is similar to magnetic motion tracking. Since other methods use cameras, they resemble optical motion tracking systems. The methods based on photo- and videooculography are similar to optical markerless motion tracking. The method based on video-based pupil and corneal reflection is similar to optical motion tracking with markers.

2.3.3   Controllers

Controllers are the most frequently used human–system interfaces, which enable rich and user-friendly interaction with XR environments. Controllers equipped with several buttons and small joysticks are called *gamepads* and *joypads*. Controllers have gained popularity mainly due to video game consoles. Game consoles are computers whose possible use focuses on gaming. Thus, they are equipped with powerful graphical processing units (GPUs) enabling efficient rendering of computer graphics. The first game consoles were produced from the seventies of the twentieth century, e.g., Magnavox Odyssey (Langshaw 2014). This console, like many others, including Nintendo (Nintendo 2020) as well as much newer Sony PlayStation (Sony Interactive Entertainment 2020) and Microsoft Xbox (Microsoft 2020), is connected to displays and uses controllers, often wirelessly linked.

Controllers may be subject to motion tracking, which is usually optical. For instance, an XBox controller with attached markers is presented in Fig. 2.3. The approach proposed by Valve Index Controllers (Valve Corporation 2020) combines a joypad with sensors responsible for finger tracking. It is an alternative to optical hand tracking and gloves.

2.3.4 Displays

Displays play a key role in XR environments in which graphical content is the
primary type of resources presented to users.

Depth Perception

Depth perception is the ability to perceive the world in three dimensions. It is
achieved in displays by presenting images from different viewpoints to the left and
right eyes, as the images of the real world are seen by the eyes. Three possible
methods implement this goal: dual screens, temporal multiplexing, and spatial
multiplexing.

A *dual screen* has separate parts for both eyes, on which corresponding yet
different images are displayed. The main advantage of this method is the resolution
of the images, which can be equal to the full resolution of the partial screens. In
addition, the frame rate can be equal to the screens frame rate. The main
disadvantage is the demand for separate screens for the individual eyes, which
prevents multiple spectators from using common screens. This approach has become
prevalent to head-mounted displays, which are discussed in Sect. 2.3.4.

In *temporal multiplexing*, images for the left eye are alternated with the images
for the right eye in a common stream displayed on a common screen. Multiple
users can watch such content at the same time. This method exists in two variants,
which determine different types of glasses necessary to watch the content. In the
first variant, shutter glasses alternately cover the eye that is not the intended receiver
of the currently displayed image (Fig. 2.4). Shutter glasses are synchronized with
the display typically using radio frequency or infrared. Second, if the interlacing
images are displayed with different polarization, polarized glasses can be used to
filter the content for the individual eyes. Temporal multiplexing permits using the

full screen resolution. The main disadvantage is the double decrease in the screen frame rate.

Fig. 2.4 Volfoni shutter glasses (Volfoni 2020) for stereovision without and with optical markers for motion tracking. ©Jakub Flotyński 2020, all rights reserved

In *spatial multiplexing*, images intended for both eyes are mixed within a common image. The image intended for the first eye is spread across even lines in the screen, while the image intended for the second eye is spread across odd lines in the screen. If both groups of lines have different polarization, multiple users equipped with polarized glasses can perceive the content displayed on a common screen in 3D at the same time. Also, the screen's full frame rate can be used, but the image resolution is twice lower than the screen resolution.

Head-Mounted Displays

VR and AR Headsets

Head-mounted displays (HMDs), also referred to as *headsets*, are displays worn on the user's head, which enable presentation of graphical content. HMDs that permit presentation of only virtual objects are suitable for VR environments, e.g., Oculus Rift (Facebook Technologies 2020) and HTC Vive (HTC Corporation 2020) (Fig. 2.5). VR headsets typically use dual screens.

Fig. 2.5 VR headsets with controllers: Oculus Rift (Facebook Technologies 2020) and HTC Vive (HTC Corporation 2020). ©Jakub Flotyński 2020, all rights reserved

HMDs that permit presentation of virtual objects superimposed on the view of the real world are suitable for AR environments, e.g., Microsoft HoloLens (Microsoft 2020), Google Glass (Google 2020c), and nVisor (NVIS 2020) (Fig. 2.6). Combining real and virtual worlds in HMDs can be achieved in two ways. First, by projecting 3D content on the transparent screen, which is the commonly used technique. Second, by capturing the real world using cameras mounted on the HMD and superimposing virtual objects on the captured images. This solution is appropriate only for static or slowly changing scenes due to the visible lag between the state of the real world and the moment of presenting the images of the world on the screen. A newer technology for AR headsets is the projection of virtual objects directly onto the retina, which has been used in Magic Leap (Magic Leap 2020).

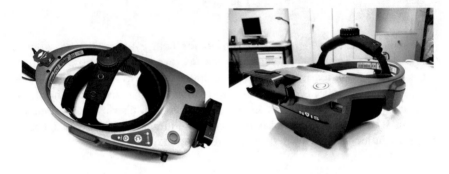

Fig. 2.6 AR headset nVisor ST50 (NVIS 2020). ©Jakub Flotyński 2020, all rights reserved

Navigating in 3D Scenes

Navigating within 3D scenes presented using HMDs is typically possible by built-in IMUs, which enable watching in different directions. In particular, while turning the head, the user is looking around. In addition, to enable precise tracking of the user's position, some HMDs are equipped with motion tracking systems, usually based on cameras (Fig. 2.7, cf. Sect. 2.3.1). In standard setups, two cameras are located in corners of the covered tracking area or on the table. If the tracking area is too restricted by the range of the cameras, controllers are used to enable user's larger movements in 3D scenes, e.g., by teleportation.

Interaction with XR Objects

HMDs are often combined with optical hand tracking systems, gloves, and controllers (cf. Sects. 2.3.1 and 2.3.3). It permits the rich interaction of users with XR environments, which is often presented as hand gestures (Fig. 2.8). Furthermore,

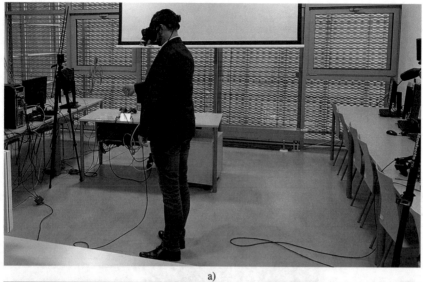

a)

b)

Fig. 2.7 Head-mounted displays with cameras tracking user's motion: HTC Vive (HTC Corporation 2020) (**a**) and Oculus Rift (Facebook Technologies 2020) (**b**). ©Jakub Flotyński 2020, all rights reserved

controllers can be subject to motion tracking, e.g., Oculus Rift controllers tracked by cameras are depicted in Fig. 2.7b. Optical hand tracking is possible by attaching a separate system (e.g., Leap Motion) to an HMD. Also, similar systems become built-in in some HMDs, e.g., HTC Vive, Fig. 2.9. Another useful functionality currently available in few HMDs are built-in eye trackers, e.g., HTC VIVE Pro Eye (HTC Corporation 2020).

Fig. 2.8 Hand gestures tracked by Bebop haptic gloves (Bebop Sensors 2020). ©Krzysztof Walczak 2019, reprinted with permission

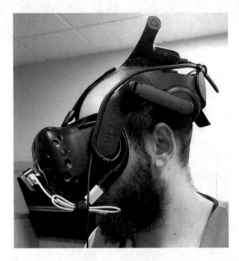

Fig. 2.9 HTC Vive (HTC Corporation 2020) with built-in optical hand tracking and attached Leap Motion (Ultraleap 2020). ©Krzysztof Walczak 2019, reprinted with permission

HMD Autonomy

Another criterion of HMD classification is their autonomy. HMDs connected to workstations, such as Oculus Rift and HTC Vive, offer the best quality of visualization of complex XR environments. The other approach are HMDs that do not need workstations. Therefore, their range is not restricted by cables. They have been enabled by common technological advances that underlie HMDs and smartphones, such as efficient processors and high-resolution displays. Oculus Go (Facebook Technologies 2020) is an HMD that needs neither an additional workstation nor a smartphone. Other HMDs use smartphones. An early solution in this field was Google Cardboard (Google 2020b). It is a simple docking station for smartphones with the Android and iOS operating systems. Further development has led to such solutions as Samsung Gear VR (Samsung 2020) and Google Daydream (Google 2020a) equipped with relatively simple controllers. Compared to workstations, the lower performance of smartphones affects the quality of visualization of complex XR environments. In turn, the advantages are better portability and lower price. A trade-off between the full autonomy and performance has been enabled by providing a wireless connection between HMDs and workstations, e.g., HTC Vive Wireless Adapter (HTC Corporation 2020). The adapter replaces wires, thereby enabling a larger area for moving with the HMD. It is mounted over the head, as shown in Fig. 2.9.

The high level of immersion, rich possibilities of combining with other XR systems, and affordable prices have made HMDs the primary approach to the presentation of XR environments to users.

Touchscreens

Touchscreens are an inextricable element of smartphones and tablets, which have been used in recent years as one of the primary interfaces for XR environments, in particular, for AR. Touchscreens are typically based on LCD and OLED displays, extending them to advanced input–output human–system interfaces. In contrast to the other interfaces, e.g., motion trackers, gloves, and controllers, touchscreens enable physical contact of users with XR objects displayed on the screens. A review of touchscreen technologies has been presented in Walker (2012). In terms of the applied method of sensing touch, the most frequently used are resistive touchscreens, capacitive touchscreens, optical touchscreens, surface acoustic wave touchscreens, dispersive touchscreens, and acoustic pulse touchscreens. Besides, different types of touchscreens are sensitive to touching by fingers or by special pens (styluses). Also, touchscreens differ in the number of touch points that may be simultaneously recognized (single point or multi-touch).

Resistive touchscreens comprise two parallel surfaces, each covered with a conductive material. There is an air gap between the surfaces. As a user touches the upper (outer) layer, it starts to adjoin the lower (inner) layer, which triggers the current flow. It is detected by sensors, which localize the touched point on the screen. Since resistive touchscreens require the layer's deformation to detect a touch, they can be used with any type of rigid touching objects, including fingers (also in gloves) and pens. Such screens are also relatively cheap and not sensitive to contamination. However, they typically have lower contrast in comparison to other touchscreens.

Capacitive touchscreens include an inductive layer covered by conductor. It enables the maintenance of electrostatic field on the surface of the screen. A touch of a finger or a capacitive pen disrupts the field, which is detected by sensors as a change of the capacitance. The use of capacitive screens is often problematic with gloves. Such screens are popular in smartphones and tablets.

Optical touchscreens include image sensors (e.g., CMOS) and light sources (e.g., infrared) located on the screen borders. Sensors detect light emitted by the sources located on the opposite screen side. A touch by an object prevents light from reaching some sensors, which enables the detection of the touch position. This technology is affordable and used for larger screens. It does not depend on the type of touching objects. Optical touchscreens that recognize many touch points at the same time are suitable for multi-user collaborative XR environments, e.g., Fig. 2.10.

Fig. 2.10 Multi-touch screen PQ Labs G5 4K (PQ Labs 2019).

Dispersive touchscreens use the effect of piezoelectricity in the glass of the screen. Piezoelectricity relies on collecting electric charge in some solid materials in response to mechanical stress. This method of sensing touch can be used with any object. Moreover, it is not sensitive to contamination. A drawback is that a dispersive touchscreen cannot detect a motionless finger after the touch.

Surface acoustic wave touchscreens are medium for ultrasonic waves that pass through the screen. As a screen is touched, the waves are affected, allowing sensors to detect the touch position. This method is sensitive to contamination, which also can modify the waves.

Acoustic pulse touchscreens are equipped with sensors of acoustic waves, which are registered upon a touch. The signal is compared to pattern signals from a given list, which enables the system to determine the touch position. Like a dispersive touchscreen, an acoustic pulse touchscreen cannot detect a motionless finger after the touch.

Touchscreens enable interactions using various touch gestures, such as tap, hold, pinch, stretch, rotate, slide, scroll, and swipe. Collected data describing such gestures can help infer various user's characteristics, such as gender, age, and identity (Al-Showarah, Al-Jawad, & Sellahewa 2015; Bevan & Fraser 2016; Acien, Morales, Fiérrez, Vera-Rodríguez, & Hernandez-Ortega 2019).

Chapter 3
Knowledge Representation with Logical Systems

3.1 Foundations of Logical Systems

Logical systems are formal organizations of concepts and relations between them that enable reasoning. A logical system consists of the following main elements:

1. A *language*, which enables expression of concepts using symbols permitted in the system.
2. *Axioms*, which are statements considered true without being derived from other statements.
3. *Rules of inference*, which enable deriving new statements (also called *theorems*) from axioms and other already derived theorems.

Logical systems have gained large attention in mathematics and computer science as independent abstract theories for proofs, particularly deduction, as well as the foundation of knowledge representation, which is widely disseminated in various fields of artificial intelligence, robotics, expert systems, and games. Logical systems allow for assertion of facts and rules that describe arbitrary applications or domains. Hence, they are also especially interesting in the context of this book.

3.1.1 Statements and Knowledge Bases

Sentences

One of the basic logical systems is propositional logic. Plenty of publications have focused on its mathematical properties, e.g., Cunningham (2012), as well as computational properties and possible applications in IT systems, e.g., Russell &

© The Author(s), under exclusive license to Springer Nature Switzerland AG 2020
J. Flotyński, *Knowledge-Based Explorable Extended Reality Environments*,
https://doi.org/10.1007/978-3-030-59965-2_3

Norvig (2009). One of the basic concepts of propositional logic is *atomic sentence* (*atom* for short).

Definition 3.1 An *atom* is a textual constant.

An atom may be given *semantics* (meaning), thereby expressing a *statement* about a possible *world* (also called a *model*) with its objects, their properties, and relationships, e.g., *an avatar is jumping*, and *there are ten buildings in a virtual housing estate*. The semantics specifies rules that allow us to consider a statement *true* or *false* in every possible world. For instance, the semantics of the aforementioned statement about buildings determines that the statement is true for the world representing Manhattan. In contrast, it is false for a world representing a desert. In propositional logic, statements represented by atoms are indivisible. It means that a statement is treated as a whole without distinguishing its elements, such as buildings, avatars, and jumping. However, such statements can be combined into *complex statements* using logical operators, such as: $\wedge$ (*and*—conjunction), $\vee$ (*or*—disjunction), $\neg$ (*not*—negation), $\Leftarrow$ (*if*—implication), and $\Leftrightarrow$ (*if and only if*—equivalence).

It is practical to group statements describing a particular application or use cases related to a world, e.g., an organization or an avatar that performs some tasks in an environment. It leads to the following definition:

Definition 3.2 A *knowledge base* is a set of statements.

Satisfiability and Validity

An essential property of a statement is *satisfiability*.

Definition 3.3 A statement is *satisfiable* if and only if it is true for some worlds.

If a statement is satisfiable in a world, we say that it is *satisfied* or *holds* in the world. Statements that are false in all possible worlds are *unsatisfiable*. Satisfiability of statements (SAT) is one of the main problems in logical systems, which can be stated as the question: *are there any possible worlds in which the statements are true?* In particular, satisfiability may be verified by checking all possible worlds until one satisfies the statements. It has been proven that the SAT problem in propositional logic, in general, is NP-complete because it demands the verification of all possible combinations of true and false values assigned to the particular atomic sentences that form the statement.

Statements that are always true are called *tautologies* or *valid statements*.

Definition 3.4 A *valid statement* is a statement that is satisfied in all possible worlds.

Valid statements are especially important to describe general properties of and relations between users and objects in systems, which we use in more complicated theories, such as first-order logic presented in Sect. 3.2.

Horn Clauses

A specific type of complex statement is *clause*.

Definition 3.5 A *clause* is a disjunction of statements.

A clause has the form: $s_1 \lor s_2 \lor \ldots \lor s_n$, where $s_1, \ldots, s_n$ are statements. We call s a *positive statement*, while $\neg s$ a *negative statement*. A special form of clause is a *Horn clause*.

Definition 3.6 A *Horn clause* is a clause in which at most one statement is positive.

A Horn clause with exactly one positive statement is called a *definite clause*. A definite clause has the form: $\neg s_1 \lor \neg s_2 \lor \neg s_3 \lor \ldots \lor s_n$, which can also be rewritten in the equivalent form: $s_n \Leftarrow s_1 \land s_2 \land \ldots \land s_{n-1}$. Definite clauses are referred to as *rules* in this book. The conjunction $s_1 \land s_2 \land \ldots \land s_{n-1}$ is referred to as the *body* (also called *premise* or *antecedent*) of the rule, while s_n is referred to as the *head* (also called *conclusion* or *consequent*) of the rule. A *rule* is an implication, whose *head* is true if the *body* is true. Thus, the body of a rule expresses a condition for its head. In this book, we use the syntax of rules based on the left-pointing arrow. It emphasizes the conclusion and complies with Prolog (Clocksin & Mellish 1984; Bramer 2014), one of the main languages for logic programming. A Horn clause with no positive statement is called a *goal clause*. The last type of horn clause we define in this book is *fact*.

Definition 3.7 A *fact* is a Horn clause that consists of one statement, which is positive.

Unlike the head of a rule, a fact is unconditional—its fulfillment does not depend on the fulfillment of other statements.

Definition 3.8 A *rule set* is a set of facts and rules.

The following is an example rule set consisting of Horn clauses built upon predicates.

$$
\begin{aligned}
&(arm\ includes\ triceps).\\
&(arm\ includes\ biceps).\\
&(burpees\ stimulates\ triceps).\\
&(pull\_up\ stimulates\ biceps).\\
&(burpees\ sculpt\ arm) \Leftarrow (arm\ includes\ triceps)\\
&\qquad \land\ (burpees\ stimulates\ triceps).
\end{aligned} \tag{3.1}
$$

The first four clauses are facts, while the last one is a rule. The facts designate different muscles as elements of different body parts. In addition, muscles are stimulated by different exercises. An exercise that stimulates a muscle also sculpts the body part that includes the muscle. A rule set is a specific type of knowledge base.

The satisfiability of horn clauses (HORNSAT) can be verified in polynomial time depending on the number of clauses in the rule set. Hence, it is in the P class (Papadimitriou 1994). It is an important advantage compared to other types of clauses, which makes the processing of Horn rule sets relatively efficient, scalable, and feasible in practical applications (*tractable*).

3.1.2   Reasoning in Logical Systems

Logical Entailment

Reasoning in logical systems is the process of drawing conclusions from statements included in a knowledge base. One of the basic terms associated with reasoning is logical *entailment*.

Definition 3.9 Statement s_1 *entails* statement s_2 if and only if s_2 is true in all worlds in which s_1 is true.

Entailment is denoted by $\models$. In other words, we say that s_2 *is entailed by* or *logically follows* s_1 ($s_1 \models s_2$). The term entailment is also frequently used in reference to knowledge bases. A knowledge base entails a statement if the statement logically follows statements included in the knowledge base. Entailment constitutes deductive reasoning, which we use in this book.

Statements asserted in a knowledge base on which we are working are called *explicit statements*. Statements that are not asserted in the knowledge base but are entailed by other statements are called *implicit statements*.

Rules of Inference

Deriving implicit statements from other (implicit or explicit) statements is referred to as *inference*. Inference is essential to reasoning, which leads to the acquisition of new knowledge from explicitly specified knowledge. Practical usage of inference is broad and includes proofs, decision making, knowledge acquisition, and query answering. The latter two are of particular importance and are frequently addressed in this book.

The main rule of inference in deductive reasoning is Modus Ponens (Latin for "mode that affirms"). It is the following tautology:

$$s_2 \Leftarrow ((s_2 \Leftarrow s_1) \wedge s_1) \tag{3.2}$$

It means that if the rule $s_2 \Leftarrow s_1$ is in a knowledge base and we know that statement s_1 is true, we infer that statement s_2 is also true. Rule set (3.1) can serve as an example.

Soundness and Completeness

A property that is crucial to inference algorithms used in practical applications is *soundness*.

Definition 3.10 An inference algorithm is *sound* if and only if it infers only entailed statements.

In other words, every statement inferred by an algorithm is entailed. Sound algorithms are also called *truth-preserving*. Such algorithms neither draw false conclusions based on true premises nor draw true conclusions based on false premises. For example, a sound algorithm infers that *burpees sculpt arm* from rule set (3.1) because this statement is entailed by the conjunction of asserted statements 1 and 3. Unlike, a sound algorithm does not infer that *burpees sculpt leg* as no statements in the rule set entail such a conclusion.

Another essential property of inference algorithms is *completeness*.

Definition 3.11 An inference algorithm is *complete* if and only if it can infer every statement that is entailed.

It means that a complete algorithm allows for acquisition of full knowledge that can potentially be inferred from a given knowledge base. Finally, sound and complete algorithms can infer all true and only true statements from a knowledge base. For example, an algorithm that cannot infer statement *burpees sculpt arm* from rule set (3.1) is not complete.

Inference Algorithms

One of the most frequently used algorithms for inference in propositional logic is resolution. Resolution is based on proof by contradiction. If a statement s is to be verified against a knowledge base KB, i.e., it is checked whether KB entails s, the satisfiability of $(KB \wedge \neg s)$ is verified. The algorithm checks pairs of statements that include contradictory atomic sentences and adds the resolved clauses to KB. If two clauses give the empty clause, KB entails s. Otherwise, if no new clauses can be added, KB does not entail s. Resolution is sound and complete.

Other inference algorithms are forward chaining and backward chaining, which apply only to knowledge bases that consist of Horn clauses. The algorithms are intuitive. Forward chaining starts with an empty knowledge base, gets bodies of rules, and infers their heads using Modus Ponens. Next, it considers the inferred heads asserted and tries to infer the heads of other rules. If the body of a rule includes only entailed statements, the head of the rule is inferred. These steps are repeated until there are no rules in the rule set whose bodies are satisfied. The algorithm is sound and complete, and it is especially useful when all entailed statements should be found. However, in case of issuing a query, the algorithm also infers irrelevant statements. It demands extra time and memory for computations.

The problem of inferring irrelevant statements does not appear in backward chaining, which is goal oriented and verifies rules in the opposite direction to the forward chaining algorithm. For a statement whose satisfiability is checked, rules whose heads include the statement are found. For these rules, the satisfiability of their bodies is verified. If a rule body is a conjunction of statements, every conjunct is recursively verified. Like forward chaining, backward chaining can infer only entailed statements and every entailed statement can be inferred. However, it is more efficient in terms of time and memory when answering to specific queries. The inference algorithms are described in more detail in multiple publications, including Russell & Norvig (2009), Papadimitriou (1994).

Monotonicity

An important property of reasoning in logical systems is *monotonicity*.

Definition 3.12 A logical system is **monotonic** if and only if for every knowledge base *KB* that can be created with the system: if *KB* entails a statement s_1, also *KB* extended with any statement s_2 entails s_1.

In monotonic systems, it is impossible to negate a fact that has already been asserted. For instance, while reasoning on rule set (3.1) in a monotonic logical system, we cannot assert that *burpees do not stimulate triceps* as it would be contradictory to statement 3. In everyday life, the non-monotonicity of logical systems resembles changing one's mind.

3.1.3 Computational Properties of Logical Systems

Computability

Computability is an important property of functions, which is also related to logical systems. Much attention has been paid to computability in the literature, e.g., Papadimitriou (1994), O'Regan (2020), where computation is typically explained using the Turing machine, a prevalent mathematical model of computation.

Definition 3.13 A function is **computable** if and only if there exists an algorithm that computes the function for every possible set of parameters in the function domain.

The crucial point in the definition is that for a computable function, a single algorithm can compute the result for any permitted set of parameters. For instance, the function $f(x, y) = x + y$ for $x, y \in R$ is computable as the algorithm that calculates the sum of two values can be used for any pair of real numbers.

If there is no common algorithm that computes a function for every possible set of its parameters, the function is *uncomputable*. For example, there is no single algorithm that solves any mathematical formula.

Decidability

If the result of computing a particular problem is true or false, we can consider the problem in terms of decidability.

Definition 3.14 A problem is *decidable* if and only if there exists an algorithm that solves the problem for any possible input case (set of input parameters).

Like in the case of computability, it is key whether a common algorithm applies to all possible parameters of the problem. For instance, the problem of determining whether $x > y$ for $x, y \in R$ is decidable as an algorithm common to all pairs of real numbers exists.

If no algorithm solves the problem for every possible input case, the problem is **undecidable**. Hence, the undecidability of a problem means that there is no one general solution to the problem that would be appropriate for all possible cases. For example, there is no common algorithm that verifies whether an arbitrary mathematical proposition is true or false. From the practical point of view, for an undecidable problem and a particular input case, we cannot be sure whether an algorithm will stop and give an answer, or it will never stop and we will never get an answer.

Between decidable and undecidable problems, *semidecidable* problems exist. A problem is **semidecidable** if there exists an algorithm that answers for every possible formula that belongs to the theory, but there is no algorithm that answers for every possible formula that is not in the theory. Hence, semidecidable problems cause less severe difficulties than undecidable problems but also have no common algorithm to solve all possible cases.

In logical systems multiple practical problems require the true/false (yes/no) answer, e.g., *are the statements in a knowledge base satisfiable*? Therefore, decidability plays a prominent role in the solutions proposed in this book.

Computational Complexity

For decidable problems, classes of computational complexity may be specified. A comprehensive analysis of computational complexity classes has been presented in Papadimitriou (1994). In this section, we present the most important concepts. Complexity classes are related to time and space (memory) needed to solve a problem depending on the size of its input parameters. A complexity class related to time or space determines the type of *function* (e.g., logarithmic, polynomial, and exponential) as well as the type of the *Turing machine* (deterministic or non-deterministic), which solves the problems of the class in time or space with an upper bound limited by the function. For example, checking the satisfiability of a formula in propositional logic can be done by a non-deterministic Turing machine in polynomial time depending on the formula size. The most frequently used complexity classes, also referred to in this book, are the following.

Definition 3.15 *LSPACE/NLSPACE* is the class of problems that can be solved by a deterministic/non-deterministic Turing machine using at most logarithmic space depending on the size of the input parameters.

It is denoted as $O(log(n))$, where n is the size of input parameters.

Definition 3.16 *P/NP* is the class of problems that can be solved by a deterministic/non-deterministic Turing machine at most in polynomial time depending on the size of the input parameters.

It is denoted as $O(n^c)$, where c is a constant.

Definition 3.17 *PSPACE* is the class of problems that can be solved by a deterministic Turing machine using at most polynomial space depending on the size of the input parameters.

Like *P* and *NP*, it is denoted as $O(n^c)$.

Definition 3.18 *EXPTIME/NEXPTIME* is the class of problems that can be solved by a deterministic/non-deterministic Turing machine at most in exponential time depending on the size of the input parameters.

It is denoted as $O(2^n)$.

Definition 3.19 *N2EXPTIME* is the class of problems that can be solved by a non-deterministic Turing machine at most in double exponential time depending on the size of the input parameters.

It is denoted as $O(2^{2^n})$.

The classes include problems of increasing complexity, which is reflected by the following relation $LSPACE \subseteq NLSPACE \subseteq P \subseteq NP \subseteq PSPACE \subseteq EXPTIME \subseteq NEXPTIME \subseteq N2EXPTIME$ (Papadimitriou 1994; Thorne & Calvanese 2010).

In addition, postfixes can be added to the names of the classes to specify related larger or smaller classes. An *X-hard* is a class of problems that are at least as complex as any problem from class X. An *X-complete* is a class of problems that are in both class X and X-hard.

Studying different classes of computational complexity leads to an important property of algorithms, which is *tractability*. A **tractable** algorithm solves a problem in time lower than exponential. Hence, tractable algorithms fall into classes that are below EXPTIME.

3.2 First-Order Logic

In this section, we explain the fundamentals of a well-established logical system—first-order logic, also referred to as first-order predicate calculus. First-order logic is more powerful than propositional logic. It provides a comprehensive formalism enabling knowledge representation, programming, and proving theorems, which has been used to create logic programming languages, e.g., Prolog and Datalog. A comprehensive discussion of first-order logic in the context of artificial intelligence systems and mathematical proofs has been presented in multiple publications, e.g., Russell & Norvig (2009), Cunningham (2012).

3.2.1 Syntax and Semantics of First-Order Logic

Expressivity

A fundamental concept related to logical systems is *ontological commitment*, which is the assumption of what and how we can say about the world. Propositional logic enables statements on facts, which are true, false, or unknown, whereas first-order logic enables statements on objects represented by quantified variables and described by properties and relations—which are also true, false, or unknown. It permits conclusions about individual objects based on statements that are general—applicable to different objects. For instance, if we assert that every avatar in a virtual crowd has a cap on the head, and John is a crowd member, we can infer that John has a cap on his head. In this regard, first-order logic resembles how people think when making general statements about the world.

Following Dantsin, Eiter, Gottlob, & Voronkov (2001), we define *expressivity*, also called *expressive power* or *expressiveness*, of a logical system as the set of all statements that can be expressed using the system. We say that first-order logic is more *expressive* or has higher *expressivity* than propositional logic because all statements expressible in propositional logic can be expressed in first-order logic. Moreover, first-order logic enables generalization of statements on individual objects by statements on objects' classes, which is unattainable in propositional logic. Finally, the specification of a property of all objects of an infinite class in first-order logic cannot be replaced with a finite number of statements in propositional logic.

Terms

In Sect. 3.1.1, we have introduced atoms as basic statements in propositional logic. However, we need more elements to express statements in first-order logic. Atoms are a specific type of *terms*.

Definition 3.20 A *term* is a number, an atom, a variable, or a compound term.

Hence, terms may also serve as the values of variables.

Definition 3.21 A *compound term* is a named ordered tuple that consists of terms.

It is denoted as $functor(argument_1, \ldots, argument_n)$, where $functor$ is an atom, which is the name of the compound term, and $argument_1, \ldots, argument_n, n \geq 1$ are terms. Compound terms represent *relations*, which may be, in general, arbitrarily complex and recursive. In this book, atoms and compound terms begin with small letters, whereas variables begin with capital letters. An example compound term— $hasWheels(Car)$—means that every car (represented by a variable) has wheels. Compound term $numberOfWheels(car, 4)$ means that a particular car (atom) has 4 wheels (number). Compound term $frontLeftWheel(car)$ denotes the front left wheel of the car.

Predicates

Along with terms, the second key element of statements are predicates.

Definition 3.22 A *predicate* is a boolean-valued function.

Predicates are used to evaluate conditions. As a sort of relations, predicates are represented by compound terms. Therefore, they use the same syntax:

$$predicate(argument_1, \ldots, argument_n) \Rightarrow \{true, false\}, \qquad (3.3)$$

where $n \geq 0$ is called *arity*, and $argument_1, \ldots, argument_n$ are terms. Hence, predicates express *statements* about objects that may be *satisfied* (true) for some sequences of terms. Predicates with arity equal to 1 are called *unary predicates*. Unary predicates are used to express statements about assignment of objects to *classes*. For example, the statements $driver(john)$ and $car(cabriolet)$ are true in worlds in which *John* is a *driver* and the *cabriolet* is a *car*, and false in other worlds. Predicates with arity equal to 2 are called *binary predicates*. Such predicates are used to express statements about relations on objects, e.g., connections between objects as well as objects' properties. For instance, the statement $drives(john, cabriolet)$ is true in worlds in which *John* drives *cabriolet*. In turn, the statement $canDrive(driver(X), car(Car))$ is true in worlds in which every driver can drive any car. For a statement that consists of a predicate with arguments, we say that it is *based on* the predicate. In contrast to statements in propositional logic, predicates enable building structured statements with elements that can be individually respected while reasoning.

Due to compatibility with the Semantic Web approach, which is discussed in Sect. 3.4, we mostly use unary and binary predicates in this book. It does not, however, restrict the proposed ideas.

Quantifiers

The generalization of statements in first-order logic in comparison to propositional logic is possible due to *quantifiers*. In first-order logic, we distinguish two types of quantifiers: the *universal quantifier* and the *existential quantifier*, which are intensively used to specify statements in this book.

The *universal quantifier* (denoted as $\forall$) is used to make statements about all objects in the world. For instance, the statement $\forall X: canJump(X) \Leftarrow avatar(X)$ means: *for every X, if X is an avatar, X can jump*, for short: *every avatar can jump*. Universal quantification liberates us from enumerating statements with individual objects that satisfy some relations.

The *existential quantifier* (denoted as $\exists$) is used to make statements that there is at least one object in the world that satisfies a relation. For instance, the statement $\exists X: avatar(X) \wedge king(X)$ means: *there is an X such that X is an avatar and X is the king*, or *there is at least one avatar that is the king*. Existential quantification allows us to state that a relation is satisfied by an object without indicating the object.

Axioms

An **axiom** is a statement that is considered true in all possible worlds, which does not have to be proven within a given theory. Axioms are statements that we presume about a domain without deriving from other statements. In this regard, axioms typically provide fundamental knowledge about a domain. Axioms should be selected in such a way to enable inference of all other useful statements that are true in the theory. Examples of axioms are

$$\forall X, Y: father(X, Y) \Leftrightarrow male(X) \wedge parent(X, Y).$$
$$\forall X, Y: parent(Y, X) \Leftarrow son(X, Y). \tag{3.4}$$

Statements entailed from axioms are referred to as **theorems**. For example, from the axioms mentioned above, we can infer that if X is a son of Y who is a male, Y is the father of X.

Knowledge expressed by axioms and theorems can fall into two main categories: *definitions* and *partial specifications*. A definition specifies the necessary and sufficient condition for a statement to be true. Hence, we state a definition if we have comprehensive knowledge about the property or relation that we specify. A definition has the form of an equivalence, e.g., the abovementioned definition of the *father* relation. In contrast to a definition, a partial specification only designates a sufficient condition for a statement to be true, which does not prevent other premises from making the statement true. Thus, we state a partial specification if we have some knowledge about a property or relation, which, nonetheless, does not encompass all possible cases in which the statement is satisfied. Thereby, it is insufficient to form a definition. A partial specification is denoted by an implication, e.g., the specification of the *parent* relation mentioned above.

3.2.2 Queries and Reasoning on Knowledge Bases

Queries to knowledge bases expressed in first-order logic enable the retrieval of information about objects and their relations, which are described in the knowledge base.

Definition 3.23 A *query* is a statement that is:

1. An atom, or
2. A statement *based on* a predicate, or
3. A conjunction of queries, or
4. A disjunction of queries.

For instance, the query $hob(H) \land serviceman(S) \land (repairs(S, H, Time) \lor tests(S, H, Time))$ issued to a knowledge base initiates reasoning to find a serviceman and time when the serviceman repairs or tests a hob.

A specific type of query is *conjunctive query*, which is a query built in line with Definition 3.23, except point 4—it does not include disjunctions.

The processing of a query yields a *query result*, which is an answer to the question posed in the query.

Definition 3.24 A *query result* for a given *query* is:

1. If the *query* does not include variables—one of the atoms: *true* (if *query* is satisfied) or *false* (if *query* is not satisfied).
2. If the *query* includes variables—a set of ordered tuples $(var_1, var_2, \ldots, var_n)$, where $var_1, var_2, \ldots, var_n$ for $n \geq 1$ are values of all the variables included in the *query*, listed in the order in which they appear in the *query*, such that the values satisfy the *query*. The set is empty if no values satisfy the *query*.

Like queries, reasoning in first-order logic may be related to individual objects, their groups, and relations. For example, if a knowledge base stores information about cooking hobs, we can ask what power consumption categories of the hobs produced by a particular manufacturer are. Even if such a class has not been explicitly distinguished, it can be created on demand while reasoning based on the values of hobs' properties.

3.2.3 Knowledge Engineering

The concepts of first-order logic presented in the previous subsections enable *knowledge engineering*, which is the process of creating knowledge bases. Knowledge engineering relies on the selection of objects and relations that describe a particular domain as well as the specification of the objects and relations using a formal language. In Russell & Norvig (2009), the following steps of the process are distinguished:

1. *Task identification*, in which the main use cases and potential questions for the intended knowledge base are specified. For example, a knowledge base describing a virtual town should specify its structure, including main elements and spatial relations between them.
2. *Assembly of relevant knowledge*, in which objects and relations in the domain should be identified and comprehended. For example, towns include buildings, streets, and green areas with size, position, and orientation.
3. *Selection of a formalism*, in which a logical system that will be used to represent the knowledge is chosen. Its expressivity should correspond to possible types of objects and relations identified in the previous step.
4. *Encoding terminological knowledge*, in which general knowledge related to classes and relations of objects is encoded using the formalism. Such knowledge should be described using axioms from which all desirable theorems will be achievable in the inference process. For example, we specify common properties and relations for particular classes of buildings: single-family houses, apartment buildings, and skyscrapers.
5. *Encoding a specific instance of the problem*, in which a world is described using the terminology prepared in the previous step. For example, we specify housing estates consisting of individual houses with given values of spatial relations.
6. *Posing queries to an inference algorithm* that is compatible with the formalism to provoke reasoning and get answers about interesting objects and relations. For instance, *what is the highest building in the town?*
7. *Verification, debugging, and correction of the knowledge base*, in which the obtained query results are checked. Results of reasoning that are inconsistent with the intended understanding of the domain are analyzed and enable improvement of the terminology (axioms). Thus, this step may launch a cycle of improvements starting from Step 4. For example, if a single-family house is regarded as the highest building in Manhattan, the definition or partial specification of the *height* property needs a revision, or the property has been incorrectly assigned to the buildings.

3.2.4 Representation of Spatial–Temporal Entities

In the previous subsections, we have shown that first-order logic can be used to express arbitrary relations of objects, including objects' properties as well as assignment of objects to classes. Hence, first-order logic is sufficiently expressive to represent spatial–temporal entities (objects and relations). A few solutions have been developed to organize the representation of temporal entities in first-order logic. The main of them are the situation calculus (Reiter 1991, 2001), the fluent calculus (Thielscher 1998), and the event calculus (R. Kowalski & Sergot 1989; Shanahan 1999). The two former solutions represent states, which are situations in which relations of objects hold. The latter approach represents events, which determine time points and intervals in which relations of objects hold.

In XR environments, local states of different objects are associated with (possibly) parallel time intervals designated by concurrent events, which may be independent and not necessarily related to global situations of the scenes. Therefore, the event calculus is presented in more detail as a potentially appropriate solution to represent the behavior of XR environments. An extensive comparison of these solutions has been presented in R. A. Kowalski & Sadri (1994).

The event calculus enables reasoning on events and time. The concept of the calculus was slightly evolving in the successive publications. In this chapter, we explain the main ideas essential to the approach proposed in this book. The concepts of the event calculus are depicted in Fig. 3.1.

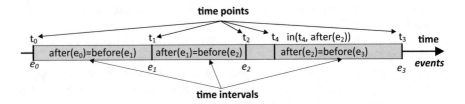

Fig. 3.1 The concept of event calculus

Definition 3.25 A *time point* is a temporal entity whose duration is equal to zero.

An *event* occurs at a time point.

Definition 3.26 A *time interval* is a temporal entity whose duration is larger than zero.

An interval is started by an event and finished by an event.

Definition 3.27 A *fluent* is a predicate whose value changes over time.

Fluents use the notation of predicates. For instance, $isFalling(ball)$ is false until the *ball* is on the edge of the table when the fluent starts to be true.

The event calculus consists of several application- and domain-independent predicates that can be used to express fulfillment of application- or domain-specific fluents in points and intervals of time.

Definition 3.28 The *time* predicate is a predicate that is true for a given *event* and a *time point* if and only if the *event* occurs at the *time point*.

It is denoted as $time(event, tp)$, where tp is a time point.

Definition 3.29 The *after* compound term is a compound term that specifies the *time interval* started by the occurrence of a given *event*.

It is denoted as $after(event)$.

Definition 3.30 The *before* compound term is a compound term that specifies the *time interval* finished by the occurrence of a given *event*.

It is denoted as $before(event)$.

Definition 3.31 The *start* predicate is a predicate that is true for a given *time interval* and an *event* if and only if the *time interval* is started by the *event*.

It is denoted as $start(ti, event)$, where ti is a *time interval*.

Definition 3.32 The *end* predicate is a predicate that is true for a given *time interval* and an *event* if and only if the *time interval* is finished by the *event*.

It is denoted as $end(ti, event)$. It is also possible to evaluate whether a time point belongs to a time interval.

Definition 3.33 The *in* predicate is a predicate that is true for a given *time point* and a *time interval* if and only if the *time point* is within the *time interval*.

It is denoted as $in(tp, ti)$.

Definition 3.34 The *holdsAt* predicate is a predicate that is true for a given *fluent* and a *time point* if and only if the *fluent* is true at the *time point*.

It is denoted as $holdsAt(fluent, tp)$. For instance, *holdsAt(reached(ball, edge), '24sec')* evaluates whether the *ball reached* the *edge* at time point 24*sec*.

Definition 3.35 The *holds* predicate is a predicate that is true for a given *fluent* and a *time interval* if and only if the *fluent* is true within the *time interval*.

It is denoted as $holds(fluent, ti)$. For instance, *holds(isFalling(ball), after(reachedEdge))* evaluates whether the *ball is falling* since it reached the *edge*.
On the basis of Definitions 3.33–3.35, we can conclude that:

Theorem 3.1 *If a fluent is satisfied within a time interval, it is satisfied at every time point that is in the time interval.*

$$\forall fluent, tp, ti: holdsAt(fluent, tp) \Leftarrow holds(fluent, ti) \wedge in(tp, ti)$$
(3.5)

3.2.5 Logic Programming

Separation of Knowledge Bases and Inference Procedures

First-order logic, which enables general as well as specific statements on objects, has become the foundation for logic programming. Logic programming separates two essential elements of an application: *logic* and *control* (R. Kowalski 1979).

Logic is knowledge encoded by statements in a knowledge base that conform to a selected logical system (formalism). It describes what we know about the domain addressed by the application, e.g., what the cars in a virtual car showroom are, and what functions of the cars can be demonstrated to visitors. *Control* is an algorithm of solving a problem expressed using the logical system. In particular, control is an inference procedure checking satisfiability of queries issued to a knowledge base. Strategies for problem solving enabled by the control are generic—do not depend on particular applications and domains, providing that the knowledge bases comply with the selected logical system. Thereby, the same control can be used across different application domains. Control depends only on the logical system selected to represent the processable knowledge bases and determines the performance of knowledge processing. This component typically implements a well-known inference algorithm, e.g., resolution (for knowledge bases using first-order logic), backward or forward chaining (for knowledge bases using Horn clauses rather than full first-order logic).

The separation of knowledge bases from inference procedures imposes an important property of logic programming. Development of an application relies on the implementation of a knowledge base and the selection of an inference algorithm, which typically has to be neither designed nor implemented. Therefore, logic programming is a sort of *declarative programming*. It has been intensively used in multiple expert systems in medicine, finance, and robotics. It differs from *imperative* (*procedural*) programming, which is currently the prevalent approach to building IT systems in popular languages, such as Java and C#. In imperative programming, both logic and control are designed and implemented by developers, thus being specific to a particular application. A comprehensive review of various approaches to logic programming has been presented in Baral & Gelfond (1994).

Prolog

One of the most frequently used languages for logic programming is Prolog, which has been addressed in a numerous publications, e.g., Clocksin & Mellish (1984), Bramer (2014). Prolog enables specification of knowledge bases that consist of Horn clauses (cf. Sect. 3.1.1), thereby complying with a fragment of first-order logic. Processing of knowledge bases by the available Prolog interpreters has a few important properties, which influence the style of programming (Russell & Norvig 2009):

1. Inference in Prolog is based on the backward chaining algorithm, which starts from conclusions to be verified and tries to prove their premises. Statements are verified in the order in which they appear in the knowledge base. The used depth-first strategy determines the exploration of the statements as deeply as possible before backtracking.

2. Built-in math functions are proven in reasoning by execution, like in imperative programming, rather than by inference. For example, the *max* function is proven by returning the larger of two given arguments.
3. It enables assertion and retraction of statements in knowledge bases using the *assert* and *retract* predicates in rule bodies. Processing these predicates can be seen as providing additional conclusions of the rule, in addition to the rule head, which is inferred in the standard way.

A variety of concepts and examples presented in this book are specified using Horn clauses. Although they are independent of particular programming languages and parsers, they can be verified using available Prolog implementations, e.g., SWI Prolog (2020).

Parallel Reasoning

Since knowledge bases consist of statements, which can be, in particular, Horn clauses, two types of parallel processing can improve the performance of reasoning, which has been summarized in Russell & Norvig (2009).

1. Rules with the same head can be simultaneously verified by evaluating their bodies in parallel. It is a relatively simple solution, which launches the inference algorithm in different threads for different clauses.
2. The statements that are conjuncts in the body of a rule can be simultaneously verified. It is, however, a relatively more complex solution. First, in logic programming, e.g., in Prolog, statements in a rule body may depend on other statements, e.g., by expecting calculated variable values. Second, results of processing conjuncts, including inferred variable values or satisfiability answers, should be notified to the threads processing other related conjuncts.

The presented types of parallel reasoning can be applied to knowledge processing in any application and domain, including solutions proposed in the next chapters of this book.

3.3 Description Logics

Description logics (DLs) are knowledge representation languages, which are widely used in knowledge engineering. Most of the description logics are fragments of first-order logic that are decidable (cf. Definition 3.14) in solving various problems related to classification. In this regard, description logics provide a trade-off between expressivity and computational properties. Description logics have formal semantics specified, which enables their unambiguous understanding by humans and reasoning by computers. Plenty of publications have been devoted to description logics. In Baader, Calvanese, McGuinness, Nardi, & Patel-Schneider (2010), a comprehensive study of description logics is presented. In Sikos (2017b), a variety of description logics are analyzed in the context of multimedia applications, such as images and movies. A concise introduction to the fundamentals of description logics is presented in Krötzsch, Simancik, & Horrocks (2012).

3.3.1   Semantics of Description Logics

Types of Entities

The semantics of description logics is related to three types of *entities*: *individuals*, *concepts*, and *roles*. An *individual* is an object in a modeled world, e.g., a car, an avatar, and a building. A *concept* is a set of objects in a world. It typically collects objects with similar properties, e.g., separate concepts collect cars, avatars, and buildings. A *role* is a binary predicate (relation) on two individuals in a world, e.g., a car *is on* a street, an avatar *is wearing* a body armor, and a building *is equipped with* an elevator. We denote concepts, roles, and individuals with lowercase to maintain consistency of naming with first-order logic.

Interpretation

Individuals are elements of the *domain* (also called the *universe of discourse*) of a described world (Rudolph 2011). A domain is denoted by $\triangle^{I}$. For the further definitions, we also distinguish the set of the names of all individuals in the world—N_I, the set of the names of all concepts to which the individuals belong—N_C, and the set of the names of all roles specified for the individuals—N_R. The semantics of a description logic is determined by the connection between the sets of names and the entities of the worlds (elements of worlds' domains), which can be described using the logic. An *interpretation function* establishes this connection.

Definition 3.36 An *interpretation function* is a function that:

1. For each individual name $a \in N_I$ determines an individual $a^{I} \in \triangle^{I}$.
2. For each concept name $A \in N_C$ determines a set of individuals $c^{I} \subseteq \triangle^{I}$.
3. For each role name $r \in N_R$ determines a set of pairs of individuals $r^{I} \subseteq \triangle^{I} \times \triangle^{I}$ that are in the role.

An interpretation function is denoted by $.^{I}$.

Definition 3.37 An *interpretation* is a pair of a domain and an interpretation function.

It is denoted by $I = (\triangle^{I}, .^{I})$. An example interpretation includes the set of all avatars in a virtual world, which is the domain, and an interpretation function that links the avatars with the players.

In the following sections, unless otherwise stated, we operate on individuals, concepts, and roles with regard to the semantics of the described worlds rather than on the entities names.

Open and Closed World Assumptions

Other terms related to the semantics of description logics are the closed and open world assumptions. In the *closed world assumption*, the statements that are not explicitly asserted are considered false. In particular, unspecified individuals are considered nonexistent. The closed world assumption is specific to the semantics of databases and logic programming (e.g., in expert systems), in which the whole world we work on is fully described. For example, only the explicitly specified avatars are members of a 3D scene.

In the *open world assumption*, the statements that are not asserted are not considered false but unknown. Likewise, we cannot assume that unspecified individuals do not exist, but we can only say that we do not know whether they exist. The open world assumption is common to the semantics of resources on the Web, in which we respect that there may always be additional information about a resource that we do not know now. For instance, even if we do not know the author of a book, one may be specified in another knowledge base available on the Web, and we cannot state that the book has no author.

Since the approach proposed in this book enables development of XR environments, in which final results can reflect what has been specified (explicitly or implicitly), we mostly use the closed world assumption.

3.3.2 Types of Statements

Statements describing concepts, roles, and individuals fall into three categories of *components* that form knowledge bases: terminological box, relational box, and assertional box, which have been precisely defined in Sikos (2017b). Assuming that statements in any of the components are not redundant, we treat them as *axioms* (cf. Sect. 3.2.1), which entail (cf. Definition 3.9) other statements (*theorems*). We also present possible entailments, which determine what can be inferred from the statements while reasoning. The following definitions of different types of statements are relevant to all possible worlds to which knowledge bases are potentially applicable.

Terminological Box

A terminological box (TBox) describes terminology related to concepts, which is typically shared by different knowledge bases representing different cases of a common domain. A TBox encompasses concept inclusion axioms and concept equivalence axioms.

Definition 3.38 A *concept inclusion statement* is a statement that expresses that every individual that belongs to a concept c_1 also belongs to a concept c_2.

It is denoted as $c_1 \sqsubseteq c_2$. We say that concept c_1 is a *specialization* of concept c_2 and c_2 is a *generalization* of c_1. We also say that c_2 includes c_1. It is equivalent to the subset relation. For example, $model3D \sqsubseteq geometrical Object$ as every individual 3D model has a geometry.

Definition 3.39 A *concept equivalence statement* is a statement that expresses that a concept c_1 includes a concept c_2, and concept c_2 includes concept c_1.

It is denoted as $c_1 \equiv c_2$. It means that both concepts consist of the same individuals, and the names of the concepts may be used as aliases. From a concept equivalence statement, we can infer that if an individual belongs to c_1, it also belongs to c_2 and vice versa, e.g., $mesh3D \equiv mesh$. Hence, concept equivalence is a counterpart to the set equality.

Definition 3.40 A *terminological box (TBox)* is a finite set of concept inclusion axioms and concept equivalent axioms.

Relational Box

A relational box (RBox) describes terminology related to roles, which is typically shared by different knowledge bases representing different cases of a common domain. An RBox encompasses the following types of statements: role inclusion axioms, role equivalence axioms, complex role inclusion axioms, and role disjointedness axioms.

Definition 3.41 A *role inclusion statement* is a statement that expresses that every two individuals that are in a role r_1 are also in a role r_2.

It is denoted as $r_1 \sqsubseteq r_2$. We say that role r_1 is a *specialization* of role r_2 and r_2 is a *generalization* of r_1. We also say that r_2 includes r_1. For example, $hasMotionTrajectory \sqsubseteq hasAnimationDescriptor$ as every motion trajectory assigned to a 3D object is considered an animation descriptor of the object. There are also, however, other types of animation descriptors such as interpolators and timers.

Definition 3.42 A *complex role inclusion statement* is a statement that expresses that for every three individuals i_1, i_2, and i_3: if i_1 and i_2 are in a role r_1 and i_2 and i_3 are in a role r_2, i_1 and i_3 are in a role r_3.

It is denoted as $r_1 \circ r_2 \sqsubseteq r_3$. Such axioms enable the specification of *transitive roles* of the form $r \circ r \sqsubseteq r$. For example, $nextFrame \circ nextFrame \sqsubseteq nextFrame$ permits the inference of the order between arbitrary two frames that appear in a sequence of frames determined by the $nextFrame$ role. The part of a complex role inclusion statement $r_1 \circ r_2$ is called a *role composition*. It always appears on the left side of a complex role inclusion statement to maintain decidability when reasoning on the knowledge base.

Definition 3.43 A *role equivalence statement* is a statement that expresses that a role r_1 includes a role r_2, and role r_2 includes role r_1.

It is denoted as $r_1 \equiv r_2$. It means that both roles connect the same pairs of individuals, and the names of the roles may be used as aliases. For example, both of the roles $includes \equiv contains$ can be used to indicate elements of hierarchical objects in 3D scenes.

Definition 3.44 A *role disjointedness statement* is a statement that expresses that arbitrary two individuals that are in a role r_1 are not in a role r_2.

It is denoted as $r_1 \neq r_2$. For example, $isPlayerIn \neq isUmpireIn$ means that it is impossible to be both a player and umpire in a game at the same time.

Definition 3.45 A *relational box (RBox)* is a finite set of role inclusion axioms, role equivalence axioms, complex role inclusion axioms, and role disjointedness axioms.

Assertional Box

An assertional box (ABox) describes assertions related to individuals typically specific to a knowledge base representing a particular case of a domain. An ABox encompasses the following types of statements: concept membership axioms, role membership axioms, negated role membership axioms, individual equality axioms, and individual inequality axioms.

Definition 3.46 A *concept membership statement* is a statement that expresses that an individual belongs to a concept.

It is denoted as $c(i)$, where c is a concept, and i is an individual. For example, $avatar(john)$.

Definition 3.47 A *role membership statement* is a statement that expresses that two individuals are in a role.

It is denoted as $r(i_1, i_2)$, where r is a role. For example, $isLookingAt(john, alice)$.

Definition 3.48 A *negated role membership statement* is a statement that expresses that two individuals are not in a role.

It is denoted as $\neg r(i_1, i_2)$. For example, $\neg isLookingAt(john, robert)$.

Definition 3.49 An *individual equality statement* is a statement that expresses that two individuals are equal.

It is denoted as $i_1 = i_2$. For example, $john = john\_kowalski$. Individual equality statement can be used to define aliases for individuals.

Definition 3.50 An *individual inequality statement* is a statement that expresses that two individuals are different.

It is denoted as $i_1 \neq i_2$. For example, $john \neq robert$.

Definition 3.51 An *assertional box (ABox)* is a finite set of concept membership axioms, role membership axioms, negated role membership axioms, individual equality axioms, and individual inequality axioms.

Knowledge Bases in Description Logics

With regard to the definitions above, we can redefine knowledge bases (cf. Definition 3.2) to build upon axioms expressed using description logics.

Definition 3.52 A *knowledge base* is a triple consisting of a TBox, an RBox, and an ABox.

This definition categorizes statements of different types. It is important from the practical point of view as tools for reasoning (reasoners) implemented for description logics are usually optimized for processing different components when solving typical reasoning tasks, which are discussed in Sect. 3.3.4.

3.3.3 Constructors of Concepts and Roles

The types of statements presented in the previous subsection enable limited possibilities of modeling complex domains in practical applications. Extending the expressivity of knowledge representation is enabled by *constructors*, which correspond to set and logical operators. Four types of operators are distinguished: concept constructors, role restrictions, nominals, and role constructors. We discuss them along with possible entailments.

Concept Constructors

Definition 3.53 The *intersection* of concepts $c_1, \ldots, c_n$, for $n \geq 2$, is the concept that consists of the individuals that belong to all of $c_1, \ldots, c_n$.

It is denoted as $c_1 \sqcap \ldots \sqcap c_n$ and also referred to as the *conjunction* of concepts. If an individual belongs to a concept intersection, we infer that it belongs to all of the conjuncts. For example, a painted sculpture in a 3D scene belongs to the concept $mesh3D \sqcap texturedObject$.

Definition 3.54 The *union* of concepts $c_1, \ldots, c_n$, for $n \geq 2$, is the concept that consists of the individuals that belong to any of $c_1, \ldots, c_n$.

It is denoted as $c_1 \sqcup c_2$ and also referred to as the *disjunction* of concepts. If an individual belongs to any of the disjuncts of a concept union, we infer that it belongs to the union. For example, a geometrical object in a 3D scene belongs to the concept $object2D \sqcup object3D$.

Definition 3.55 The *complement* of a concept c is the concept that consists of all individuals that do not belong to c.

It is denoted as $\neg c_1$ and also referred to as the *negation* of a concept. If an individual belongs to the negation of a concept, we infer that it does not belong to the concept. An *atomic negation* is the negation of a single concept. For example, objects of 3D scenes that do not have geometry belong to the concept $\neg geometrical Object$. A *complex concept negation* is the negation of the intersection or union of concepts. For example, $\neg(geometrical Object \sqcup animated Object)$ are all objects with no geometry and no animation.

   We also introduce distinguished concepts that are used in the following definitions.

Definition 3.56 The *top concept* is the concept that includes all individuals in the world.

It is denoted as $\top$. For instance, $\top$ includes all objects that build a particular XR environment. In general, $\top \equiv c \sqcup \neg c$, for an arbitrary concept c.

Definition 3.57 The *bottom concept* is the concept that includes no individuals.

It is denoted as $\bot$. In general, $\bot \equiv c \sqcap \neg c$, for an arbitrary concept c.

Role Restrictions

Role restrictions enable combining concepts with roles. They provide higher expressivity for modeling and enable reasoning on concepts interrelated with roles.

Existential and Universal Restrictions

Existential and universal restrictions (also called quantification) are related to concepts whose individuals appear in roles.

Definition 3.58 An *existential restriction* ($\exists r.c$) is a concept that consists of such individuals that each of them is in role r with an individual that belongs to concept c.

If an individual belongs to an existential restriction concept, we infer that it appears in at least one role r with an individual that belongs to concept c. If $c \equiv \top$, we obtain a *limited existential restriction*, which has the form $\exists r.\top$. Otherwise, we have a *full existential restriction.* For example, $structural Object3D \equiv \exists includes.object3D$ means that every structural object includes at least one 3D object as an element. Since the statement is a definition, the inclusion of a 3D object is necessary and sufficient to classify an individual as a 3D structural object.

Definition 3.59 A *universal restriction* ($\forall r.c$) is a concept that consists of such individuals that if an individual is in role r with an individual i, i belongs to concept c.

If an individual i is used in role r with an individual that belongs to a universal restriction concept, we infer that i belongs to concept c. An individual of $\forall r.c$ does not have to appear in role r, but if it appears, we infer that the connected individual belongs to c. For instance, $scene3D \sqsubseteq \forall isIlluminatedBy.lightSource$ means that a 3D scene can be illuminated by 0 or more light sources. It cannot be in role $isIlluminatedBy$ with individuals that are not light sources. Since the statement is a partial specification, we know that every 3D scene may have light sources, but linking light sources is insufficient to classify an individual as a 3D scene.

Unqualified Cardinality Restrictions

Unqualified cardinality restrictions express in how many memberships of roles individuals of a concept appear. Three types of cardinality restrictions are distinguished: *at-least cardinality restrictions, at-most cardinality restrictions*, and *exact cardinality restrictions*.

Definition 3.60 An *at-least cardinality restriction* ($\geq n\ r.\top$) is a concept that consists of such individuals that each of them appears at least n times in role r with some individuals.

In cardinality restrictions, it does not matter to what concepts the linked individuals belong. For example, $table \sqsubseteq\ \geq 3\ hasLeg.\top$ means that every table has at least three legs. No matter what the legs are.

Definition 3.61 An *at-most cardinality restriction* ($\leq n\ r.\top$) is a concept that consists of such individuals that each of them appears at most n times in role r with some individuals.

For example, $material \sqsubseteq\ \leq 2\ hasSide.\top$ means that every material has at most two sides.

Definition 3.62 An *exact cardinality restriction* ($= n\ r.\top$) is a concept that consists of such individuals that each of them appears exactly n times in role r with some individuals.

For example, $pipe \sqsubseteq\ = 2\ hasEnd.\top$ means that every pipe has exactly two ends.

Qualified Cardinality Restrictions

Qualified cardinality restrictions express how many memberships of roles individuals of a concept appear with individuals that belong to a particular concept. Three types of qualified cardinality restrictions are distinguished: *at-least qualified cardinality restrictions*, *at-most qualified cardinality restrictions*, and *exact qualified cardinality restrictions*.

Definition 3.63 An *at-least qualified cardinality restriction* ($\geq n\ r.c$) is a concept that consists of such individuals that each of them appears at least n times in role r with some individuals that belong to concept c.

For example, $woodenTable \sqsubseteq\ \geq 3\ hasLeg.woodenLeg$ means that every wooden table has at least three wooden legs.

Definition 3.64 An *at-most qualified cardinality restriction* ($\leq n\ r.c$) is a concept that consists of such individuals that each of them appears at most n times in role r with some individuals that belong to concept c.

For example, $texturedMaterial \sqsubseteq\ \leq 2\ hasSide.texturedSide$ means that every textured material has at most two textured sides.

Definition 3.65 An *exact qualified cardinality restriction* ($= n\ r.c$) is a concept that consists of such individuals that each of them appears exactly n times in role r with some individuals that belong to concept c.

For example, $spatialObject \sqsubseteq\ = 1\ hasPosition.vector$ means that every spatial object has exactly one vector that determines its position in the scene.

Domains and Ranges

Domains and ranges of roles enable the specification of what concepts of individuals the roles link.

Definition 3.66 The *domain* of a role r is such a concept that it consists of all individuals i_1 for which $r(i_1, i_2)$ holds.

The domain of role r is concept c in the following statement: $\exists r.\top \sqsubseteq c$. It means that the concept of all individuals that are in role r with some individuals (the left side of the statement) is included in concept c (the right side). For example, $\exists hasCamera.\top \sqsubseteq scene$ means that the $hasCamera$ role is used only for scenes.

Definition 3.67 The *range* of a role r is such a concept that it consists of all individuals i_2 for which $r(i_1, i_2)$ holds.

The range of role r is concept c in the following statement $\top \sqsubseteq \forall r.c$. It means that the top concept (the left side) is included in the concept of all individuals such that in every specified role r they appear with an individual of concept c

(the right side). In other words, all individuals satisfy this restriction. For example, $\top \sqsubseteq \forall hasCamera.camera$ means that the *hasCamera* role indicates only cameras.

Reflexivity

Reflexivity represents individuals that are related to themselves by a role.

Definition 3.68 A *reflexive role* is a role in which every individual appears with itself.

For a reflexive role r, the statement $\top \sqsubseteq \exists r.self$ holds. For example, $human \sqsubseteq \exists knows.self$ means that every human knows oneself.

Definition 3.69 An *irreflexive role* is a role in which no individual appears with itself.

For an irreflexive role r, the statement $\top \sqsubseteq \neg \exists r.self$ holds. For example, $\top \sqsubseteq \exists isParentObjectOf.self$ means that no object in a hierarchical 3D model can be the parent of itself.

Nominals

Nominals permit the creation of concepts by enumerating their individuals by names.

Definition 3.70 A *nominal* is a concept that consists of one individual.

Nominals can be merged by union to create an enumeration, which is the concept that consists of individuals of all the merged nominals:

$$enum \equiv \{i_1\} \sqcup \ldots \sqcup \{i_n\}, \text{ for } n \geq 1$$

For example, possible basic types of light sources in 3D scenes can be enumerated as: $lightSource \equiv \{point\} \sqcup \{directional\} \sqcup \{area\} \sqcup \{spot\} \sqcup \{omni\}$.

Role Constructors

The most important role constructor is inverse role.

Definition 3.71 A role r_1 is *inverse* to a role r_2 if and only if: $r_1(i_1, i_2)$ holds for arbitrary individuals i_1 and i_2 iff $r_2(i_2, i_1)$ holds.

It is denoted as $r_1 \equiv r_2^-$. In XR environments, the specification of inverse roles makes sense for a variety of relations. For instance, $isCameraOf \equiv hasCamera^-$.

The availability of inverse roles can improve the flexibility of representation and reasoning on environments.

Likewise for concepts, the universal and empty roles are specified. The universal role, which corresponds to the top concept, holds for all pairs of individuals in a knowledge base. The empty role, which corresponds to the bottom concept, holds for no pairs of individuals in a knowledge base.

The semantics of all the presented types of concept and role constructors, with regard to their interpretations, has been discussed in detail in Sikos (2017b). Typically, the interpretation of the result of an operation on entities is equal to the result of the operation on the entities' interpretations, e.g., $(c_1 \sqcap \ldots \sqcap c_n)^{\mathcal{I}} = c_1^{\mathcal{I}} \sqcap \ldots \sqcap c_n^{\mathcal{I}}$.

3.3.4 Reasoning Tasks in Description Logics

The constructors and possible entailments presented in the previous subsections enable automated reasoning on knowledge bases, which can be used to solve different tasks related to verification of relationships between concepts, roles, and individuals. Before the discussion of the tasks, we introduce an important relation between interpretations and knowledge bases.

Definition 3.72 An interpretation *models* a knowledge base if and only if it satisfies the TBox, RBox, and ABox of the knowledge base.

It is denoted by $\mathcal{I} \models KB$. We also say that the interpretation *is a model of* the knowledge base.

The main tasks of reasoning in description logics have been thoroughly investigated in terms of decidability and computational complexity and presented in numerous publications, e.g., Sikos (2017b). They are the following.

Instance checking is the task of verifying whether an *individual* belongs to (is an instance of) a *concept*.

Definition 3.73 An individual $a^{\mathcal{I}}$ *is an instance of* a concept $c^{\mathcal{I}}$ in a knowledge base *KB* if and only if $a^{\mathcal{I}}$ belongs to $c^{\mathcal{I}}$ in every possible interpretation $\mathcal{I}$ that models *KB*.

For example, check whether a particular game avatar (individual) is a knight (concept).

Checking *concept satisfiability* is the task of verifying whether there is at least one individual that is an instance of the concept.

Definition 3.74 A concept $c^{\mathcal{I}}$ *is satisfiable* in a knowledge base *KB* if and only if there exists an interpretation that models *KB* and its domain includes an individual that belongs to $c^{\mathcal{I}}$: $\exists \mathcal{I}: \mathcal{I} \models KB \wedge \exists a^{\mathcal{I}} \in \Delta^{\mathcal{I}}: a^{\mathcal{I}} \in c^{\mathcal{I}}$.

For example, check whether there is an avatar (individual) in the battlefield who is the king (concept).

Checking *concept subsumption* is the task of verifying whether one concept is included in another concept.

Definition 3.75 A concept $c_1^{\mathcal{I}}$ *subsumes* a concept $c_2^{\mathcal{I}}$ in a knowledge base *KB* if and only if for every interpretation that models *KB*: $c_2^{\mathcal{I}} \subseteq c_1^{\mathcal{I}}$.

For example, check whether all knights (concept) in a battlefield are horse riders (another concept).

Checking *knowledge base consistency* is the task of verifying whether no entailments of axioms included in the knowledge base are contradictory.

Definition 3.76 A knowledge base is *consistent* if and only if there exists an interpretation that models the knowledge base.

Since every interpretation represents a world, if a knowledge base is modeled by an interpretation, we know that the knowledge base is consistent. For instance, a consistent knowledge base representing a virtual training session cannot state that the training was running and finished at a particular moment.

Conjunctive query answering is the task of verifying whether a knowledge base satisfies a given query according to Definition 3.3. For example, is there such a moment in a virtual training that the instructor launches the repaired device and it starts working?

3.3.5   Families of Description Logics

Various description logics have been proposed depending on the supported constructors of concepts and roles discussed in Sect. 3.3.3, which, in turn, determine the expressivity of the logics. The supported constructors are reflected by the names of description logics, comprised of the symbols listed in Table 3.1.

The $(\mathcal{D})$ symbol is typically related to *concrete domains*, which are sets of objects with predefined semantics, e.g., numbers and dates, which are essential in multiple practical applications.

The $\mathcal{AL}$ family of description logics are appropriate for application domains that require expressive representations with reach terminology (concepts and roles, and relations between them), e.g., complex 3D scenes and behavior-rich XR environments. The $\mathcal{EL}$ family of description logics are suitable for large knowledge bases that can be built upon limited terminology. Limited expressivity, in comparison to $\mathcal{AL}$, reduces the computational complexity of common reasoning tasks. The third well-established family of description logics is *DL-LITE*, which, like $\mathcal{EL}$, do not support disjunction and universal quantification. *DL-LITE* logics have been designed to optimize the time required for processing queries to knowledge bases.

Table 3.1 Naming conventions for description logics

Symbol	Supported constructors
$\mathcal{AL}$	Attributive languages—atomic negation, concept intersection, universal quantification, and limited existential quantification
$\mathcal{C}$	Complex concept negation
$\mathcal{S}$	$\mathcal{ALC}$ with transitive roles
$\mathcal{E}$	Full existential quantification
$\mathcal{EL}$	Existential language—concept intersection and full existential quantification
$\mathcal{F}$	Functional roles, which are a special case of at-most qualified cardinality restriction ($\top \sqsubseteq \, \leq 1 \, r.c$)
$\mathcal{U}$	Concept union
$\mathcal{H}$	Role hierarchy (role inclusion)
$\mathcal{R}$	Complex role inclusion, role disjointness, reflexivity, and irreflexivity
$\mathcal{O}$	Nominals
$\mathcal{I}$	Inverse roles
$\mathcal{N}$	Unqualified cardinality restrictions
$\mathcal{Q}$	Qualified cardinality restrictions
$(\mathcal{D})$	Datatypes, datatype properties, data values
DL-LITE	Atomic negation, concept intersection, existential quantification, and inverse roles

Different description logics can be labeled using the presented symbols. For instance, the $\mathcal{SHIF}(\mathcal{D})$ description logic enables atomic negation, concept intersection, universal quantification, and limited existential quantification ($\mathcal{AL}$) with transitive roles ($\mathcal{S}$), inverse roles ($\mathcal{I}$), functional roles ($\mathcal{F}$), and datatypes ($\mathcal{D}$). The $\mathcal{SROIQ}(\mathcal{D})$ description logic extends $\mathcal{SHIF}(\mathcal{D})$ with complex role inclusion, role disjointness, reflexivity and irreflexivity ($\mathcal{R}$), nominals ($\mathcal{O}$), and qualified cardinality restrictions ($\mathcal{Q}$).

3.3.6 Spatial and Temporal Description Logics

Several description logics that enable reasoning on spatial and temporal entities have been developed. They have been extensively summarized in Sikos (2017b) in the context of modeling multimedia resources. Spatial and temporal description logics are typically created by adding some concrete domains and predicates to description logics created using the standard constructors presented in the previous subsection. However, extended expressivity is often achieved at the expense of decidability. A comprehensive survey of temporal description logics has been presented in Artale & Franconi (2001).

The $\mathcal{ALCRP}(\mathcal{D})$ description logic is $\mathcal{AL}$ extended with a concrete domain for polygons ($\mathcal{D}$). It also enables predicates based on the region connection calculus

(Randell, Cui, & Cohn 1992), e.g., disjoint, touching, overlapping, and contains. $\mathcal{ALCRP}(\mathcal{D})$ is undecidable unless some restrictions are applied to the terminology of the logic. In the paper, the authors present examples of spatial knowledge representation and reasoning.

The $\mathcal{T\text{-}ALC}$ description logic (Liu, Xu, Wang, Liu, & Zhang 2012) is $\mathcal{ALC}$ extended with time intervals. The $\mathcal{TL\text{-}ALCF}$ description logic encompasses the temporal logic $\mathcal{TL}$, which enables temporal operators (roles) proposed in Allen & Ferguson (1997), such as before, meets, overlaps, starts, during, finishes, equals as well as their inverse operators. They enable the representation of individuals that vary over time (Artale & Lutz 2004). *DL-LITE* description logics have been extended with temporal constructors such as since, until, next time, previous time, always in the future, and always in the past (Artale, Kontchakov, Ryzhikov, & Zakharyaschev 2011).

Little attention in the literature is paid to spatiotemporal description logics, which combine domains and constructors related to space and time. In Sotnykova, Vangenot, Cullot, Bennacer, & Aufaure (2005), the spatiotemporal description logic $\mathcal{ALCRP}(S_2 \oplus \mathcal{T})$ has been proposed. It provides a concrete domain (S_2) for polygons based on the region connection calculus (Randell et al. 1992). Moreover, it enables time intervals and relations between them proposed in Allen & Ferguson (1997).

3.4   Semantic Web

The Semantic Web is one of the predominant trends in the development of the current Web and the primary approach to describe the semantics of web resources of various types, such as web pages, images, audio, video, and 3D content. The research on the Semantic Web was initiated by the World Wide Web Consortium (W3C) in 2001 (Berners-Lee, Hendler, & Lassila 2001). It aims at the evolutionary development of the current Web toward a distributed database linking structured content with descriptions of its semantics. On the Semantic Web, knowledge bases describing resources are referred to as *ontologies* (cf. Definition 3.52). Ontologies are *specifications of conceptualization* encompassing *objects, concepts, and other entities that are assumed to exist in some area of interest and the relationships that hold among them* (Gruber 1995; Genesereth & Nilsson 1987). Ontologies constitute the foundation of the Semantic Web across diverse domains and applications (W3C 2020). Ontology-based description of content makes it understandable for humans and processable by computers. It enables new functionality of web-based systems, which can "understand" the meaning of particular elements of content as well as their relationships, leading to improved methods of searching, reasoning, combining, and presenting the content.

3.4.1 Standards for Building Ontologies

Resource Description Framework

The primary Semantic Web standard for building ontologies for different content types is the Resource Description Framework (RDF) (W3C 2014a). RDF is a data model that enables creation of *statements* on resources.

Definition 3.77 An *RDF statement* is an ordered triple: *(subject, predicate, object)*, where the *subject* and the *object* are resources, and the *predicate* is a binary relation.

As opposed to first-order logic statements in general, RDF statements use only binary predicates. As we did in the previous sections, also in the rest of this book, we use RDF-compliant statements based on binary predicates expressed using the Prolog-based notation: *predicate(subject, object)*.

RDF organizes the foundation for describing resources, including datatypes (e.g., HTML and XMLLiteral), blank nodes (resources with only local identifiers), containers (unconstrained structures of resources), and lists (constrained structures of resources).

RDF Schema and Web Ontology Language

The collection of entities specified by RDF is limited, which confines the expressivity of possible descriptions of resources. The RDF Schema (RDFS) (W3C 2014b) and the Web Ontology Language (OWL) (W3C 2012) are Semantic Web standards based on RDF, which significantly extend the formal semantics for RDF-based descriptions.

OWL is a language for modeling ontologies, which implements description logics. Different OWL profiles have been developed to support different constructors (cf. Sect. 3.3.3) and achieve desirable computational complexity of reasoning tasks (cf. Sect. 3.3.4). The main OWL profiles, which correspond to different description logics, are the following (W3C 2012b):

1. OWL Lite, which is based on $\mathcal{SHIF}(\mathcal{D})$,
2. OWL DL, which is based on $\mathcal{SHOIN}(\mathcal{D})$,
3. OWL 2 DL, which is based on $\mathcal{SROIQ}(\mathcal{D})$,
4. OWL 2 EL, which is based on $\mathcal{ELRO}$ (also called $\mathcal{EL}^{++}$),
5. OWL 2 QL, which is based on *DL-LITE*.

However, there are many other possible OWL profiles, which are variants of the ones above.

RDF, RDFS, and OWL provide slightly modified names of description logics' entities and constructors, summarized in Table 3.2. On the Semantic Web, *concepts* are referred to as *classes*, *roles—properties* (object and datatype properties, depending on the type of the range), *individuals* are also called *objects* and *instances* of classes, and *concrete objects* (with predefined semantics) are called *literal values*. We focus on the main fragment of the Semantic Web terminology used to express the elements of description logics presented in the previous subsection. The full specification of the notation can be found in the documentation of the Semantic Web standards. In the next chapters, we use the Semantic Web-based notation of concepts related to description logics. We believe it simplifies the implementation and practical verification of the proposed ideas.

Although description logics are underpinning OWL, it specifies a few additional features not offered by description logics. First, OWL enables keys, which are specific properties with unique values vastly used in databases to ensure the uniqueness of objects. If two individual names are associated with the same key, they indicate the same individual. Second, OWL enables annotation of entities, which resembles comments in programming and is not taken into account in reasoning. Furthermore, OWL permits import of ontologies, which facilitates exchange and reuse of entities. OWL itself does not allow for the specification of rules. However, they are enabled by the Semantic Web Rule Language (SWRL) (W3C 2004a), which is an extension to OWL. Finally, OWL-base ontologies can be queried using the SPARQL language (W3C 2013), which has syntax similar to SQL.

3.4.2   Representation of Temporal Entities

Overview of Available Approaches

Semantic temporal representation of content has been studied in the Semantic Web domain and leads to the development of several solutions. The most important of them encompass temporal description logics (cf. Sect. 3.3.6) (Artale & Franconi 2001), Temporal RDF (Gutierrez, Hurtado, & Vaisman 2005), versioning of ontologies (Klein & Fensel 2001), n-ary relations (Natasha Noy 2006), and 4D-fluents (Batsakis, Petrakis, Tachmazidis, & Antoniou 2009).

Temporal description logics, which have been presented in more detail in Sect. 3.3.6, extend OWL with concrete domains, enable time intervals and temporal predicates, such as *always* and *sometimes*. The crucial advantage of temporal description logics is the possibility of temporal reasoning on objects and properties that vary over time. The main problem with temporal description logics is undecidability and incompatibility with the primary Semantic Web standards and tools, which hinders the use of the logics in practical applications.

Another approach, Temporal RDF, extends RDF with information about time (Gutierrez et al. 2005). Every RDF triple is labeled with time, which leads to quadtuples. The main problem with this solution is that it modifies RDF in a non-standard way. It is also incompatible with RDFS and OWL, thereby its possible practical application is limited both in terms of creating ontologies with available tools as well as temporal queries and reasoning.

Table 3.2 Semantic Web terminology corresponding to description logics

Description logics	Semantic Web (RDF, RDFS, and OWL)
Concept	Class (`owl:Class`)
Individual/abstract object	Individual/object (`owl:NamedIndividual`)
Concrete object	Literal value/data (`rdfs:Literal`)
Role	Predicate/property (`rdf:Property`)
Role with an abstract object	`owl:ObjectProperty`
Role with a concrete object	`owl:DatatypeProperty`
Concept inclusion	`rdfs:subClassOf`
Concept equivalence	`owl:equivalentClass`
Role inclusion	`rdfs:subPropertyOf`
Complex role inclusion	`owl:propertyChainAxiom`
Transitive role	`owl:TransitiveProperty`
Role equivalence	`owl:equivalentProperty`
Role disjointedness	`owl:propertyDisjointWith`
Concept membership	`rdf:type`
Role membership	`ns:property`
Negated role membership	`owl:NegativePropertyAssertion`
Individual equality	`owl:sameAs`
Individual inequality	`owl:differentFrom`
Concept intersection	`owl:intersectionOf`
Concept union	`owl:unionOf`
Concept complement	`owl:complementOf`
Existential restriction	`owl:someValuesFrom`
Universal restriction	`owl:allValuesFrom`
At-least cardinality restriction	`owl:minCardinality`
At-most cardinality restriction	`owl:maxCardinality`
Exact cardinality restriction	`owl:cardinality`
Functional role	`owl:FunctionalProperty`
At-least qualified cardinality restriction	`owl:minQualifiedCardinality`
At-most qualified cardinality restriction	`owl:maxQualifiedCardinality`
Exact qualified cardinality restriction	`owl:qualifiedCardinality`
Role domain	`rdfs:domain`
Role range	`rdfs:range`
Role reflexivity	`owl:ReflexiveProperty`
Role irreflexivity	`owl:IrreflexiveProperty`
Nominals	`owl:oneOf`
Inverse role	`owl:inverseOf`

Versioning of ontologies is an approach in which new versions of an ontology are created every time the described state of affairs changes (Klein & Fensel 2001). This solution is feasible with the available semantic tools. Nevertheless, versioning of ontologies does not provide links between the successive versions of objects stored in different versions of an ontology, which prevents temporal reasoning on the objects. Also, the management of different versions of ontologies is difficult and would require additional links and software to be efficient.

In the approach based on n-ary relations, for every temporal relation, an additional object is created and linked with a time interval (Natasha Noy 2006). Furthermore, for every property that linked the primary objects, much additional data is required, including new properties and inverse properties that must be created to link the primary objects with the additional object expressing the temporal relation. Since linked to the intermediate objects, such properties have different domains or ranges than those used in the primary ontology. This approach is compatible with the available standards and tools. However, as it does not extend the semantics and possible entailments of the standards, n-ary relations do not enable temporal reasoning.

To summarize, the approaches introduce data redundancy and require remarkable changes in the available Semantic Web standards. It leads to the loss of possibilities of queries and reasoning with the standardized languages, in particular, SPARQL. For this reason, they are not implemented by the well-established tools. The problems associated with the use of these approaches have been discussed in detail in Welty & Fikes (2006), Batsakis et al. (2009).

4D-Fluents

Another solution, which avoids those shortcomings, are 4D-fluents (Welty & Fikes 2006). 4D-fluents introduce less additional data than n-ary relations, do not require extension of the primary Semantic Web standards (RDF, RDFS, OWL, SWRL, and SPARQL), and can be used with the available tools. Hence, they also respect the classes of computational complexity and possible problems that may be described and solved using OWL (W3C 2012b). Therefore, we explain 4D-fluents in more detail in this section. The definition of 4D-fluent is similar to the definition of *fluent* in the event calculus respecting the binary nature of RDF predicates.

Definition 3.78 A *4D-fluent* is an RDF predicate whose value changes over time.

The concept of 4D-fluents is depicted in Fig. 3.2. The approach specifies how to transform an RDF statement, which is time-independent, into a time-dependent statement. For example, the result of transforming an RDF statement *two objects are linked by a predicate* is statement *two objects are linked by a property at a time point or within a time interval*. It is achieved using *time slices*, which are temporal counterparts to the primary time-independent objects, associated with *time points* or *time intervals*. Due to the compatibility with the Semantic Web standards, we specify the following definitions.

Definition 3.79 *TimePoint* is the class of all *time points*.

Every time point is an instance of the *TimePoint* class.

Definition 3.80 *TimeInterval* is the class of all *time intervals*.

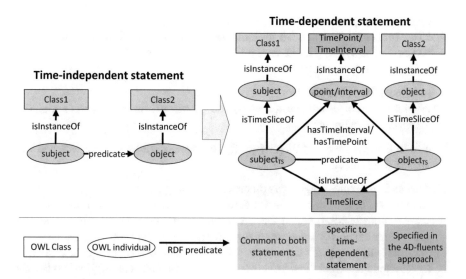

Fig. 3.2 The concept of 4D-fluents

Every time interval is an instance of the *TimeInterval* class.

Definition 3.81 A *temporal statement* is an RDF statement that is true only at some *time points* or within some *time intervals*.

Hence, predicates used in temporal statements are 4D-fluents.

Definition 3.82 A *time slice* is an individual that is an *RDF subject* or an *RDF object* in a *temporal statement*.

Definition 3.83 *TimeSlice* is the class of all *time slices*.

Every time slice is an instance of the *TimeSlice* class.

Like in first-order logic and the event calculus, time points are used to express instant states, whereas time intervals are used to express temporary states. The representation of an object with several different values of a property in different time points or intervals includes several distinct time slices of the object (one for every point/interval) that are associated with the points/intervals and are assigned the proper property values.

The following steps must be completed to add temporal information to the statement: a *subject* is linked to an *object* by a *predicate*, where the *subject* is an individual and the *object* is an individual, a class, or a literal value, such as string, integer, and float.

1. For the *subject*, create an instance of the *TimeSlice* class ($subject_{TS}$) and set the *isTimeSliceOf* object property of $subject_{TS}$ to the *subject*.
2. Set $subject_{TS}$ as instances of all the classes to which the *subject* belongs.

3. Create a *time point* or a *time interval* that is an instance of the *TimePoint* or *TimeInterval* class and set the *hasTimePoint* or *hasTimeInterval* object property of *subject*$_{TS}$ to the *time point* or the *time interval*.
4. If the *object* is an individual:

   a. Repeat Steps 1–3 for the *object*,
   b. Link *subject*$_{TS}$ and *object*$_{TS}$ by the *predicate* as the *subject* and the *object* were linked,

   else link *subject*$_{TS}$ and the *object* by the *predicate* as the *subject* and the *object* were linked.

For instance, to express that a customer was watching a car for 10 min in a virtual car showroom, create time slices for both customer and car, and link them by the *watches* predicate. Next, create the interval representing those 10 min and assign it to the time slices. The presented steps permit us to represent both unary and binary relations. Unary relations appear if *object* is an OWL class, e.g., a car was being repaired for 1 week (assignment to the *RepairedObject* class). Binary relations appear if *object* is an OWL named individual or a literal value, e.g., the speed of a train was 100 mph for 2 min.

Time Ontology in OWL

The Time Ontology in OWL (World Wide Web Consortium 2020b) has been developed to enable the temporal description of resources on the Semantic Web. The ontology specifies diverse types of *temporal entities* and relations between them, such as instants (time points), intervals, time zones as well as temporal datatypes related to days, months, and years. Semantic temporal properties can be expressed using different temporal reference systems, including the Gregorian calendar and clock.

Chapter 4
Ontology-Based Creation of Extended Reality

4.1 Role of Ontologies in Extended Reality

Knowledge-based 3D modeling has a relatively long but not very rich history. It has covered tools for designing AR applications (Feiner, Macintyre, & Seligmann 1993), the influence of semantically organized XR spaces on the users' cognition, interpretation, and interaction (Chen, Thomas, Cole, & Chennawasin 1999), modeling of historical monuments using geometrical components combined with semantic structures (Grussenmeyer, Koehl, & Nourel 1999), automatic configuration of interior scenes based on constraints (Gosele, Stuerzlinger, et al. 1999) as well as semantic representation of events and actions in XR environments (Cavazza & Palmer 2000). Although the approaches have been developed before the advent of the Semantic Web, they use schemes with domain- and application-specific concepts that could be implemented as ontologies in follow-up developments.

With the large dissemination of web-based systems, the Semantic Web has influenced XR to the largest extent of various approaches based on logical systems, which enable knowledge representation. The most recent advances in this domain are related to photogrammetry (Ben Ellefi et al. 2019), molecular visualization (Trellet, Férey, Flotyński, Baaden, & Bourdot 2018; Trellet, Ferey, Baaden, & Bourdot 2016), content description and retrieval (Sikos 2017a,b), design of industrial spaces (Perez-Gallardo, Cuadrado, Crespo, & Jesús 2017), and archeology (Drap, Papini, Sourisseau, & Gambin 2017). A comprehensive overview of ontologies, methods, and tools for 3D modeling based on the Semantic Web has been presented in the state-of-the-art report (Flotyński & Walczak 2017b). In this chapter, we present concepts and conclusions from that review that are key to ontology-based creation of XR.

Ontologies created with the Semantic Web standards: RDF, RDFS, and OWL have been mostly used to represent 3D content in XR environments. In particular, ontology-based annotation, extraction, exchange, retrieval, and creation of content

J. Flotyński, *Knowledge-Based Explorable Extended Reality Environments*,
https://doi.org/10.1007/978-3-030-59965-2_4

(De Floriani & Spagnuolo 2007; Spagnuolo & Falcidieno 2009; Latoschik & Blach 2008) have been regarded as the main issues related to modern XR environments (De Floriani & Spagnuolo 2007; Spagnuolo & Falcidieno 2009; Latoschik & Blach 2008) and an essential step toward building the 3D internet (Alpcan, Bauckhage, & Kotsovinos 2007). Research has also been conducted in ontology-based modeling of 3D content behavior and relationships between 3D models in 3D scenes (Tutenel, Bidarra, Smelik, & De Kraker 2008).

Ontologies are used in two different ways in computer graphics—to *describe* 3D content metadata and to *model* and *represent* 3D content. Ontologies used to describe content metadata (e.g., topic, author, and creation date), e.g., Arndt, Troncy, Staab, Hardman, & Vacura (2007), Arndt, Troncy, Staab, & Hardman (2009), W3C (2012a), can be considered as advanced metadata schemes (TBox and RBox) and metadata descriptions (ABox), which have been widely used, in particular, for 3D content annotation and retrieval (ARCO accessed March 24, 2015; Wojciechowski, Walczak, White, & Cellary 2004; White et al. 2004; Daras et al. 2011; Walczak, Chmielewski, Stawniak, & Strykowski 2006). In 3D modeling, ontologies comprised of TBox and RBox are typically schemes for representation of 3D scenes and components at different levels of specificity. For instance, a TBox specifies different classes of virtual museum artifacts, such as statues, stamps, and coins, while an RBox specifies spatial properties of the artifacts (Flotyński & Walczak 2016). In general, such a schema can be fulfilled by multiple 3D scenes. ABox statements usually describe particular 3D scenes and scene components. For instance, an ABox describes a particular virtual museum exhibition with artifacts located in different rooms.

In both cases—metadata description and content representation—the main advantage of ontologies over standard metadata and 3D formats is the formal semantics, which enables queries and reasoning. A ***3D ontology***, which we frequently refer in this review, is a pair of a TBox and an RBox specifying classes and properties that enable representation of 3D content at particular levels of specificity. ABox that complies with a 3D ontology is referred to as an ***ontology-based 3D representation***.

Ontologies can be used to represent 3D content *internally* and *externally*. An internal ontology-based 3D representation is associated with the primary content encoded in a specific 3D format (e.g., VRML, X3D, COLLADA). In some cases, it is syntactically built-in into the content, e.g., Flotyński & Walczak (2013c,a,d). Taking into account that the primary representation is sufficient for content visualization (includes all necessary content components), an internal ontology-based representation incorporates redundant information, e.g., Falcidieno et al. (2004), Albertoni et al. (2005). Such representations enable access to 3D content with semantic tools, in particular, in semantic annotation, search, and retrieval. For instance, an internal representation specifies such properties of 3D content as the number of triangles, vertices, and edges to facilitate its search and retrieval (De Floriani, Hui, Papaleo, Huang, & Hendler 2007). An external ontology-based content representation replaces the primary content in a 3D format or extends it by adding new content components, e.g., Bille, Pellens, Kleinermann, & De Troyer

(2004), Vasilakis et al. (2010), Albrecht, Wiemann, Günther, & Hertzberg (2011). External representations add interpretation (cf. Sect. 3.3.1) to components of 3D content. For instance, an ontology links particular meshes in 3D scenes to particular pieces of furniture in a virtual shop to enable intuitive search and presentation of domain-specific objects to customers (De Troyer, Kleinermann, Mansouri, et al. 2007).

4.2 Ontology-Based 3D Modeling

4.2.1 Concept

Ontology-based 3D modeling is performed with respect to the semantics of 3D content components, their classes, and properties, which are specified in 3D ontologies. Typically, the result of ontology-based modeling is *final 3D content* encoded in a 3D format or language (e.g., VRML, X3D, JavaScript) understandable to 3D browsers (e.g., Cortona, BS Contact, or an internet browser). Ontology-based modeling emphasizes the specification of desirable presentational effects to be achieved instead of a sequence of instructions that must be performed to achieve such effects. Hence, ontology-based 3D modeling, along with *modeling by constraints*, e.g., Xu, Stewart, & Fiume (2002), Le Roux, Gaildrat, & Caube (2004), can be regarded as a specific kind of *declarative modeling* (Gaildrat 2007)—cf. *declarative programming* explained in Sect. 3.2.5.

Ontology-based 3D modeling is a specific type of broader *semantic 3D modeling*, which has been introduced in Falcidieno & Spagnuolo (1998) as a sequence of transitions between four universes: *shape universe and knowledge domain*, *mathematical universe*, *representation universe*, and *implementation universe*. In the first universe, components of 3D content are coupled with domain knowledge to provide a *conceptual 3D world* that is represented at an arbitrarily chosen level of specificity. A conceptual world may be directly associated with an application domain, e.g., XR museum, building information models, and interior design. In the mathematical universe, a *mathematical model* is used to represent the content. For instance, terrain may be modeled using bi-dimensional scalar fields. A mathematical model may be transformed into different *representation models*, e.g., solids may be represented using constructive solid geometry or boundary representation. Finally, a representation model may be transformed into different *implementation models* (data structures), e.g., a mesh is encoded using a structure with fields containing the coordinates of the vertices. Concerning the characteristics mentioned above, semantic modeling of 3D content can be seen as an extension of geometric modeling. While in geometric modeling users employ entities that are directly related to computer graphics, in semantic modeling, users employ entities that are directly related to a selected application or domain. In semantic modeling, the linkage of such application- or domain-specific entities to graphical entities (which are necessary for final visualization) is provided in advance, or the transformation is performed transparently from the users' point of view.

Interrelating domain- or application-specific knowledge with 3D content, which occurs in semantic modeling, is one of the main elements of building intelligent XR environments, which may be explored with regard to the meaning of their components. It exceeds the capabilities of 3D formats and requires new methods of mapping domain objects onto structures of graphical components (Luck & Aylett 2000). A semantic representation of an XR environment can be created as an additional level of the application, enabling conceptual processing of 3D content at a domain-related level of specificity (Aylett & Cavazza 2001), e.g., actors, actions, and features.

4.2.2   Preliminary Steps

Ontology-based 3D modeling, in which ABox representing 3D models and scenes is created, is typically preceded by the design of a TBox and RBox, which provide a scheme for the content. The design of an ontology used for 3D modeling covers similar steps to those of the general knowledge engineering process (cf. Sect. 3.2.3): specification of a target domain, identification of applications, gathering developers' requirements for the content to be created with the ontology, identification of the critical concepts to be included in the ontology, elicitation of competency questions for the ontology, and the initial design of the ontology (Papaleo, Albertoni, Marini, & Robbiano 2005). The design of 3D ontologies is usually performed using ontology editors, such as Protégé (Stanford University 2020). The 3D modeling process is restricted by the entities specified in the used 3D ontology. The more specific to 3D graphics and animation the ontology is, the more potential use cases it has. However, such general-purpose graphical ontologies do not incorporate domain-specific elements and thereby are unsuitable for content creation by domain experts. Therefore, a 3D ontology should balance the expected level of domain representation and the level of content details that can be manipulated with the ontology. It is crucial to consider the preferences of the target users of the ontology to satisfy this requirement. Such preferences should cover the planned use cases as well as classes and properties of content components, which will enable modeling of 3D content for the intended use cases. For instance, a 3D ontology for modeling XR museum exhibitions by curators should include classes and properties of artifacts and skip entities specific to their graphical representation (Flotyński 2014).

4.2.3   Activities of Ontology-Based 3D Modeling

On the basis of the available literature, ontology-based 3D modeling can be considered as a process encompassing the following four activities: *semantic reflection, semantic selection, semantic configuration,* and *semantic transformation* of 3D content. Semantic reflection and semantic transformation are the activities in which 3D content changes the format of representation—from a format readable by 3D browsers to an ontology-based format and vice versa. These activities are necessary because 3D ontologies are not processable by the available 3D browsers. In turn, semantic selection and semantic configuration are the activities in which 3D content is modified using the entities specified in the used 3D ontology. Some approaches enable only single modeling activities, e.g., Kaloger-akis, Christodoulakis, & Moumoutzis (2006), De Floriani et al. (2007), Papaleo, De Floriani, Hendler, & Hui (2007), whereas other approaches enable several modeling activities combined into a content creation pipeline, e.g., Albrecht et al. (2011). The individual activities are described in the following subsections. 3D scenes and components represented using ontologies and 3D formats are called semantic and syntactic, respectively.

Semantic Reflection

In semantic reflection, semantic 3D components corresponding to syntactic compo-nents expressed in a 3D format are created (e.g., shapes, materials, and animations). Syntactic components may be obtained from different sources and encoded in different formats and languages (e.g., VRML, X3D, MPEG-4) (Walczak 2012a). The created semantic components are parts of an ontology-based representation, and they are typically parametrized to enable further semantic configuration, e.g., Walczak, Cellary, & White (2006). For example, some works have been devoted to reflecting different parts of a human body (Attene, Robbiano, Spagnuolo, & Falcidieno 2007) and indoor scenes (Albrecht et al. 2011). If other modeling activities follow semantic reflection, the semantic components are encoded using a common Semantic Web standard to preserve cross-compatibility in the further configuration and transformation (Walczak 2012b). Semantic components may represent different features of 3D content, such as geometry, structure, space, appearance, animation, and behavior at different levels of specificity (Flotyński & Walczak 2013a, 2014). In general, semantic components can modify, extend, and gather the meaning of their prototype syntactic components, e.g., a set of meshes reflect furniture; different textures and shininess reflect different kinds of wood (Flotyński & Walczak 2013b).

Semantic Selection

In semantic selection, semantic components are chosen for inclusion in the target 3D representation. Semantic selection indicates a subset of all semantic components that are available in a repository (Kleinermann et al. 2005; De Troyer, Kleinermann, Mansouri, et al. 2007; Kapahnke, Liedtke, Nesbigall, Warwas, & Klusch 2010). Selection is performed using entities at the specificity level determined during the reflection. The level may be either related to 3D graphics—its geometry, structure, space, appearance, animation, and behavior, e.g., Spagnuolo & Falcidieno (2008), or related to an application or domain, e.g., factory simulation (Kapahnke et al. 2010) and interior design (Albrecht et al. 2011). Semantic selection typically precedes semantic configuration in the ontology-based 3D modeling process.

Semantic Configuration

In semantic configuration, values are assigned to semantic properties of selected components, and the components are combined into an ontology-based representation that is a coherent 3D scene. Configuration is performed at the level of specificity that has been used in the previous activities. It may be related to graphics, e.g., Kalogerakis et al. (2006), related to an application or domain, e.g., Kapahnke et al. (2010), or related to both of them, e.g., De Troyer, Kleinermann, Pellens, & Bille (2007).

Semantic Transformation

In semantic transformation, configured ontology-based 3D scenes are encoded in particular 3D formats. Therefore, semantic transformation can be seen as inverse to semantic reflection. However, in contrast to reflection, transformation produces a coherent 3D representation consisting of content components with determined properties, which enables its presentation (Flotyński, Dalkowski, & Walczak 2012; Flotyński & Walczak 2014a,b). Transformation is often performed without the use of Semantic Web ontologies, e.g., Buche, Querrec, Loor, & Chevaillier (2003), Buche, Bossard, Querrec, & Chevaillier (2010), Chevaillier et al. (2012), De Troyer, Bille, Romero, & Stuer (2003). In such cases, transformation is not a part of semantic modeling. However, it is undeniably a part of a broader 3D modeling process.

Summary of Modeling Activities

In the approaches to semantic modeling that are discussed in this book, semantic reflection, selection, and configuration are performed either manually (by developers) or automatically (by specific software). Automatic reflection usually requires analysis of content components (Albrecht et al. 2011), e.g., the context of use and connections with other components. In particular, when it follows 3D content segmentation. Automatic selection and configuration are often used in contextual content adaptation, which may take into account such elements as interaction, user preferences, and profiles (Walczak, Rumiński, & Flotyński 2014).

4.2.4 Taxonomy of Ontology-Based Approaches

Numerous research works have been devoted to ontology-based representation and modeling of 3D content. The approaches vary in several aspects. In this section, a taxonomy, along with a classification of the available approaches, is presented. The taxonomy has been elaborated taking into account the aspects mentioned in the previous sections. Together with classification, it also enables identification of the main challenges and open issues in the area of knowledge-based creation of XR environments.

The taxonomy is depicted in Fig. 4.1, which has been prepared based on results presented in Flotyński & Walczak (2017b). Every approach is either a 3D *ontology* or a *method/tool* for ontology-based 3D modeling. The distinction between ontologies and methods/tools corresponds to the distinction between data representing 3D content and logic—activities and software used to create the content. The parallel branches in the taxonomy tree represent independent classification criteria, e.g., features and semantic technologies used. However, some criteria are closely related to one another, and they need to be discussed together. For instance, the discussion of specificity levels requires referring to the features represented at these levels. Such criteria have been commonly addressed in the following sections.

4.3 Ontologies of 3D Content

The classification of the ontologies based on the taxonomy is outlined in Table 4.1 prepared based on Flotyński & Walczak (2017b). In the following subsections, 3D ontologies are summarized according to the particular classification criteria (Fig. 4.1).

4.3.1 Specificity Levels and Represented Features

The semantics of 3D content components and properties may be represented at different (concrete and conceptual) levels of specificity, which is the primary distinction of 3D ontologies in the proposed taxonomy.

Concrete Representation

Concrete 3D representations are based on entities whose meaning is specific to 3D graphics and animation, e.g., texture, dimensions, coordinates, and LODs (Kalogerakis et al. 2006; Bille, Pellens, et al. 2004; Falcidieno et al. 2004; Albertoni

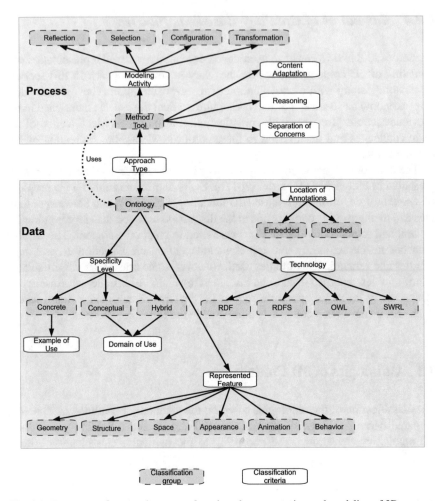

Fig. 4.1 Taxonomy of approaches to ontology-based representation and modeling of 3D content

et al. 2005; Spagnuolo & Falcidieno 2008) as well as XR environments, e.g., interfaces, markers, and models (Rumiński & Walczak 2014; Rumiński 2015). Since such ontologies specify widely accepted classes and properties of 3D content, their use is not limited to particular domains, although some of them have been presented in particular contexts, e.g., human simulation (Gutiérrez 2005; Attene et al. 2007) and tourist guide (Reitmayr & Schmalstieg 2005). Examples of use of concrete 3D ontologies are given in Table 4.1. Concrete 3D representations enable low-level access to 3D content components and properties using Semantic Web tools, such as Protégé (Stanford University 2020; Chu & Li 2008, 2012), which is not permitted by the available 3D content formats and programming languages.

In concrete representations, features of 3D content are directly described—using entities borrowed from widely used 3D content formats, languages, and libraries,

Table 4.1 Classification of 3D ontologies

Ontology	Specificity Level	Location of Annotations	Semantic Technique	Geometry	Structure	Space	Appearance	Animation	Behaviour	Domain / Example of Use
1 (De Troyer et al., 2003; Bille, Pellens, et al., 2004; Bille, 2006-2007; De Troyer, Kleinermann, Pellens, & Bille, 2007; Pellens, De Troyer, Bille, Kleinermann, & Romero, 2005)	Hybrid	Detached	OWL	✓	✓	✓	✓	✓	✓	game design
2 (Falcidieno et al., 2004; Albertoni et al., 2005; Spagnuolo & Falcidieno, 2008; AIM@SHAPE, 2017)	Concrete		OWL	✓	✓	✓	✓	✓		shape representation
3 (Gutiérrez, 2005; García-Rojas et al., 2006; Gutiérrez et al., 2007; Mortara, Patané, & Spagnuolo, 2006)	Conceptual		OWL	✓	✓	✓	✓	✓	✓	human simulation
4 (Otto, 2005b, 2005a)	Conceptual	Detached	RDFS		✓	✓				interior design
5 (Reitmayr & Schmalstieg, 2005)	Concrete		OWL	✓		✓				tourist guide
6 (Kalogerakis et al., 2006)	Concrete	Detached	OWL, Access-Limited Logic	✓	✓	✓	✓	✓		compounds, genome and cell visualization
7 (Pittarello & De Faveri, 2006)	Conceptual	Embedded	RDF		✓	✓				virtual museum
8 (Attene et al., 2007; Robbiano, Attene, Spagnuolo, & Falcidieno, 2007)	Conceptual	Detached	OWL		✓	✓				human simulation
9 (De Floriani et al., 2007; Papaleo et al., 2007)	Concrete	Detached	OWL	✓	✓	✓				shape representation
10 (Chu & Li, 2008, 2012)	Concrete		OWL	✓		✓		✓	✓	human simulation
11 (Zaid, Kleinermann, & De Troyer, 2009)	Conceptual	Detached	SWRL	✓						order process
12 (Kapahnke et al., 2010)	Conceptual	Detached, Embedded	RDFa, OWL		✓	✓				factory simulation
13 (Vasilakis et al., 2010)	Concrete		OWL	✓	✓	✓		✓		human simulation, product work-flow
14 (Albrecht et al., 2011)	Conceptual		OWL		✓	✓				interior design
15 (Latoschik & Tramberend, 2011; Wiebusch & Latoschik, 2012)	Conceptual	Detached	OWL				✓	✓		game design
16 (Flotynski & Walczak, 2013c, 2013a; Flotynski, 2013; Flotynski & Walczak, 2013d)	Hybrid	Embedded	RDFa, OWL	✓	✓	✓	✓	✓	✓	virtual museum
17 (Flotynski & Walczak, 2013b, 2014; Flotynski, 2014)	Conceptual	Detached	OWL, SWRL	✓	✓	✓	✓			interior design, virtual museum
18 (Flotynski & Walczak, 2013b, 2014; Flotynski & Walczak, 2014)	Concrete	Detached	OWL, SWRL	✓	✓	✓	✓	✓		virtual museum
19 (Flotynski, Brutzman, et al., 2019; Flotynski, Malamos, et al., 2020)	Concrete	Detached	OWL	✓	✓	✓	✓	✓		cultural heritage

such as COLLADA, X3D, and OpenGL. Therefore, concrete representations can be translated to equivalent final 3D content (Flotyński & Walczak 2013b, 2014a) (cf. Sect. 4.4.1). The features that are most frequently covered by ontologies of 3D content are geometry, structure, and space, which are inherent to all 3D models and scenes. Appearance, animation, and behavior are the less addressed features. Animation and behavior require more complex semantic description (e.g., rule-based) than other features (Zaid et al. 2009). The particular solutions are described in more detail below.

The model proposed in the AIM@SHAPE project (*AIM@SHAPE* 2017) combines 3D content with its corresponding concrete representations (Falcidieno et al. 2004; Albertoni et al. 2005; Spagnuolo & Falcidieno 2008). The model introduces four levels of content representation. The raw level covers basic properties related to such features as space and appearance, e.g., dimensions and colors. The geometric level covers diverse geometrical components, e.g., polygons, parametric surface models, and structured point sets. The structural level organizes both raw and geometrical levels by enabling, e.g., multi-resolution geometry, multi-scale models, and topological decomposition. Finally, the semantic level associates concrete content components specified at the lower levels with their semantic equivalents.

The ontology proposed in Reitmayr & Schmalstieg (2005) includes entities linking geometrical models with spatial properties. An example use of the ontology is related to the representation of buildings in a tourist guide.

The ontology proposed in De Floriani et al. (2007), Papaleo et al. (2007) permits concrete representation of non-manifold 3D shapes, e.g., a spider web on a window, an umbrella with wires, a cone touching a plane at a single point. The ontology includes such properties as the number of vertices, the number of non-manifold vertices, the number of edges, the number of non-manifold edges, and the number of connected components. The Common Shape Ontology (Vasilakis et al. 2010) also stresses the representation of shapes. It is focused on geometry, structure, and animation of 3D content and provides such entities as manifold and non-manifold shapes, point sets, hierarchically structured groups of models, position, orientation, and keyframe animations.

The ontologies described in Chu & Li (2008, 2012) enable representation of multi-user XR environments and avatars. The ontologies focus on the geometry, space, animation, and behavior of 3D content. The included entities are semantic equivalents to entities incorporated in widely used 3D content formats, such as VRML and X3D. Environmental objects, which are the main entities of 3D content, are described by translation, rotation, and scale. Avatars are described by names, statuses, and UIs, while their behavior is described by code bases.

In Flotyński, Brutzman, et al. (2019), Flotyński, Malamos, et al. (2020), an approach to generating ontology-based counterparts to available 3D formats has been proposed. The X3D Ontology (Web3D Consortium 2020a), which is a semantic equivalent of the Extensible 3D (X3D) (Web3D Consortium 2020b) format, has been presented. It gathers all concepts of X3D, including animation and interaction. The ontology has been automatically generated from the X3D XML Schema combined with the X3D Unified Object Model (X3DUOM), which complements the schema with information about classes of and relationships between X3D nodes.

Conceptual Representation

Conceptual 3D representations are based on entities whose meaning is not directly related to 3D graphics and animation, but it is specific to an application or domain, e.g., XR museum (Pittarello & De Faveri 2006) and interior design (Otto 2005b,a; Albrecht et al. 2011). Conceptual 3D representations describe content at a domain level of specificity, which is especially useful for users operating with well-known entities, e.g., Attene et al. (2007), Robbiano et al. (2007), or domain-specific entities, e.g., Kapahnke et al. (2010), without experience in computer science.

In conceptual representations, features of 3D content are indirectly described, e.g., different pieces of furniture represent different geometry (Albrecht et al. 2011). In such cases, the generation of final 3D content is performed using format-specific algorithms implemented in software, e.g., Bille, De Troyer, Kleinermann, Pellens, & Romero (2004), or it requires additional mapping of ontologies to content formats and languages to enable more generic semantic transformation (Flotyński & Walczak 2014b). Widespread demand for 3D representations that hide technical details of content has stimulated the development of ontologies for conceptual 3D representation more than ontologies for concrete and hybrid representation. The most specific solutions are described in more detail below.

Several ontologies have been designed for the representation of human body. The ontology proposed in Gutiérrez (2005), Gutiérrez et al. (2007) includes entities enabling the representation of virtual humans: geometrical descriptors of vertices and polygons, structural descriptors of articulation levels, 3D animations of face and body, and behavior controllers (animation algorithms). The extension of virtual humans with semantically represented emotional body expressions is possible by applying the ontology proposed in García-Rojas et al. (2006). The ontology is built upon the Whissel's wheel activation–evaluation space (Whissel 1989). It includes entities combining passive/active and negative/positive adjectives related to human emotions, e.g., despairing (very passive and very negative), furious, terrified and disgusted (very active and very negative), serene (very passive and very positive), exhilarated, delighted, and blissful (very active and very positive). Other ontologies of the human body have been described in Attene et al. (2007), Robbiano et al. (2007).

An ontology for conceptual 3D representation that can be used in game design has been proposed in Wiebusch & Latoschik (2012), Latoschik & Tramberend (2011). The ontology represents 3D content using actors. They are the main elements of the created scenes, which manage entities—collections of semantic properties describing different 3D models. Communication between actors is based on events and shared variables.

In Zaid et al. (2009), an OWL- and SWRL-based ontology for modeling features of 3D models in different application domains has been proposed. The ontology specifies compositions of features (conjunction and alternative), attributes of features (variables associated with features), relations between features (mandatory or optional), and constraints on features (e.g., excludes, implies, extends, equal, greater, and lesser). Furthermore, the created ontology-based 3D representations may be verified in terms of consistency, e.g., an object required by another object cannot exclude the use of that requiring object.

Hybrid Representation

Hybrid 3D representation is a combination of the previous two types of representation. It covers 3D content at both concrete and conceptual levels of specificity. Both types of representations are typically combined via a mapping (De Troyer et al. 2003; Bille, Pellens, et al. 2004; Pellens et al. 2005; Bille 2006–2007; Flotyński & Walczak 2013b; Flotyński & Walczak 2014). Therefore, the elaboration of hybrid 3D ontologies demands more effort, and it still gains little attention from the research community. Hybrid representations are convenient for 3D content that needs to be represented at different specificity levels. For instance, primitive actions (move, turn, and rotate) are combined to represent composite behaviors understandable to end users without knowledge of 3D graphics (De Troyer, Kleinermann, Pellens, & Bille 2007). The combined concrete and conceptual 3D representations proposed in Flotyński & Walczak (2014a,b) are mapped to templates encoded in 3D formats (e.g., VRML, X3D, and ActionScript), which enables automatic generation of final 3D scenes.

4.3.2 Knowledge Representation Technologies Used

Every ontology can be classified in terms of the Semantic Web technologies used for its implementation. Since the RDF, RDFS, OWL, and SWRL technologies are related to consecutive stages of the Semantic Web development, the ontologies based on the latter technologies are also based on the former ones.

The Semantic Web technologies are based on description logics (OWL) and logic programming (SWRL), which have been devised long before the advent of the Semantic Web (cf. Chap. 3). It enables reasoning on ontologies and knowledge bases on the Semantic Web. A summary of the role of different Semantic Web entities, including classes, roles, individuals, statements, and description logic constructors, in the context of 3D modeling is outlined in Table 4.2, which is based on the discussion presented in Flotyński & Walczak (2017b). The mapping between the Semantic Web entities and description logics entities has been presented in Table 3.2. The list covers the most frequently used entities in the reviewed approaches. The table provides information about the expressivity of the particular ontologies of 3D content (described in Table 4.1), which have been implemented using different Semantic Web technologies. Of course, the more description logics constructors (cf. Sect. 3.3.3) a 3D ontology supports, the more expressive the 3D representations built with the ontology are.

Table 4.2   Role of Semantic Web entities in 3D modeling

Semantic web technology	Entity	Usage	Example
RDF	rdf:Statement	Expresses properties of 3D content components.	*Mouse shape includes nose* is a statement (Robbiano et al., 2007).
	rdf:type	Assigns properties associated with classes to content components.	A *ball* is of the type entity of a *virtual world* (Wiebusch&Latoschik, 2012).
RDFS	rdfs:domain rdfs:range	Denote applicability of properties to components of a particular class.	The *hasStructuralDescriptor* property has domain *shape representation* and range *descriptor* (Vasilakis et al., 2010).
	rdfs:subClassOf rsfs:subPropertyOf	Denote inheritance of components and properties assigned to super-classes and super-properties.	*Table* and *chair* are subclasses of *furniture* in a 3D scene (Albrecht et al., 2011), thus they are made of the same material.
OWL	owl:Class	Represents content components with common properties.	Virtual *rooms* in a 3D scene are connected by a *component* of the *door* class (Kapahnke et al., 2010).
	owl:NamedIndividual	Represents a content component	
	owl:equivalentClass	Denotes an alias to a class that may be at a different specificity level.	The *painting* class is an equivalent to a class describing a *texture* on a surface.
	owl:sameAs	Denotes an alias to an component.	An avatar has multiple names.
	owl:differentFrom	Designates different components.	Artifacts in a virtual museum are different objects.
	owl:DatatypeProperty	Represents content properties described by literal values.	Components of the *Transform* have x, y and z coordinates in 3D scenes (Chu&Li, 2012).
	owl:ObjectProperty	Represents content properties content components.	*HasOutput* is an object property that links *reconstructions* to *annotated meshes* (Vasilakis et al., 2010).
	owl:TransitiveProperty	Represents structures of components linked by properties of the same semantics.	A *non-manifold* is a *mesh*, which is a *geometry*, thus a *non-manifold* is a *geometry* (Papaleo et al., 2007).
	owl:FunctionalProperty	Represents a property that has a single value.	A material has only one value of transparency.
	owl:equivalentProperty	Denotes an alias to a property that may be at a different specificity level.	The *made of* property is an equivalent to the *hasMaterial* property (Walczak et al., 2014).
	owl:inverseOf	Represents inverse properties linking components.	*Before* is inverse to *after* (De Troyer, Kleinermann, Pellens, & Bille, 2007).
	existential and cardinality restrictions	Represents obligatory sub-components in the non-empty structure of an component.	Every *loggia has some walls* (a least one) (Pittarello&De Faveri, 2006).
	universal restriction	Represents uniform structure of components, comprised of sub-components of a common class.	All *objects* in a *virtual museum room* are *placed on stands* (Walczak&Flotyński, 2014).
	owl:complementOf	Represents components that do not have some properties.	Every round *road sign* that is not an *order road sign* is white and has red circuit (Flotynski&Walczak, 2016).
	owl:intersectionOf	Represents components that inherit prop	Every round *road sign* that is blue is an *order road sign* (Flotynski, 2014).
SWRL	ruleml:Imp	Represents semantic rules (implications).	If two component properties are dependent but also exclude themselves (body), an exception is raised (head) (Zaid et al., 2009).
	ruleml:body	Represents the antecedent (premise) of a rule.	
	ruleml:head	Represents the consequent (conclusion) of a rule.	
	Built-Ins	Operations on variables and calculations.	Present only the objects between which the distance in the scene is maximal (Walczak & Flotynski, 2015).

4.3.3 Location of Semantic Annotations

Another classification criterion is the location of ontology-based annotations that constitute the 3D representation. *Detached* semantic annotations create content representations separated from the content. For example, different knowledge bases can represent separate 3D models, e.g., Kalogerakis et al. (2006). In turn, *embedded* semantic annotations are included in the represented 3D content. In comparison to detached annotations, embedded annotations are more concise, reduce specification of redundant data (e.g., object IDs in both representations), and facilitate management of content that is inextricably linked with its ontology-based representation. For instance, annotations based on RDFa (W3C 2013) may be embedded in X3D documents (Flotyński & Walczak 2013c,a,d). The majority of ontologies are used to create detached representations. The most specific embedded representations are described below.

A model combining conceptual 3D representations with X3D documents has been proposed in Pittarello & De Faveri (2006). Three types of entities are used within the ontologies to specify the relative positions of 3D models: contained, shared, and bounded. The entities are mapped to particular nodes of X3D representations using X3D nodes for metadata description (MetadataSet and MetadataString). X3D metadata nodes enable creation of ontology-based representations that are directly embedded in the 3D content.

In Kapahnke et al. (2010), conceptual representations may be either detached or embedded in the represented content. Ontology-based 3D representations are encoded in XML using the RDFa and OWL standards and linked to 3D content encoded in XML3D. Another approach using RDFa to annotate 3D documents has been proposed in Flotyński & Walczak (2013c,a,d). Ontology-based representations are directly embedded in 3D content using X3D metadata nodes and attributes. The embedded representations can be extracted from the content and combined into detached representations depending on the structure, types, and roles of the content components (Flotyński 2013).

4.4 Methods and Tools for Ontology-Based 3D Modeling

In some works, e.g., Buche et al. (2003, 2010), Chevaillier et al. (2012), the focus is on the methods and tools for 3D modeling rather than 3D ontologies, though some underlying ontologies are necessary to make the approaches working. Such methods and tools are reviewed in this section and summarized in Table 4.3, which is based on results presented in Flotyński & Walczak (2017b). Not all of the methods and tools have corresponding ontologies in Table 4.1.

A *method of ontology-based 3D modeling* is a set of generic activities accomplished sequentially or in parallel, which produce 3D content, e.g., Flotyński &

Table 4.3 Classification of methods and tools for ontology-based 3D modeling

#	Approach	Method (M)/Tool (T)	Reflection	Selection	Configuration	Transformation	Separation of Concerns	Reasoning	Content Adaptation
1	(Buche et al., 2003, 2010; Chevaillier et al., 2012)	T		✓	✓		✓		
2	(De Troyer et al., 2003; Bille, Pellens, et al., 2004; Bille, De Troyer, et al., 2004; Bille et al., 2005; Kleinermann et al., 2005; Mansouri, 2004-2005; Pellens et al., 2005; De Troyer, Kleinermann, Pellens, & Bille, 2007; De Troyer, Kleinermann, Mansouri, et al., 2007)	M		✓	✓		✓		
3	(Gutiérrez, 2005; Gutiérrez et al., 2005)	M				✓			-
4	(Coninx et al., 2006; Pellens et al., 2006; Pellens, 2006-2007; Vanacken et al., 2007; Pellens et al., 2008, 2009)	T			✓				-
5	(Kalogerakis et al., 2006)	M			✓			✓	-
6	(Attene et al., 2007; Robbiano et al., 2007; Attene et al., 2009)	M	✓					✓	-
7	(Bilasco et al., 2007)	M,T		✓	✓				✓
8	(De Floriani et al., 2007; Papaleo et al., 2007)	M	✓						-
9	(Lugrin & Cavazza, 2007; Lugrin, 2009)	T			✓		✓	✓	-
10	(Kapahnke et al., 2010)	T		✓	✓		✓		
11	(Albrecht et al., 2011)	M	✓	✓	✓		✓	✓	
12	(Fischbach et al., 2011; Latoschik&Tramberend, 2011;Wiebusch&Latoschik, 2012)	T		✓	✓				
13	(Cao&Klusch, 2013; Zinnikus et al., 2013)	M	✓						-
14	(Flotynski & Walczak, 2013b; Flotynski & Walczak, 2013a, 2014; Flotynski, 2014; Flotynski & Walczak, 2014, 2014)	M	✓	✓	✓	✓	✓	✓	
15	(Walczak & Flotynski, 2014; Walczak et al., 2014; Flotynski&Walczak, 2015;Walczak & Flotynski, 2015)	M,T		✓	✓			✓	✓
16	(Pelkey & Allbeck, 2014)	T	✓						-
17	(Flotynski & Sobocinski, 2018a; Flotynski & Nowak, 2019; Flotynski, Englert, et al., 2019)	M	✓					✓	-

Walczak (2014). Typically, in the activities, 3D ontologies are used. Some activities may be performed manually—by a human using specific hardware or software tools, while other activities may be performed automatically—by software. For instance, a graphic designer can perform content reflection, while a query-processing engine can perform content selection (Walczak & Flotyński 2015; Flotyński & Walczak 2016).

A tool for ontology-based 3D modeling is a set of interconnected software modules that permit interaction with users as well as storage, retrieval, and processing of knowledge bases in order to produce 3D content. For instance, a modeling tool may be based on the client–server architecture with a client based on a 3D browser and a server comprised of several services, e.g., Kapahnke et al. (2010). Tools implement methods of modeling, but in several works, methods are not explicitly presented as the focus is on software modules instead of the activities performed by the modules to produce 3D content. In the following sections, methods and tools of ontology-based 3D modeling are summarized according to the particular classification criteria.

4.4.1 Supported Modeling Activities

Methods and tools are classified in terms of the supported modeling activities, which may be one or several of semantic reflection, semantic selection, semantic configuration, and semantic transformation (cf. Sect. 4.2.3). Several supported activities within a method or a tool form a content creation pipeline, e.g., Bille, De Troyer, et al. (2004), Bille et al. (2005), Kleinermann et al. (2005).

The methods and tools usually support only subsets of all the modeling activities. The largest group encompasses approaches supporting content selection and configuration. The second group comprises approaches that support only semantic reflection and do not support other modeling activities. Semantic transformation gains little attention from the research community. The most specific solutions are described in more detail below.

The method proposed in De Troyer et al. (2003), Bille, Pellens, et al. (2004), Bille, De Troyer, et al. (2004), Bille et al. (2005), Kleinermann et al. (2005), Mansouri (2004-2005), Pellens et al. (2005), De Troyer, Kleinermann, Pellens, & Bille (2007), De Troyer, Kleinermann, Mansouri, et al. (2007) enables content selection and configuration at the conceptual level using domain-specific ontologies, which are mapped to a concrete 3D ontology. The method proposed in Flotyński & Walczak (2013a) also uses mapping between 3D ontologies at the concrete and conceptual levels. The method also enables semantic reflection, in which reusable semantic 3D content components and properties are created, and semantic transformation. Final 3D content, which can be encoded in different languages (e.g., VRML, X3D, and ActionScript), is automatically generated by linking templates of code in particular languages to statements included in the ontology-based 3D representation. The transformation is described by an ontology indicating templates of code and their corresponding statements.

The method proposed in De Floriani et al. (2007), Papaleo et al. (2007) enables reflection of non-manifold 3D shapes using concrete 3D properties. The method reflects geometrical properties of shapes: non-manifold singularities (e.g., isolated points and curves), one-dimensional parts, connected components, and maximally connected components. Once identified, the properties are mapped to a shape ontology and form a concrete ontology-based 3D representation of the shape.

In some works, semantic reflection is performed after content segmentation, in which different components of the content are distinguished based on their properties (geometry, colors, and relative positions). In Attene et al. (2007, 2009), Robbiano et al. (2007), after automatic segmentation of 3D content, the distinguished components are semantically reflected. Two modes of reflection have been developed. Automatic reflection is performed by software considering topological relations between content components (e.g., orientation, size, adjacency, and overlapping). Manual reflection is performed by a user equipped with a graphical tool. Moreover, an example of semantic reflection based on an ontology of the human body is presented.

The method of modeling 3D content based on point clouds proposed in Albrecht et al. (2011) involves several activities. First, in semantic selection, an input point cloud is analyzed to discover planar patches, properties (e.g., locations), and relationships. Then, a reasoner processes a domain-specific ontology including conceptual elements that potentially match the analyzed patches. Next, matching elements are selected and configured to build a conceptual representation. The created representation is an ontology-based equivalent to the input point cloud.

In the Simulator X (Fischbach et al. 2011; Latoschik & Tramberend 2011; Wiebusch & Latoschik 2012), the selection of 3D content elements is performed by a user. The selected elements (actors and entities) are configured using state variables, which can be shared by different actors in the content.

iRep3D (Cao & Klusch 2013; Zinnikus et al. 2013) enables semantic reflection of 3D models by analyzing its syntactic, conceptual, functional, and geometrical features. The method is used for 3D models encoded in X3D, XML3D, and COLLADA.

4.4.2   3D Content Adaptation

The methods and tools that implement several modeling activities can be classified in terms of *support for 3D content adaptation*. The methods and tools supporting content adaptation enable 3D modeling with respect to individual users' preferences expressed in ontology-based queries (Bilasco et al. 2007; Walczak & Flotyński 2014). Ontology-based adaptation facilitates sharing and reusing content in comparison to modeling 3D content from scratch. Content adaptation can be performed across the whole modeling process and can affect the results of different modeling activities. The methods and tools that do not support content adaptation enable modeling of content in its final form, in which it will be presented to end users, e.g., De Troyer et al. (2003), Bille, Pellens, et al. (2004), Bille, De Troyer, et al. (2004), Bille et al. (2005), Kleinermann et al. (2005), Mansouri (2004-2005), Pellens et al. (2005), De Troyer, Kleinermann, Pellens, & Bille (2007).

Currently, few approaches permit content adaptation. In 3DAF (Bilasco et al. 2007), once queries are issued by users invoking methods of the communication interface, the invocations are translated into SQL-like queries and processed by a query manager. Next, 3D components are retrieved from an annotation repository, and a final 3D scene is generated. For example, trees are excluded from a 3D scene, and the geometry of buildings in the scene is simplified.

In Walczak et al. (2014), Walczak & Flotyński (2015), Flotyński & Walczak (2016), selection and composition of content are performed in response to users' queries. Queries are ontologies that are—on demand—combined and processed with generalized ontology-based 3D representations (3D meta-scenes). The method has been implemented as a service-oriented tool based on Blender (Flotyński & Walczak 2015; Walczak & Flotyński 2015; Flotyński & Walczak 2016). In the other analyzed approaches, 3D content is created in its final form without possibilities of further adaptation. An ontology-based approach to semantic contextual personalization of virtual stores has been presented in Walczak, Flotyński, & Strugała (2019).

4.4.3   Reasoning in 3D Content Creation

Due to the use of ontologies, every method and tool can be classified in terms of the *support for reasoning* in the modeling process. In case of methods and tools that do not support reasoning on 3D representations, final 3D content is based only on the statements explicitly specified while modeling. For instance, in De Troyer et al. (2003), Bille, Pellens, et al. (2004), the mapping of domain-specific entities to 3D-specific entities is explicitly specified and further used in modeling. In case of methods and tools that support reasoning, final 3D content is based on the explicit and implicit (inferred) statements. For instance, in Kalogerakis et al. (2006), software processes rules and statements to visualize a planetary system using inferred knowledge.

Although reasoning is one of the Semantic Web principles, this is still used in less than a half of the approaches. The approaches that support reasoning require less users' effort in modeling than the approaches that only make use of the explicit knowledge, like in the case of typical metadata (Flotyński & Walczak 2014; Walczak & Flotyński 2019). For instance, in Lugrin & Cavazza (2007), Lugrin (2009), ontology-based representations of events and actions are used to infer their effects in 3D scenes. The approach proposed in Flotyński & Sobociński (2018a), Flotyński & Nowak (2019), Flotyński, Englert, et al. (2019) uses reasoning to investigate customers' interests and preferences in virtual showrooms and to classify stages of city design processes. Moreover, such approaches are more flexible in terms of which users define which statements for the content.

4.4.4 Separation of Concerns in 3D Content Creation

Encompassing different modeling activities and enabling 3D representation at different specificity levels usually permits separation of concerns between different modeling users. Such users may have different skills and experience and be equipped with different hardware and software tools, e.g., ontology editors, graphical editors, and scanners. For instance, basic content components may be scanned, manipulated, and mapped to high-level entities by a developer; next, the high-level entities may be used to create 3D representations by a domain expert (Walczak et al. 2014; Flotyński & Walczak 2015).

In a few of the available approaches, the modeling process is separated into activities that may be accomplished by different users. Examples are the methods of ontology-based modeling with mapping between concrete and conceptual specificity levels (Bille, De Troyer, et al. 2004; Bille et al. 2005; Kleinermann et al. 2005; Flotyński & Walczak 2013a, 2014). In the methods, conceptual 3D representations are created by domain experts equipped with domain ontologies, while concrete 3D representations are created by graphic designers.

Separation of concerns is addressed more often in tools than in methods of modeling. In tools, different modeling activities are typically related to different software modules, which, in turn, can be used by users with different skills in 3D modeling. In MASCARET (Buche et al. 2003, 2010; Chevaillier et al. 2012), selection and configuration of 3D components are performed by experts in the Semantic Web and computer graphics equipped with a 3D modeling tool.

In the simulation tool presented in Lugrin & Cavazza (2007), Lugrin (2009), the Unreal Tournament game engine (for rigid-body physics and content presentation), a reasoner (for updating 3D scenes upon events occurrence) and a behavioral engine (for recognizing actions and changing objects in conceptual terms) are used. Combining different engines within one tool creates opportunities for separation of concerns between users with different skills.

An example of a division of responsibilities between different software modules in a client–server architecture has been presented in Kapahnke et al. (2010). The tool leverages semantic entities, services, and hybrid automata to describe the behavior of 3D components. The client is based on a 3D content presentation tool, e.g., an XML3D browser, while the server is built of several services enabling content selection and configuration. A graphical module maintains and renders 3D scene graphs. A scene module manages global scene ontologies, which represent the created simulations. A verification module checks spatial and temporal requirements against properties of content components. An agent module manages intelligent avatars, e.g., their perception of the scene. The user interface communicates with web-based and immersive XR reality platforms.

4.5   Open Challenges

The following conclusions may be drawn from this survey. 3D ontologies form a shared space for representing the semantics of 3D content at concrete and conceptual levels of specificity. Ontologies are used within methods and tools for modeling 3D content. The available methods and tools typically do not cover the whole modeling process but enable only selected modeling activities. The available approaches still do not fully benefit from the possibilities of knowledge inference from content representations, and many of them use ontologies like metadata descriptions of 3D components and scenes.

Some problems may be indicated in the field of ontology-based representation and modeling of 3D content. The creation of a TBox and an RBox is the preliminary step that must be finished before 3D content can be semantically modeled. In specific applications and domains, it may be challenging to find appropriate ontologies that provide entities sufficient for the analyzed area and use cases. In such cases, it may be necessary that content authors are also involved in the creation of the appropriate ontology. Another limit in the use of 3D ontologies are frequently changing use cases for which 3D content should be created. In such cases, the elaborated TBox and RBox may be used few times, making their creation unreasonable. Finally, exponential computational complexity in case of modeling based on some reasoning tasks and families of description logics (cf. Sects. 3.3.4 and 3.3.5) may significantly increase the time required for modeling, making the solution intractable.

So far, hybrid 3D representation has gained less attention. Hybrid representation enables more flexible 3D content creation and management (indexing, searching, and analyzing) in comparison to separated concrete and conceptual 3D representations because it combines these two specificity levels and benefits from the synergy of such multi-level content representation.

Likewise, the inference of implicit knowledge from ontology-based 3D representations is hardly used. It can potentially reduce the time and costs of modeling by liberating users from specifying all components of the created 3D content.

Only a few of the available methods and tools permit semantic transformation of content to different 3D formats languages. In contrast to syntactic transformation, semantic transformation can potentially provide better results by taking into account the meaning of particular content components and properties, e.g., transformation of selected functional subsets of ontology-based 3D scenes.

Other related ideas are automatic reflection of semantic representations from 3D content, semantically oriented content synthesis, documenting the life cycle of 3D models as well as semantically described visualization and interaction with 3D content (Catalano, Mortara, Spagnuolo, & Falcidieno 2011).

Chapter 5
E-XR: Explorable Extended Reality Environments

The main contribution of this book is the *E-XR approach to creation of explorable XR environments*. The approach addresses challenges that are discussed in Sect. 5.1 in the context of limitations of the available approaches to XR development. The challenges provide the main motivations for this work and determine functional and non-functional requirements for the E-XR approach, which are specified in Sect. 5.2.

5.1 Problem Statement

The increasing involvement of experts and users in the development of IT systems in different domains as well as the rapid progress of XR, artificial intelligence, and the Web demands new approaches to the creation and functionality of XR environments. The new solutions should reflect the need for collaboration of multiple users with different knowledge, skills, requirements, interests, and preferences, who access environments directly or indirectly—using intermediate systems. In this regard, the available approaches to XR development have serious deficiencies limiting their possible applications. The following subsections summarize different approaches regarding the essential criteria discussed in Chaps. 2–4. The summary is outlined in Table 5.1.

5.1.1 Domain Terminology in XR Environments

The available approaches require knowledge of technical concepts specific to 3D graphics and animation, or they are limited to a particular application or domain without the possibility to be used in other applications and domains. The available

© The Author(s), under exclusive license to Springer Nature Switzerland AG 2020
J. Flotyński, *Knowledge-Based Explorable Extended Reality Environments*,
https://doi.org/10.1007/978-3-030-59965-2_5

Table 5.1 Summary of approaches to XR development in the context of explorable XR

Approach \ Criteria	Domain terminology	Declarative	On-demand XR composition	XR behavior representation	Knowledge exploration
3D formats	-	✓	-	-	-
Object-oriented programming	✓	-	-	-	-
3D modeling tools	-	✓	-	-	-
Game engines	✓	-	-	-	-
Knowledge-based technologies	✓	✓	-	-	✓
Semantic 3D content	✓	✓	-	-	✓

solutions do not enable flexible—applicable to different domains—connection between users' and 3D objects' properties, and domain terminology.

Although object-oriented programming languages, which are used in multiple game engines (cf. Chap. 2), enable representation of 3D content with domain-specific terminology, such as classes and properties, they do not offer standardized solutions for knowledge exploration with reasoning and queries (discussed in Sect. 5.1.5). It is an important deficiency for practical usage of these solutions.

In comparison to object-oriented programming languages, declarative programming languages, description logics, and the Semantic Web approach (cf. Chap. 3) are more suitable for domain knowledge representation as they leverage widely known algorithms for reasoning and query processing together with query languages (cf. Chap. 3). However, these technologies have not been employed for development of behavior-rich XR environments so far.

XR development with domain terminology opens new opportunities for creating and using XR by domain experts, who rarely have advanced technical skills. In addition, knowledge-based XR environments can also foster application of analytical systems that process domain knowledge yet are incapable of extracting it from XR on their own. For instance, marketing specialists can use analytical tools to investigate customers' behavior based on the information provided by XR stores.

5.1.2   Declarative Specification of XR Behavior

The available solutions use technical concepts to design XR behavior (e.g., keyframes and interpolation) or require imperative programming of instructions that must be executed to achieve desirable goals. Both solutions are strictly related to computer science, including 3D graphics, animation, and programming.

3D formats, such as VRML, X3D, and XML3D (cf. Sect. 2.2.2), enable specification of desirable 3D effects, as opposed to imperative programming languages and libraries, which express steps of processing (cf. Sect. 2.2.1). However, they use 3D-specific concepts and are unsuitable for domain knowledge representation. This problem also applies to 3D modeling tools and game engines (cf. Sect. 2.2.3), which use such 3D formats and also enable modeling of animations with state diagrams. Unlike 3D formats, knowledge representation technologies (cf. Chap. 3) and approaches to semantic 3D content (cf. Chap. 4) enable declarative specification of requirements and goals, thus being a potential candidate for development of explorable XR environments.

Declarative syntax of 3D formats and knowledge representation technologies, including logic programming, description logics, and the Semantic Web, is relatively simple compared to imperative syntax in terms of the available instructions. Therefore, it could facilitate the development of visual domain-oriented modeling tools, which are comprehensible to non-IT specialists. For example, basic animations of dancing figures could be composed into a complex sequence in a declarative visual way using a knowledge-based behavior editor.

5.1.3   On-Demand Composition of XR Environments

The available approaches do not enable efficient on-demand composition of customized XR environments. 3D content formats (cf. Sect. 2.2.2) and programming languages (cf. Sect. 2.2.1) have been designed for developing XR environments in their final form, without special support for 3D content customization. Likewise, 3D modeling tools and game engines (cf. Sect. 2.2.3) enable modeling and design of environments in their final form.

On-demand composition could be especially useful for distributed collaborative web-based XR environments. Such environments are accessed ad hoc by different users with different knowledge, skills, expectations, interests, and preferences, who want to use XR for different purposes. For instance, different guides presenting different functions of appliances can be composed on demand for different target groups of users—customers, service technicians, and salesmen.

5.1.4   Representation of Past, Current, and Future XR Behavior

The available solutions do not enable knowledge-based comprehensive representation of XR behavior, incorporating users' and objects' past, current as well as possible future actions and interactions. Although a variety of knowledge representation technologies are available, yet their potential has not been used to build XR environments.

Representation of past, current, and possible future behavior of XR environments could incorporate logs of demonstrated behavior as well as the specification of potential behavior. Hence, XR environments could be explored within simulations without the need to run. It can enable efficient analysis of behavior descriptors stored in shared repositories. For instance, medical students can watch and learn about the consecutive parts of virtual surgery and ask about possible faults at particular stages.

5.1.5   *Knowledge Exploration in XR Environments*

The available knowledge-based approaches to development of XR do not enable exploration of temporal users' and 3D objects' properties with reasoning and queries about different moments and periods in time. Metadata frameworks in the available 3D formats and tools offer no strict formalism of classes, individuals, and relations between them, which limits their expressivity and accuracy. Thereby, unstructured and semi-structured metadata are unsuitable for unambiguous reasoning as well as complex and precise queries, which narrows their possible practical applications.

Furthermore, object-oriented languages, which can represent users and 3D objects with domain-specific terminology, are intended for programming workflow and unsuitable for knowledge representation and exploration. It is a noticeable difference compared to logic-based approaches. The object-oriented approach demands the explicit implementation of additional software functions for knowledge exploration. It typically requires advanced technical skills, which hinders contribution from domain experts, whose knowledge is essential to the development of the environment. Moreover, special effort is needed to decouple the new functions responsible for knowledge exploration from the previous functions responsible for XR management, e.g., by refactoring the former code and applying apt design patterns. It may be time consuming and expensive, especially if an environment must be extended by programmers who have not developed it.

Exploring users' and objects' behavior can be valuable in multiple application domains to acquire knowledge about users' experience, preferences, and interests, characterize 3D objects, and understand objects' actions and interactions. Reasoning has essential advantages in the context of developing XR environments. First, it enables the authors to focus on fundamental features of the environment while skipping features that can be implicated by the fundamentals. For example, classifying a man as a crowd member imposes his behavior to be similar other crowd members' behavior. Second, it allows XR users to infer arbitrarily rich knowledge about the environment when combining the environment with additional, contextual knowledge bases provided independently of the original one associated with the environment. For instance, an educational XR garden can be used to reason about the development of different plants and animals living there using various knowledge bases attached to particular courses. In turn, queries can enable flexible access to users' and 3D objects' properties using complex and precise conditions while skipping properties irrelevant to a particular use case. Content exploration with reasoning and queries can be especially useful to develop shared (e.g., web-based) explorable XR environments. For example, repositories of interactive 3D cars can be queried for particular models demonstrating the behavior of specific new components.

5.2   Requirements

Taking into account the limitations of the available approaches in the context of building XR environments mentioned in Sect. 5.1, functional and non-functional requirements for the E-XR approach have been stated. The requirements emphasize representation and exploration of behavior, which encompasses users' and 3D objects' actions and interactions, as these aspects receive particularly little attention in the projects and literature devoted to XR development (cf. Chaps. 2–4).

5.2.1   Functional Requirements

Functional Requirement 1: Knowledge-Based Representation of XR Behavior Oriented to Domain Semantics

Wide use of XR demands domain experts' involvement in the XR development process, which requires focus on domain knowledge and semantics of objects rather than technical concepts. The approach should be general (application and domain independent), yet applicable to different applications and domains when equipped with specific terminology. Features as well as the behavior of users and objects should be represented using domain knowledge. For instance, 3D objects in a VR store represent interacting virtual customers and products, which hides the technical specificity of both agents and objects.

Functional Requirement 2: Declarative Specification of Behavior in the XR Development Process

The XR development process should focus on the specification of domain requirements to be met and goals to be achieved rather than processing steps to be accomplished in a particular order. The goal-oriented approach can facilitate the implementation of visual tools, thereby mitigating XR development and making it more attainable to non-IT specialists. For example, to repair a VR cooker, a service technician must exchange its fan and controller, which are independent activities to be done in any order.

Functional Requirement 3: On-Demand Composition of XR Behavior

The on-demand composition of behavior can be considered as the process of building customized environments that satisfy individual requirements of users and services. Such requirements can cover the selection of 3D objects, their properties, and behavior. For instance, animated training guides can be composed of selected exercises with specific equipment. The results of behavior composition should be suitable for further indexing, searching, and processing by search engines and analytical tools.

Functional Requirement 4: Representation of the Past, the Current, and the Potential Future XR Behavior

The approach should enable the representation of past, current, and possible future users' and 3D objects' behavior. XR behavior can include any kind of autonomous activities of users and objects as well as arbitrary interactions between users, users and objects, and between different objects. Users' and objects' behavior should be logged (registered) in a form that enables its further presentation and knowledge-based exploration, thereby allowing environment users to watch past and current actions and interactions and gain knowledge about them. Possible environment behavior should be known in advance, including potential states and events that can occur as well as the necessary conditions. For instance, a VR gym training represents demonstrated exercises, lasting exercises as well as potential exercises, including their names and duration, which are available for searching and analyzing, as well as interactions between avatars in the exercises.

Functional Requirement 5: Knowledge-Based Exploration of XR Behavior

The approach should enable exploration of environment behavior, including reasoning on and queries to ontologies and rule sets describing past, current, and possible future users' and objects' actions and interactions. For example, customers of VR stores can be classified according to their preferences inferred from selecting products while shopping.

Functional Requirement 6: Development of New as well as Transformation of Existing XR Environments

The approach should enable building new XR environments and transformation of existing environments into the explorable form. In case of transformation, the original functionality of the environment should be maintained.

5.2.2 Non-functional Requirements

Non-functional Requirement 1: Compatibility with Prevalent Tools and Languages

It should be possible to integrate the approach with prevalent imperative programming languages, libraries, 3D modeling tools, and game engines. Although the available solutions are continually evolving, integration at the conceptual and general implementation levels should be possible. Such levels are mostly immutable to a variety of solutions. In particular, the approach should extend the dominant solutions, which are development environments that enable XR creation using imperative programming languages.

Non-functional Requirement 2: Low Delay in Logging XR Behavior While Using XR Environments

The environment behavior should be logged systematically while the environment is running—with minimal delay between actions and interaction occurred and their registration in behavior logs. Minimal delay might permit systematically tracking of behavior logs, the flexibility of using logging functions in the same or distinct threads with XR rendering and control, and optimization for use over networks.

Non-functional Requirement 3: Maintaining Performance of the Original XR Environments

The impact of extending XR environments on their performance, in particular FPS, should be minimized. Furthermore, adding new functions should introduce minimal redundancy and modifications to the original implementation. The complexity of introducing potential future extensions of the environment should be maximally reduced. Moreover, the increase in the overall environment size after injecting the additional code should be minimized. These are to minimize the programmers' effort, time spent, and risk of undesirable side effects for the primary presentation and behavior of the environment.

Non-functional Requirement 4: Efficient Reasoning and Query Processing

Reasoning and query processing on the behavior of XR environments should satisfy important properties that are well known in the domain of logical systems. The approach should enable the application of sound and complete reasoning algorithms. In addition, main tasks of reasoning should be decidable with limited computational complexity.

5.3 Concept and Scope

The main contribution of this book is the *E-XR approach to creation of explorable XR environments*. The approach is a solution to the problems described in Sect. 5.1, which satisfies the requirements specified in Sect. 5.2. The E-XR approach is a set of formal data and workflow models as well as methods and algorithms for creating explorable XR environments and exploring such environments. The approach is on the intersection of the following main disciplines in computer science:

1. Extended reality, in particular: interactive and component-based environments;
2. Artificial intelligence: knowledge representation and exploration, logic programming, description logics, and Semantic Web;
3. Software design and development: modular and service-oriented architectures as well as imperative object-oriented and procedural programming;
4. Data engineering and data modeling: rule sets, ontologies, and knowledge bases.

The main aspects of the concept as well as the scope of E-XR are presented in Fig. 5.1. Explorable XR environments are XR systems based on interrelated knowledge and visualization related to particular application domains. Explorable environments allow for knowledge exploration and visualization with reasoning and queries. Knowledge exploration covers users' and objects' behavior at different moments and in different periods, including past, current, and possible future behavior. Users' and objects' activities include arbitrary autonomous actions and interactions. In general, subject to exploration may be time-dependent and time-independent properties of XR users and objects and their arbitrary elements. Users and objects as well as their elements can be given domain-specific semantics that hides their 3D-specificity, including geometry, structure, space, appearance, and animation. Reasoning enables inference of tacit knowledge, which has not been explicitly specified by the environment authors, to make it available for exploration along with the explicitly specified knowledge. The collected knowledge may be a target for queries, which enable selection of elements and properties that are interesting in a particular use case while filtering out irrelevant knowledge. In E-XR, exploration is possible due to the use of knowledge representation specific to a particular application domain for which the environment has been created. The employed knowledge representation technologies are programming in first-order logic and the Semantic Web, derived from description logics.

To enable the creation of explorable XR environments, we propose new structured models that specify formal semantics for data and workflow and use them for XR development and exploration. We propose a development pipeline, in which explorable XR environments are composed of reusable service-oriented XR components. XR components include geometrical shapes, hierarchical objects, spatial properties, presentational elements, and animations. They may be prepared using 3D and animation modeling tools as well as game engines. The basic requirement for the design of XR components is object-oriented or procedural implementation and interface, which enable the combination of the components by invoking their methods. Due to the composition, explorable environments are customized to their authors' demands, reflecting expected functionality, use cases, and needs of potential users. Possible application and usage of explorable XR environments is broad and covers: monitoring, analyzing, comprehending, examining and controlling users' and objects' behavior, analysis of users' skills, experience, interests, and preferences as well as features of XR users and objects.

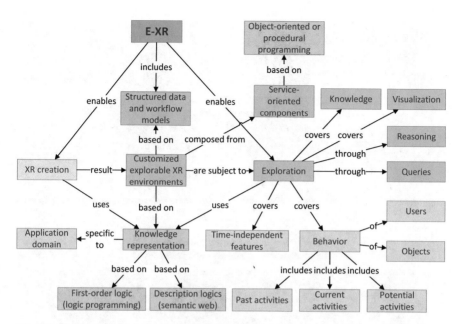

Fig. 5.1 The concept and scope of E-XR approach

5.4 Architecture

The E-XR approach consists of four main elements, which correspond to the goal of this book and form a stack (Fig. 5.2). Every element that is higher in the stack is built upon the lower elements. The foundation is technologies for knowledge representation and imperative programming. On their basis, we have elaborated structured data and workflow models, which are used by the proposed method and algorithms for the development of XR environments. Finally, the created environments can be used by the methods and algorithms for knowledge exploration that we propose. The main elements of E-XR are the following:

1. The *visual knowledge-based behavior model* enables representation of the behavior of XR components and environments as well as their time-independent properties, which express immutable features of the environments. The behavior of an XR environment covers activities of its users and objects. The model consists of two main elements based on distinct knowledge representation technologies, which differ in expressivity. Therefore, they are used by different elements located higher in the E-XR architecture stack.

   a. The *ontology-based component for behavior representation* provides the foundation for representing the behavior of explorable XR environments. The component encompasses classes and properties specified in ontologies

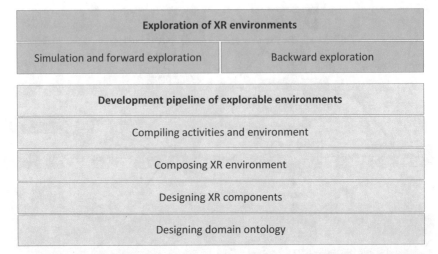

Exploration of XR environments	
Simulation and forward exploration	Backward exploration

Development pipeline of explorable environments
Compiling activities and environment
Composing XR environment
Designing XR components
Designing domain ontology

Semantic link model				
Representation of activities and features		Workflow representation	Mapping		Code templates
Activity ontology	Activity knowledge bases		Class mapping	Event mapping	
Object-oriented and procedural programming languages					

Visual knowledge-based behavior model			
Ontology-based component			Rule-based component
Domain ontologies	Fluent ontology	Visual semantic behavior logs	Fluent rule set
Description logics and semantic web			Programming in first-order logic

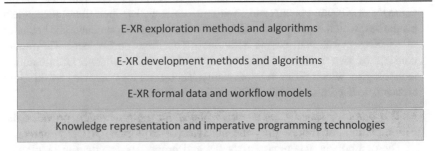

E-XR exploration methods and algorithms
E-XR development methods and algorithms
E-XR formal data and workflow models
Knowledge representation and imperative programming technologies

Fig. 5.2 Architecture of E-XR approach with technology stack and main elements

based on Semantic Web standards, which implement description logics. The component consists of three main elements:

  i. *Domain ontologies*, which are formal specifications of conceptualization of particular application domains for which explorable XR environments are created.
  ii. The *fluent ontology*, which specifies domain-independent classes and properties of temporal entities as well as relations between them. The ontology also specifies entities for the visual representation of the behavior of XR components and environments. The ontology enables visualization interrelated with knowledge exploration.
  iii. Specification of *visual semantic behavior logs*, which represent knowledge about and visualization of users' and objects' behavior demonstrated during sessions of using explorable XR environments.

  b. The *rule-based component for behavior representation* provides complex relations between temporal entities specified in the *fluent ontology* of the *ontology-based component*. In particular, the component enables transitions between events and states, which are essential to describe the behavior of XR components and environments. The entities and relations are specified in the *fluent rule set*. The rule set has been specified using logic programming, which enables relations between properties of individual objects.

2. The *semantic link model* enables connection of the *visual knowledge-based behavior model* with object-oriented and procedural XR implementations. Imperative programming languages and libraries, which enable implementation of XR, are the second key group of technologies employed by E-XR, besides knowledge representation technologies. The goal of the semantic link model is to enable knowledge representation with its full potential while maintaining the possibility to develop XR using object-oriented and procedural programming, which is the prevalent solution in this area. The model consists of a few elements devised for different purposes:

  a. The *representation of activities and features*, which enables annotation of imperative object-oriented and procedural XR implementations to make them suitable for composition and exploration. The annotated elements of implementations are classes, methods, parts of methods as well as variables. The representation is specified by the *activity ontology*, which is used to create *activity knowledge bases* describing particular XR components and environments.
  b. The *workflow representation*, which enables the imperative implementation of XR components and environments to be represented by the behavior model. In particular, it represents methods of classes and objects using events, states, and transitions. Thereby, it is vital for the composition and exploration of environments.
  c. *Mapping*, which associates object-oriented and procedural implementations with domain knowledge of the behavior model. In particular, it represents

    application classes using domain classes, and methods invocation, finalization, and completion using domain-specific events and properties.

    d. *Code templates*, which are associated with events, states, and transitions, enable knowledge-based composition of explorable environments based on components implemented with imperative languages.

3. The *development pipeline of explorable XR environments* is a method and set of algorithms for creating explorable XR environments with the *visual knowledge-based behavior model* and the *semantic link model*. The models describe data and workflow in a knowledge-based semantic way in the pipeline. XR environments are composed of reusable service-oriented components, whose behavior and features are described by the behavior model and are linked to imperative implementations by the semantic link model.

4. The *exploration methods for XR environments* with exploration algorithms enable visual and knowledge-based exploration of XR environments developed using the pipeline. Exploration is based on reasoning and queries and includes users' and objects' features and behavior regarding their past, current, and potential future activities. XR behavior can be widely understood as autonomous actions and interactions between different users (e.g., in collaborative environments), objects (e.g., agents and avatars) as well as between users and objects.

Chapter 6
E-XR Visual Knowledge-Based Behavior Model

The *E-XR visual knowledge-based behavior model* (*behavior model* for short) is the first of the four main elements of the E-XR approach. It is located at the bottom of the architecture stack (Fig. 5.2) and used by the other E-XR elements. The model uses knowledge representation technologies to provide axioms that enable representation of behavior and features of XR components and environments. An *XR component* is a reusable module—a set of classes with methods—that can be composed with other XR components into an XR environment.

Definition 6.1 An **XR component** is a 11-tuple $\{\mathcal{GEOM}, \mathcal{TRAN}, \mathcal{PRES}, \mathcal{NAVI}, \mathcal{ANIM}, \mathcal{SCR}, \mathcal{AKB}, \mathcal{CTS}, \mathcal{MKB}, \mathcal{MRS}, \mathcal{AS}\}$, where:

1. $\mathcal{GEOM}$ is a set of hierarchically structured 2D and 3D shapes, e.g., meshes, spheres, rectangles, and arcs.
2. $\mathcal{TRAN}$ is a set of transformations, which may be applied to $\mathcal{GEOM}$ elements, e.g., rotation, scale, screw, and intersection.
3. $\mathcal{PRES}$ is a set of presentational elements, which may be applied to $\mathcal{GEOM}$ elements, e.g., textures, colors, and light sources.
4. $\mathcal{NAVI}$ is a set of elements that may be used to navigate over $\mathcal{GEOM}$ elements, e.g., viewpoints and navigation modes.
5. $\mathcal{ANIM}$ is a set of elements that may be used to animate $\mathcal{GEOM}$, $\mathcal{TRAN}$, $\mathcal{PRES}$, and $\mathcal{NAVI}$ elements, e.g., sensors, interpolators, and events.
6. $\mathcal{SCR}$ is a set of imperative scripts describing classes with methods that implement the behavior of users and $\mathcal{GEOM}$, $\mathcal{TRAN}$, $\mathcal{PRES}$, $\mathcal{NAVI}$, and $\mathcal{ANIM}$ elements in the imperative way.
7. $\mathcal{AKB}$ is an *activity knowledge base* (cf. Definition 7.1).
8. $\mathcal{CTS}$ is a *component transition set* (cf. Sect. 7.2.3).
9. $\mathcal{MKB}$ is a *mapping knowledge base* (cf. Definition 7.21).
10. $\mathcal{MRS}$ is a *mapping transition set* (cf. Definition 7.24).
11. $\mathcal{AS}$ is a set of all other related assets, e.g., sounds and temporal documents.

© The Author(s), under exclusive license to Springer Nature Switzerland AG 2020
J. Flotyński, *Knowledge-Based Explorable Extended Reality Environments*,
https://doi.org/10.1007/978-3-030-59965-2_6

For instance, in the Unity game engine, an XR component is an animated prefab including 3D shapes and C# scripts that describe the behavior of the shapes.

Whereas behavior is determined by changes in users' and objects' properties over time, features are determined by time-independent properties, which remain immutable until the environment's termination. It makes the representation of behavior more complex than the representation of features. Therefore, while discussing the proposed ideas, we focus on the behavior representation and explicitly refer to features only when they are represented and used in a specific manner.

The model permits the expression of the semantics of behavior in arbitrary domains, independently of 3D graphics and animation technologies underlying particular XR environments. Furthermore, according to functional requirement 2 for the approach (cf. Sect. 5.2.1), the specification of behavior is declarative. It permits XR designers to focus on goals to be achieved in the environment while maintaining the possibility to explore users' and objects' behavior with reasoning and queries. The behavior model consists of two main components, which are sub-models responsible for the representation of different types of behavior using different knowledge representation technologies:

1. *The ontology-based component*, which represents behavior using the Semantic Web approach derived from description logics (cf. Sects. 3.3 and 3.4). These technologies provide a formalism that is sufficient to represent past and current environment behavior. For this purpose, the component enables the creation of *behavior logs*, which are knowledge-based descriptors (knowledge bases) inter-related with visual descriptors (such as images and movies) of behavior. Hence, they allow for both knowledge and visual exploration of XR environments using reasoning and queries. As behavior logs are based on the Semantic Web, they comply with the current trends in the evolution of the Web and network-based systems. The ontology-based component is presented in detail in Sect. 6.1.

2. *The rule-based component*, which extends the explorable representation of behavior enabled by the ontology-based component using first-order logic as well as concepts derived from logic programming and the event calculus (cf. Sect. 3.2). These approaches provide formalism that is sufficiently powerful to permit the key functions of E-XR: composition of explorable environments as well as representation and exploration of the overall behavior of such environments, including past, current, and possible future activities, which meets functional requirement 4. This component of the behavior model is presented in detail in Sect. 6.2.

6.1   Ontology-Based Component

In this section, the *ontology-based component of the behavior model* is described. The component is part of the behavior model used to represent features as well as past and current behavior of XR environments in the form of behavior logs that cover users' and objects' activities described by temporal statements.

The component is based on the Semantic Web standards—RDF, RDFS, and OWL—and the 4D-fluents approach (cf. Sect. 3.4). It extends the approach proposed in Flotyński, Nowak, & Walczak (2018), Flotyński & Sobociński (2018a,b). The Semantic Web standards, which are based on description logics (cf. Sect. 3.4), offer expressivity sufficient to represent the domain-specific semantics of past and current features and behavior of XR environments in the form that enables their exploration with reasoning and queries. Moreover, these standards have been thoroughly investigated in terms of decidability and computational complexity of typical reasoning and query problems.

The ontology-based component is the pair of a *domain ontology* and the *fluent ontology*, which are pairs of TBox and RBox (cf. Definitions 3.40 and 3.45). The axioms of the ontologies permit semantic representation of users and objects, including their features and behavior, with general and domain knowledge.

6.1.1 Domain Ontologies

A *domain ontology* is a pair of a TBox and an RBox that specify the conceptualization of a particular application domain. A domain ontology specifies entities related to a particular domain, such as classes, properties, and relations between them, e.g., hierarchies of classes and properties, restrictions on classes as well as domains and ranges of properties. Hence, the use of domain ontologies in E-XR enables the fulfillment of functional requirement 1 for the approach (cf. Sect. 5.2.1). A *domain class* is an OWL class (W3C 2004b) that is specified in a *domain ontology*. A *domain property* is an OWL object property or OWL datatype property (W3C 2004b) that is specified in a *domain ontology*.

A domain ontology is determined by a particular XR application and should be comprehensible to users in the related field. For example, a domain ontology for urban planning includes such classes as villa, family house, multifamily house, street, and square, and such properties as building location and orientation, number of stages, and type of facade. A domain ontology is common to various cases of composition and exploration of XR environments in a particular application domain. Different domain ontologies are used by explorable environments developed for different application domains, e.g., virtual stores, virtual museums, and virtual tourist guides.

Although the ontology-based component may include a number of domain ontologies, in the rest of the book, we refer to the union of them similar to a single domain ontology, which does not affect the presented concepts.

6.1.2 States and Events

States

The fundamental entities for representing the behavior of explorable XR environments are *states*. A *state* is a representation of a fragment of an XR environment, in particular a collection of terms describing users and objects. States are denoted by terms, while their occurrence can be evaluated using predicates. The aforementioned definition of *state* is broad and appropriate to cover every possible situation that may occur in an environment, including permanent as well as changing situations. Examples of permanent situations are: a city has a fixed location ($hasLocation(city, coordinates(x, y))$), and a 3D scene is always illuminated ($isIlluminated(scene)$). Changing situations can be perceived as activities, which are commonly understood as *the quality or state of being active* (Merriam-Webster 2020), a change in an environment, something done by users or objects, or something that happens to them. Activities cover actions, which are autonomous (involve single objects) and interactions, which involve multiple objects. Examples of actions are: an aircraft is flying ($isFlying(aircraft)$) and an avatar is walking ($isWalking(avatar)$). Examples of interactions are: a user pushes a button ($pushes(user, button)$), and two persons communicate with one another by a mediator ($communicate(person_1, person_2, mediator)$). Activities are manifested by changes in the environment, in particular, by animations and modifying variables. For instance, a walking avatar is visualized as a 3D object with a variable structure or geometry, and position in the scene.

Two types of states are distinguished: *instant states* and *interval states*—depending on whether they happen at time points or within time intervals.

Definition 6.2 An **instant state** is a state that occurs at a *time point*.

Definition 6.3 An **interval state** is a state that occurs within a *time interval*.

Events

States are begun and finished by *events*. Like states, events are denoted by terms, while their occurrence can be evaluated using predicates.

Definition 6.4 The **begins** predicate is a predicate that is true for a given *event* and a *state* if and only if the *event* begins the *state*.

It is denoted as $begins(event, state)$, e.g., $begins(startOfRun, run)$.

Definition 6.5 The **finishes** predicate is a predicate that is true for a given *event* and a *state* if and only if the *event* finishes the *state*.

It is denoted as $finishes(event, state)$, e.g., $finishes(endOfRun, run)$.

6.1.3 Fluent Ontology

The *fluent ontology* specifies fundamental temporal entities—classes and properties—that permit representation of users' and objects' behavior. The fluent ontology augments domain ontologies with temporal terminology that can be used together with domain classes and properties. The fluent ontology is an immutable part of E-XR, which is common to all explorable XR environments, independently of particular application domains.

The fluent ontology is based on the event calculus, 4D-fluents, and the Time Ontology in OWL (cf. Sects. 3.2.4 and 3.4.2). Following the event calculus and the Time Ontology, we use *time points* (*tp* for short, also referred to as *instants* (World Wide Web Consortium 2020b)) and *time intervals* (*ti* for short). We also gather both concepts under the collective term *temporal entity*, as proposed in the Time Ontology. In this regard, we modify the *start* and *end* predicates of the event calculus (cf. Definitions 3.31 and 3.32) to make them compliant with temporal entities. We have used the following constructors of description logics: $\mathcal{ALUQ(D)}$ (cf. Table 3.1), to specify the entities of the fluent ontology. The OWL 2 DL profile is sufficiently expressive to provide such a logic (cf. Sect. 3.4.1).

Definition 6.6 The *start* predicate is a predicate that is true for a given *temporal entity* and a *time point* if and only if the *temporal entity* is started at the *time point*.

It is denoted as $start(temporalEntity, tp)$.

Definition 6.7 The *end* predicate is a predicate that is true for a given *temporal entity* and a *time point* if and only if the *temporal entity* is finished at the *time point*.

It is denoted as $end(temporalEntity, tp)$.

The fluent ontology is presented in Listing 6.1. It specifies the following entities:

1. *State* (line 9), which is an OWL class and the class of all *states*.
2. *InstantState* (lines 11–12), which is a subclass of *State* and the class of all *instant states*.
3. *IntervalState* (lines 14–16), which is a subclass of *State* and the class of all *interval states*. *IntervalState* is disjoint with *InstantState*.
4. *Event* (line 18), which is an OWL class and the class of all *events*.
5. *TemporalEntity* (cf. Sect. 3.4.2, line 20), which is an RDFS class and the class of all *temporal entities*.
6. *TimePoint* (cf. Definition 3.79, lines 22–23), which is a subclass of RDFS Datatype and *TemporalEntity* and the class of all time points. The use of RDFS datatype enables specification of time domains depending on the requirements of particular applications.
7. *TimeInterval* (cf. Definition 3.80, lines 25–26), which is a subclass of *Temporal- Entity* and the class of all time intervals. Two properties describe a time interval:

   1) *start* (lines 28–30),
   2) *end* (lines 32–34),

   which indicate time points that start and end the time interval.
8. *TimeSlice* (Definition 3.83, line 36–54), which is an OWL class and the class of all *time slices*. Every *time slice* has two obligatory properties assigned, as determined by OWL qualified cardinality restrictions:

1) *isTimeSliceOf* (lines 37–41 and 56–58), which indicates the primary object
   for which the time slice has been created,
2) *hasTimePoint* or *hasTimeInterval* (lines 42–53 and 60–66), which indicate a time point or time interval—depending on the duration of the state
   represented by *time slice*.

9. *VisualDescriptor* (lines 68–84), which is an OWL class and the class of all
   visual descriptors. Two types of properties describe a visual descriptor:

   1) At least one *visualRepresentation* (lines 69–72 and 86–88), which indi-
      cates a resource, such as an image, movie, or animated 3D model, that
      visualizes a property or a relationship.
   2) One or two *isVisualDescriptorOf* (lines 73–83 and 90–92), which indi-
      cates a time slice visualized by the descriptor. One *isVisualDescriptorOf*
      property is used if the object of the associated statement is a literal value. Two
      isVisualDescriptorOf properties are used if the object of the statement is
      a resource with URI.

Listing 6.1 Fluent ontology (RDF Turtle format)

```
 1  @base <http://semantic3d.org/e-xr/fluent-ontology> .
 2  @prefix fo: <http://semantic3d.org/e-xr/fluent-ontology#> .
 3  @prefix owl: <http://www.w3.org/2002/07/owl#> .
 4  @prefix rdf: <http://www.w3.org/1999/02/22-rdf-syntax-ns#> .
 5  @prefix rdfs: <http://www.w3.org/2000/01/rdf-schema#> .
 6
 7  <http://semantic3d.org/e-xr/fluent-ontology> rdf:type
       owl:Ontology .
 8
 9  fo:State rdf:type owl:Class .
10
11  fo:InstantState rdf:type owl:Class ;
12    rdfs:subClassOf fo:State .
13
14  fo:IntervalState rdf:type owl:Class ;
15    rdfs:subClassOf fo:State ;
16    owl:disjointWith fo:InstantState .
17
18  fo:Event rdf:type owl:Class .
19
20  fo:TemporalEntity rdf:type rdfs:Class .
21
22  fo:TimePoint rdf:type rdfs:Datatype ;
23    rdfs:subClassOf fo:TemporalEntity .
24
25  fo:TimeInterval rdf:type rdfs:Class ;
26    rdfs:subClassOf fo:TemporalEntity.
27
28  fo:start rdf:type owl:ObjectProperty ;
29    rdfs:domain fo:TimeInterval ;
30    rdfs:range fo:TimePoint .
31
```

```
32  fo:end rdf:type owl:ObjectProperty ;
33    rdfs:domain fo:TimeInterval ;
34    rdfs:range fo:TimePoint .
35
36  fo:TimeSlice rdf:type owl:Class ;
37    rdfs:subClassOf [ rdf:type owl:Restriction ;
38        owl:onProperty fo:isTimeSliceOf ;
39        owl:onClass owl:Thing ;
40        owl:qualifiedCardinality "1"^^xsd:nonNegativeInteger
41    ] ,
42    [ rdf:type owl:Class ;
43      owl:unionOf (
44        [ rdf:type owl:Restriction ;
45          owl:onProperty fo:hasTimePoint ;
46          owl:onClass fo:TimePoint ;
47          owl:qualifiedCardinality "1"^^
                  xsd:nonNegativeInteger
48        ]
49        [ rdf:type owl:Restriction ;
50          owl:onProperty fo:hasTimeInterval ;
51          owl:onClass fo:TimeInterval ;
52          owl:qualifiedCardinality "1"^^
                  xsd:nonNegativeInteger
53        ] )
54    ] .
55
56  fo:isTimeSliceOf rdf:type owl:ObjectProperty ;
57    rdfs:domain fo:TimeSlice ;
58    rdfs:range owl:Thing .
59
60  fo:hasTimePoint rdf:type owl:ObjectProperty ;
61    rdfs:domain fo:TimeSlice ;
62    rdfs:range fo:TimePoint .
63
64  fo:hasTimeInterval rdf:type owl:ObjectProperty ;
65    rdfs:domain  fo:TimeSlice ;
66    rdfs:range  fo:TimeInterval .
67
68  fo:VisualDescriptor rdf:type owl:Class ;
69    rdfs:subClassOf [ rdf:type owl:Restriction ;
70      owl:onProperty fo:visualRepresentation ;
71      owl:someValuesFrom xsd:anyURI
72    ] ,
73    [ rdf:type owl:Class ; owl:intersectionOf (
74      [ rdf:type owl:Restriction ;
75        owl:onProperty fo:isVisualDescriptorOf ;
76        owl:onClass fo:TimeSlice ;
77        owl:minQualifiedCardinality "1"^^
              xsd:nonNegativeInteger
78      ]
79      [ rdf:type owl:Restriction ;
80        owl:onProperty fo:isVisualDescriptorOf ;
81        owl:onClass fo:TimeSlice ;
```

```
82                owl:maxQualifiedCardinality "2"^^
                       xsd:nonNegativeInteger
83         ] )
84      ] .
85
86   fo:visualRepresentation rdf:type owl:DatatypeProperty ;
87      rdfs:domain fo:VisualDescriptor ;
88      rdfs:range xsd:anyURI .
89
90   fo:isVisualDescriptorOf rdf:type owl:ObjectProperty ;
91      rdfs:domain fo:VisualDescriptor ;
92      rdfs:range fo:TimeSlice .
```

6.1.4 Visual Semantic Behavior Logs

Domain ontologies and the *fluent ontology* are used to create *visual semantic behavior logs* consisting of *temporal statements*. The concept of *temporal statements* is depicted in Fig. 6.1. In the figure, every two nodes linked by a predicate denote a single RDF statement.

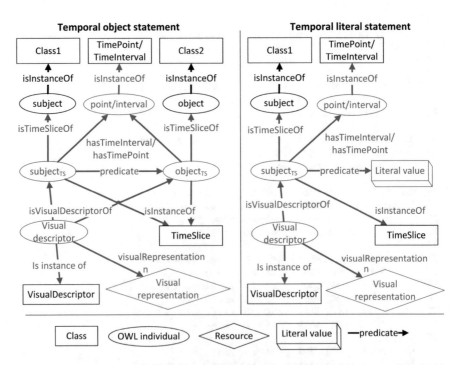

Fig. 6.1 Temporal statements (red) of visual semantic behavior log. Entities that are linked with but are not part of temporal statements are marked in black

Definition 6.8 A *temporal object statement* is an ABox that consists of the following RDF statements:

1) $rdf{:}Type(subject_{TS}, fo{:}TimeSlice)$,
2) $fo{:}isTimeSliceOf(subject_{TS}, subject)$,
3) $rdf{:}Type(object_{TS}, fo{:}TimeSlice)$,
4) $fo{:}isTimeSliceOf(object_{TS}, object)$,
5) One of the triples:

     a. *rdf:type(timePoint, fo:TimePoint), fo:hasTimePoint(subject$_{TS}$, timePoint), fo:hasTimePoint(object$_{TS}$, timePoint)* or
     b. *rdf:type(timeInterval, fo:TimeInterval), fo:hasTimeInterval (subject$_{TS}$, timeInterval), fo:hasTimeInterval(object$_{TS}$, timeInterval)*,

6) $predicate(subject_{TS}, object_{TS})$,
7) $rdf{:}type(visualDescriptor, fo{:}VisualDescriptor)$
8) $fo{:}isVisualDescriptorOf(visualDescriptor, subject_{TS})$,
9) $fo{:}isVisualDescriptorOf(visualDescriptor, object_{TS})$,
10) At least one RDF statement
    $fo{:}visualRepresentation(visualDescriptor,$
    $visualRepresentationURI)$,

where $subject, object, subject_{TS}, object_{TS}, timePoint, timeInterval,$ $visualDescriptor$, and $visualRepresentationURI$ are identifiers of resources, and entities with the fo prefix are *fluent ontology* entities.

Temporal object statements are used to express properties and relationships in which *objects* are resource with identifiers. For instance, a temporal object statement can be the following:

1. A *user* (subject) with its time slice, which is linked to a time slice of an *appliance* by the *repairs* predicate.
2. The reparation is lasting within a *time interval*.
3. Both *tile slices* link a *visual descriptor* of the activity in the form of a movie as well as an image.

Definition 6.9 A *temporal literal statement* is an ABox that consists of the following RDF statements:

1) $rdf{:}Type(subject_{TS}, fo{:}TimeSlice)$,
2) $fo{:}isTimeSliceOf(subject_{TS}, subject)$,
3) One of the pairs:

     a. *rdf:type(timePoint, fo:TimePoint), fo:hasTimePoint(subject$_{TS}$, timePoint)* or
     b. *rdf:type(timeInterval, fo:TimeInterval), fo:hasTimeInterval(subject$_{TS}$, timeInterval)*,

4) $predicate(subject_{TS}, object)$,
5) $rdf{:}type(visualDescriptor, fo{:}VisualDescriptor)$
6) $fo{:}isVisualDescriptorOf(visualDescriptor, subject_{TS})$,

7) At least one RDF statement
$fo{:}visual Representation(visual Descriptor, visual Representation URI)$,

where $subject$, $subject_{TS}$, $timePoint$, $timeInterval$, $visualDescriptor$, and $visualRepresentationURI$ are identifiers of resources, $object$ is a literal value, and entities with the fo prefix are *fluent ontology* entities.

In contrast to *temporal object statements*, *temporal literal statements* are used to express properties in which *objects* are literal values.

Definition 6.10 A *temporal statement* is a *temporal object statement* or a *temporal literal statement*.

In E-XR, a temporal statement expresses a user's or object's activity using the terminology provided by domain ontologies.

Definition 6.11 A *visual semantic behavior log* is a set of:

1) *temporal statements* and
2) *assertions* on subjects and objects that appear in the *temporal statements* such that the assertions are not related to time.

A behavior log represents a temporal state of affairs during a particular use (session) of an explorable XR environment. Logs can be processed by reasoning engines to infer tacit (implicit) users' and objects' properties based on their explicit properties. Moreover, logs can be queried by users, applications, and services to acquire visual and semantic information about activities.

6.2 Rule-Based Component

In this section, the *rule-based component of the behavior model* is described. The component is part of the behavior model used to represent past, current, and possible future behavior of explorable environments, which is determined while composing the environments. The rule-based component extends the ontology-based component with axioms that specify predicates on states, events, and time. They are required to specify the behavior of environments, which is necessary to enable their composition and advanced exploration covering complex relations.

The achievement of the goals above is possible as the component is based on first-order logic. It extends the approach proposed in Flotyński & Walczak (2017a), Flotyński, Krzyszkowski, & Walczak (2017, 2018), Flotyński, Walczak, & Krzyszkowski (2020). First-order logic offers powerful formalism, which enables rules on predicates and variables. Rules allow for description of arbitrary properties and relationships between users and objects in XR environments. In addition, first-order logic permits reasoning on numerical domains. It is key to permit spatial and temporal reasoning and relations between time points and intervals, in which users' and objects' properties and relationships are held.

In Sects. 6.2.1–6.2.3, we present the formalism of the rule-based component. Next, we describe the *fluent rule set*, which is built upon this formalism. It provides the foundation for behavior specification independently of particular applications and domains.

6.2.1 Time

Time Domain

Time points, which are the instances of the *TimePoint* class and the basic entities representing time in the behavior model, are scalars. In particular, time points may be date–time values captured while an XR environment is running, which can be useful in cases of exploring past and current behavior of the environment. Time points may also be represented by increasing real numbers—in cases of simulating and exploring possible behavior of an environment. Anyway, the *TimePoint* class, which constitutes the time domain, must enable the use of the following operators to compare time points: $=$ (*equal*), $<$ (*earlier than*), $>$ (*later than*), $\leq$ (*earlier than or equal*), $\geq$ (*later than or equal*), and $\neq$ (*different than*).

Temporal Reasoning

We also define predicates for time points and intervals based on the predicates of the event calculus and the Time Ontology (cf. Sects. 3.2.4 and 3.4.2). Such predicates permit temporal reasoning on time points and intervals.

The *start* and *end* predicates (cf. Definitions 6.6 and 6.7) can be used to complement Definition 3.33 of the *in* predicate as follows:

Definition 6.12 The *in* predicate is a predicate that is true for a given *time point* and a *time interval* if and only if the *time point* is greater than or equal to the time point that starts the *time interval*, and less than or equal to the time point that finishes the *time interval*:

$$\forall tp, ti: in(tp, ti) \Leftrightarrow$$

$$\exists tp_{start}, tp_{end}: start(ti, tp_{start}) \wedge end(ti, tp_{end}) \wedge tp \geq tp_{start} \wedge tp \leq tp_{end}.$$
$$(6.1)$$

As examples of relations between time intervals, we define three predicates of the Time Ontology (World Wide Web Consortium 2020b), which have been proposed in Allen & Ferguson (1997): *before*, *after*, and *starts*.

Definition 6.13 The *before* predicate is a predicate that is true for a given *time interval* ti_1 and a *time interval* ti_2 if and only if ti_1 finishes before ti_2 starts. $before(ti_1, ti_2)$ is equivalent to $after(ti_2, ti_1)$:

$$\forall ti_1, ti_2: before(ti_1, ti_2) \Leftrightarrow after(ti_2, ti_1)$$

$$\Leftrightarrow \exists tp1_{end}, tp2_{start}: \tag{6.2}$$

$$end(ti_1, tp1_{end}) \wedge start(ti_2, tp2_{start}) \wedge tp2_{start} > tp1_{end}.$$

Definition 6.14 The **starts** predicate is a predicate that is true for a given *time interval* ti_1 and a *time interval* ti_2 if and only if ti_1 and ti_2 start at the same time point and ti_1 finishes before ti_2 finishes:

$$\forall ti_1, ti_2: starts(ti_1, ti_2)$$

$$\Leftrightarrow \exists tp_{start}, tp1_{end}, tp2_{end}: start(ti_1, tp_{start}) \wedge start(ti_2, tp_{start}) \tag{6.3}$$

$$\wedge end(ti_1, tp1_{end}) \wedge end(ti_2, tp2_{end}) \wedge tp2_{end} > tp1_{end}.$$

The other predicates mentioned in Sect. 3.3.6 can be defined similarly.

6.2.2   Relations Between States and Events

The rule-based component extends the formal representation of states and events provided by the ontology-based component and specifies relations between them.

Definition 6.15 The **begin** compound term is a compound term that denotes the *event* that starts a *state*.

It is denoted as $begin(state)$, e.g., $begin(run) = startOfRun$. In addition, $begins(begin(state), state)$.

Definition 6.16 The **finish** compound term is a compound term that denotes the *event* that finishes a *state*.

It is denoted as $finish(state)$, e.g., $finish(run) = endOfRun$. In addition, $finishes(finish(state), state)$.

Axiom 6.2.1 Every *state* is begun by an *event* and finished by an *event*:

$$\forall state \in State: \exists event_{begin}, event_{finish} \in Event: \tag{6.4}$$

$$begins(event_{begin}, state) \wedge finishes(event_{finish}, state).$$

Hence, from the occurrence of states, we can infer the occurrence of the related events.

Theorem 6.1 *The event that begins an interval state occurs at the time point that starts the time interval of the state:*

$$\forall state \in IntervalState, tp \in TimePoint, ti \in TimeInterval: \tag{6.5}$$

$$time(begin(state), tp) \Leftarrow holds(state, ti) \wedge start(ti, tp).$$

Theorem 6.2 *The event that finishes an interval state occurs at the time point that ends the time interval of the state:*

$$\forall state \in IntervalState, tp \in TimePoint, ti \in TimeInterval:$$
$$time(finish(state), tp) \Leftarrow holds(state, ti) \wedge end(ti, tp). \tag{6.6}$$

Theorem 6.3 *The event that begins an instant state is equal to the event that finishes the state, and it occurs at the time point when the state occurs:*

$$\forall state \in InstantState, tp \in TimePoint:$$
$$(time(begin(state), tp) \wedge begin(state) = \tag{6.7}$$
$$finish(state)) \Leftarrow holdsAt(state, tp).$$

Definition 6.17 The ***event**$_{startEnv}$* atom is an atom that denotes the event that begins the XR environment.

Hence, we can conclude that:

Theorem 6.4 *No event can occur earlier than event$_{startEnv}$:*

$$\forall event \in Event, tp \in TimePoint:$$
$$tp \geq tp_{startEnv} \Leftarrow time(event, tp) \wedge time(event_{startEnv}, tp_{startEnv}). \tag{6.8}$$

Definition 6.18 The ***event**$_{stopEnv}$* atom is an atom that denotes the event that finishes the XR environment.

Hence, we can conclude that:

Theorem 6.5 *No event can occur later than event$_{stopEnv}$:*

$$\forall event \in Event, tp \in TimePoint:$$
$$tp \leq tp_{stopEnv} \Leftarrow time(event, tp) \wedge time(event_{stopEnv}, tp_{stopEnv}) \tag{6.9}$$

Events denote the beginning and finish of states, thereby determining their duration.

Definition 6.19 The ***duration of a state*** is the difference between the *time point* of the event that finishes the *state* and the *time point* of the event that begins the *state*. It is specified in the domain of time points and denoted by compound term *duration(state)*:

$$\forall state \in State: \exists x \in TimePoint$$

$$duration(state) = x$$

$$\Leftrightarrow \exists event_{begin}, event_{finish} \in Event, tp_{begin}, tp_{finish} \in TimePoint:$$

$$begins(event_{begin}, state) \wedge finishes(event_{finish}, state)$$

$$\wedge time(event_{begin}, tp_{begin}) \wedge time(event_{finish}, tp_{finish})$$

$$\wedge x = tp_{finish} - tp_{begin}.$$

$$(6.10)$$

Duration can be used to calculate how long a state lasts in a selected domain of time. As every state is begun and finished by an event, which determine the state duration (cf. Axiom 6.2.1 and Definition 6.19), we can conclude that:

Theorem 6.6 *The events that begin and finish an instant state are equal, thus the duration of an instant state is equal to zero.*

Theorem 6.7 *The events that begin and finish an interval state are different, thus the duration of an interval state is larger than zero.*

6.2.3   Behavior

In the previous subsections, we have specified relations between states and events. However, practical applications also need direct relations between states and temporal entities in which the states occur. Concepts of the event calculus (cf. Sect. 3.2.4) can be used to achieve this goal.

Occurrence of States Over Time

We specify the type of predicates that evaluate states' occurrence at time points.

Definition 6.20 An ***instant evaluation predicate*** (ISEP) is a predicate that is true for a given *state* or an *event*, and a *time point* if and only if the *state* or the *event* occurs at the *time point*.

ISEP predicates are, in particular, the *holdsAt* (cf. Definition 3.34) and *time* (cf. Definition 3.28) predicates. *holdsAt*(*state*, *tp*) evaluates whether *state* occurs at time point *tp*. The predicate can be applied to instant and interval states because every state may be evaluated at a time point (cf. Theorem 3.1). For example, *time(turnsOn(user, appliance), tp)* evaluates whether *user turns on appliance* at time point *tp*, while *holdsAt(works(appliance), tp)* evaluates whether *appliance is working* at time point *tp*.

It is possible to evaluate whether a *state* is begun or finished at a particular *time point* using an ISEP predicate. Such an evaluation can be done using the *time* predicate together with the *begin* and *finish* terms, which denote events (cf. Definitions 6.15 and 6.16). The predicates $time(begin(state), tp)$ and $time(finish(state), tp)$ evaluate whether *state* is begun and finished at time point *tp*, respectively. In a similar way, we specify the type of predicates that evaluate states' occurrence within time intervals.

Definition 6.21 An *interval evaluation predicate* (ITEP) is a predicate that is true for a given *interval state* and a *time interval* if and only if the *interval state* occurs within the *time interval*.

An ITEP predicate is $holds(state, ti)$ (cf. Definition 3.35). For example, $holds(tests(user, appliance), ti)$ evaluates whether *user is testing appliance* within time interval *ti*.

Definition 6.22 A *temporal evaluation predicate* (TEP) is an ISEP or an ITEP.

Transitions Between States

States and events can trigger other states and events. For instance, an XR environment is running (state) since it was started (event). A ball is falling (state) since it was dropped (event), whereas it is rising (state) since bounced off the floor (event). Besides, states may depend on other states, e.g., a house is fully illuminated if every room has been illuminated, no matter what was the order of switching on lamps in the particular rooms. It permits creation of arbitrary chains of cause and effect described by *transitions*, which conform to the event–condition–action model (Dittrich, Gatziu, & Geppert 1995). Two types of transitions are distinguished: *event-based transitions* and *state-based transitions*.

Definition 6.23 An *event-based transition* is a Horn clause consisting of:

- A *body* that is a conjunction of a statement based on an ISEP predicate that evaluates the occurrence of an event, and an arbitrary number of statements based on predicates that are not fluents,
- A *head* that is a statement based on a TEP predicate.

An event-based transition is denoted as

$$TEP \Leftarrow ISEP_{event} \wedge s_1 \wedge \ldots \wedge s_n, \tag{6.11}$$

where $ISEP_{event}$ is a statement that is true if and only if an event occurs at a time point, and $s_1, \ldots, s_n, n \geq 0$, are statements based on predicates that are not fluents. The TEP predicate used in the head of an event-based transition may express the occurrence of event, instant state, or interval state. The time points associated with events and states in the body and head of a transition are in the following relations:

Axiom 6.2.2 An *event* whose occurrence is asserted in the head of an *event-based transition* occurs not earlier than the *event* whose occurrence is evaluated in the body of the transition.

In such a case, one event triggers another event.

Axiom 6.2.3 An *instant state* whose occurrence is asserted in the head of an *event-based transition* occurs not earlier than the *event* whose occurrence is evaluated in the body of the transition.

Axiom 6.2.4 An *interval state* whose occurrence is asserted in the head of an *event-based transition* starts not earlier than the event whose occurrence is evaluated in the body of the transition.

In such cases, an event triggers a state.

Definition 6.24 A *state-based transition* is a Horn clause consisting of:

- A *body* that is a conjunction of statements at least one of which is a statement based on an ISEP predicate that evaluates the occurrence of a state. All the statements based on ISEP predicates use a common time point.
- A *head* that is a statement based on a TEP predicate.

A state-based transition is denoted as

$$TEP \Leftarrow ISEP_{state-1} \wedge \ldots \wedge ISEP_{state-n} \wedge s_1 \wedge \ldots \wedge s_m, \tag{6.12}$$

where $ISEP_{state-1}, \ldots, ISEP_{state-n}$ for $n \geq 1$ are statements that are true if and only if $state - 1, \ldots, state - n$ occur at a given time point, and $s_1, \ldots, s_m, m \geq 0$, are statements based on predicates that are not fluents. Like for event-based transitions, relations between the time points associated with events and states in the body and head of a *state-based transition* may be characterized.

Axiom 6.2.5 An *event* whose occurrence is asserted in the head of a *state-based transition* occurs not earlier than at the time point for which the states in the body of the transition are evaluated.

Axiom 6.2.6 An *instant state* whose occurrence is asserted in the head of a *state-based transition* occurs not earlier than at the time point for which the states in the body of the transition are evaluated.

Axiom 6.2.7 An *interval state* whose occurrence is asserted in the head of a *state-based transition* starts not earlier than at the time point for which the states in the body of the transition are evaluated.

Definition 6.25 A *transition* is an event-based transition or a state-based transition.

Transitions move XR components and environments between different states, which constitutes the behavior of the components. The body of a transition is evaluated for a particular time point, which is common to all statements of the conjunction in the body. It has two significant consequences. First, if interval states are required to trigger a new state or event, they must be evaluated at a common time point—as if they would be instant states at this time point—using the *holds At* predicate. Second, as the probability of occurring multiple events at once is infinitely low, at most one event is permitted in the body of an event-based transition.

Some transitions need to generate new facts and add them to the rule set. It is possible due to the *assert* predicate.

Definition 6.26 The *assert* predicate is a predicate that is true for a given *statement* if and only if the *statement* exists in the rule set, or it is possible to add the *statement* to the rule set.

The predicate is denoted as $assert(statement)$. In examples in this book, the predicate is frequently used to associate time points with time intervals in transitions. We assume that the *assert* predicate is satisfied unless otherwise stated. The transitions in the following example:

1. $holds(pluggedIn(Printer), ti_1) \Leftarrow time(pluggesIn(User, Printer), TP)$
   $\wedge\, assert(start(ti_1, TP)),$

2. $holdsAt(switchOnAttempt(User, Printer), TP)$
   $\Leftarrow time(switchesOn(User, Printer), TP),$

3. $holds(switchedOn(Printer), ti_2) \Leftarrow holdsAt(pluggedIn(Printer), TP)$
   $\wedge\, holdsAt(switchOnAttempt(User, Printer), TP)$
   $\wedge\, assert(start(ti_2, TP)),$

4. $holds(canPrint(Printer), ti_3) \Leftarrow holdsAt(hasPaper(Printer), TP)$
   $\wedge\, holdsAt(switchedOn(Printer), TP) \wedge assert(start(ti_3, TP)),$

$$(6.13)$$

express that the state in which a printer is plugged in is triggered by the event of plugging it in (1). Further, the event of switching on the printer triggers the state that denotes the attempt (2). If the state occurs while the printer is plugged in, it triggers the printer to be switched on, which is another state (3). Finally, a switched-on printer that has paper (states) can print (another state)—4. Nonetheless, it is unsaid when the *hasPaper* predicate is satisfied as we know nothing about an event of inserting paper into the printer, which is necessary to print. Therefore, we cannot be sure that the readiness for printing starts immediately upon switching on the printer. Hence, both *hasPaper* and *switchedOn* are states that enable *canPrint*, but none of them alone is sufficient to trigger it. In every transition, the *assert* predicate states that a *time point* starts a new *time interval*. The intervals are identified by unique atoms ti_1, ti_2, and ti_3, which are generated by the system.

If multiple events must occur to enable a final state in an environment, multiple transitions must be specified—one transition for every event, which leads to an intermediate state. Then, another transition gathers all the intermediate states to lead to the final state. For example, a cooker (which was broken) is ready to use since both its fan and heating plate are repaired. No matter which was repaired first:

$$holds(isReady(Cooker), ti_{ready}) \Leftarrow holdsAt(isRepaired(fan), TP)$$

$$\wedge\, holdsAt(isRepaired(heatingPlate), TP) \wedge assert(start(ti_{ready}, TP)).$$

$$holds(isRepaired(Element), ti_x)$$

$$\Leftarrow time(finish(repair(Serviceman, Element)), TP)$$

$$\wedge\, assert(start(ti_x, TP)).$$

$$(6.14)$$

In the bodies of the transitions, ISEP predicates are used. In the heads, ITEP predicates, which designate repaired elements and readiness for printing, are used. States, events, facts, and transitions describe the *behavior* of an XR component or environment.

Definition 6.27 The *behavior* of an XR environment is a 4-tuple $\{\mathcal{E}, \mathcal{S}, \mathcal{F}, \mathcal{T}\}$, where:

- $\mathcal{E}$ is a set of *events*,
- $\mathcal{S}$ is a set of *states*,
- $\mathcal{F}$ is a set of *facts* and rules that do not use fluents,
- $\mathcal{T}$ is a set of *transitions*.

6.2.4   Fluent Rule Set

The *fluent rule set* has been specified based on the concepts discussed in Sects. 6.2.1–6.2.3 to enable the representation of XR environments' behavior. In this regard, it extends the *fluent ontology* (cf. Sect. 6.1.3) with relations between states, events, and time entities. The formalism of the fluent rule set provides higher expressivity than the formalism of the fluent ontology in the sense of linking individual objects' properties. Therefore, it is appropriate for composition and exploration of the behavior of XR environments, including past, current, and possible future activities. The facts and rules of the fluent rule set are application and domain independent, thus the rule set is common to all environments created with the E-XR approach. The fluent rule set consists of the following facts and rules:

1. Following Definitions 3.28, 6.17, and 6.18, it includes the facts that link the environment start event and the environment stop event with their time points: $time(event_{startEnv}, t_{startEnv})$ and $time(event_{stopEnv}, t_{stopEnv})$.
2. Following Theorems 6.4 and 6.5, it includes the facts that state that $t_{startEnv}$ is the earliest possible time point in an environment, and $t_{stopEnv}$ is the latest

possible time point in an environment, i.e., every time point in an environment is
between these time points:

$$TP \geq t_{startEnv}.$$
$$TP \leq t_{stopEnv}. \tag{6.15}$$

3. Following Definition 6.12, it includes the pointing to the left part of equivalence 6.1, which specifies the necessary and sufficient condition for the *in*
   predicate.
4. Following Theorem 3.1, it includes rule 3.5, which allows us to infer the
   satisfaction of the *holds At* predicate based on the satisfaction of the *holds*
   predicate.
5. Following Theorems 6.1, 6.2, and 6.3, it includes the rules that infer events
   beginning and finishing interval and instant states.
6. Following Definitions 6.13 and 6.14, it includes the pointing to the left parts of
   the equivalences, which specify the necessary and sufficient conditions for the
   predicates on time intervals.

Chapter 7
E-XR Semantic Link Model

The *E-XR semantic link model* (*link model* for short) is the second of the four main elements of the E-XR approach. It enables representation of workflow in XR environments using the *behavior model* with its semantics and the underlying knowledge representation technologies (cf. Chap. 6). The model permits linking imperative implementations of XR components, including their classes and methods, to the *ontology-* and *rule-based components* of the behavior model. The possibility to use imperative object-oriented and procedural languages makes the E-XR approach compatible with a wide range of solutions, including programming libraries, editors, and game engines. Thereby, it enables the fulfillment of non-functional requirement 1 (cf. Sect. 5.2.2). The link between different technologies is specified in a declarative way, which conforms to functional requirement 2 for the approach (cf. Sect. 5.2.1).

Due to the link model, execution of class methods is semantically represented by domain knowledge as users' and objects' activities and features. Methods represented by activities and features are used to compose the workflow of XR environments from XR components, which are independent, reusable modules with classes and methods. Furthermore, the methods can be used to log activities and features demonstrated while the environment is running. Hence, various kinds of users' and objects' behavior in different points and intervals of time can be subject to XR composition and exploration with automated reasoning and queries. The link model consists of four main components, which enable different stages of composition and exploration of XR environments.

1. *Representation of Activities and Features*, which is a knowledge-based data model for imperative implementations of XR components. The representation is devised for object-oriented and procedural languages and libraries as the foundation of XR implementation, while maintaining the possibility of composing and exploring the implementation with knowledge representation technologies. Activities and features are described in a structured way, with explicit semantics of their elements.

J. Flotyński, *Knowledge-Based Explorable Extended Reality Environments*,
https://doi.org/10.1007/978-3-030-59965-2_7

2. *Workflow Representation*, which is a specialization of the behavior model to states and events on methods in object-oriented and procedural implementations of XR components. The representation links such states and events with time points and intervals. Finally, it specifies transitions on states and events, which are critical to compose and explore XR behavior.
3. *Mapping*, which is a data model that augments imperative implementations of XR components with domain semantics specified by the behavior model. It links application classes to domain-specific classes and events on methods to domain-specific events. Mapping is crucial to facilitate the composition and exploration of environments by users without expertise in computer science.
4. *Code Templates*, which enable transformation of explorable XR environments composed using the behavior and semantic link models to imperative implementations while preserving the knowledge that describes the XR components used in the composition.

7.1   Representation of Activities and Features

Activities and features are domain-specific states that form a link between implementations of XR components and the behavior model. The representation of activities and features is specified using the Semantic Web approach in the *activity ontology*. The *activity ontology* is a pair of a TBox and an RBox that include axioms describing how users' and objects' activities and features are implemented in XR components and environments. The activity ontology is suitable for object-oriented and procedural XR implementations. The activity ontology is based on the fluent ontology of the behavior model (Fig. 5.2). It uses the following constructors of description logics: $\mathcal{ALUHQ(D)}$ (cf. Table 3.1). The OWL 2 DL profile is sufficiently expressive to provide such a logic (cf. Sect. 3.4.1).

The hierarchies of the classes, object properties, and datatype properties of the activity ontology are presented in Figs. 7.1, 7.2, and 7.3. The visualization has been prepared with the Protégé editor (Stanford University 2020), which has been used to develop the ontology. The overall ontology is presented in Listing 7.1. We refer to the classes and properties of the ontology in the following subsections. First, we describe the organization of imperative XR implementations in Sect. 7.1.1. Second, in Sect. 7.1.2, we introduce *join points*, which permit annotation of implementations in order to specify *activities* (explained in Sect. 7.1.3) and *features* (discussed in Sect. 7.1.4).

7.1.1   Classes, Methods, and Variables

The activity ontology covers the organization of object-oriented and procedural XR implementations since both types of implementations rely on functions as the basic

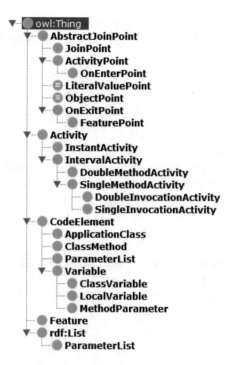

Fig. 7.1 OWL classes specified in activity ontology

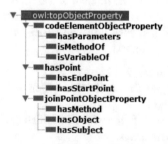

Fig. 7.2 OWL object properties specified in activity ontology

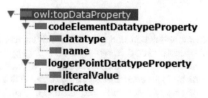

Fig. 7.3 OWL datatype properties specified in activity ontology

elements of workflow. The ontology specifies the following classes and properties related to elements of code:

CodeElement (Listing 7.1, line 14) is the class of all elements of the code of XR components. Different subclasses of *CodeElement* are distinguished.

1. *ApplicationClass* (lines 16–17) is the class of all application classes specified in the code of XR components and a subclass of *CodeElement*.
2. *Variable* (lines 19–33) is the class of all variables and a subclass of *CodeElement*. The following obligatory properties describe every variable:
   a. Exactly one *name* (lines 37–41).
   b. Exactly one *datatype* (lines 43–47).
   c. Exactly one *isVariableOf* (lines 52–56), which indicates an application class or a class method to which the variable belongs.

   Different subclasses of *Variable* are distinguished.

   a. *MethodParameter* (lines 58–59) is the class of all method parameters and a subclass of *Variable*.
   b. *LocalVariable* (lines 61–62) is the class of all local method variables and a subclass of *Variable*.
   c. *ClassVariable* (lines 64–65) is the class of all class variables and a subclass of *Variable*.

3. *ParameterList* (list 69–70) is the class of all lists of method parameters, a subclass of *CodeElement*, and a subclass of the RDF list. Every parameter list includes all parameters of a method (instances of *MethodParameter*) in the order in which they appear in the method declaration.
4. *ClassMethod* (lines 72–89) is the class of all methods specified in the code of XR components and a subclass of *CodeElement*. The following obligatory properties describe every method:
   a. Exactly one *name* (lines 37–41).
   b. Exactly one *datatype* (lines 43–47), which is the datatype of the value returned by the method.
   c. Exactly one *isMethodOf* (lines 91–92), which indicates the application class to which the method belongs.
   d. Exactly one *hasParameters* (lines 94–95), which indicates the list of parameters of the method.

Listing 7.1 Activity ontology, which represents activities and features (RDF Turtle format)

```
1  @base <http://semantic3d.org/e-xr/activity-ontology> .
2  @prefix ao: <http://semantic3d.org/e-xr/activity-ontology#>.
3  @prefix fo: <http://semantic3d.org/e-xr/fluent-ontology#> .
4  @prefix owl: <http://www.w3.org/2002/07/owl#> .
5  @prefix rdf: <http://www.w3.org/1999/02/22-rdf-syntax-ns#> .
6  @prefix rdfs: <http://www.w3.org/2000/01/rdf-schema#> .
7  @prefix xsd: <http://www.w3.org/2001/XMLSchema#> .
8
9  <http://semantic3d.org/e-xr/activity-ontology> rdf:type
```

```
10     owl:Ontology .
11
12    ##########Imperative Code Representation##########
13
14    ao:CodeElement rdf:type rdfs:Class .
15
16    ao:ApplicationClass rdf:type rdfs:Class ;
17       rdfs:subClassOf ao:CodeElement .
18
19    ao:Variable rdf:type owl:Class ;
20       rdfs:subClassOf ao:CodeElement ,
21       [ rdf:type owl:Restriction ;
22         owl:onProperty ao:name ;
23         owl:qualifiedCardinality "1"^^xsd:nonNegativeInteger ;
24         owl:onDataRange xsd:string ] ,
25       [ rdf:type owl:Restriction ;
26         owl:onProperty ao:datatype ;
27         owl:qualifiedCardinality "1"^^xsd:nonNegativeInteger ;
28         owl:onDataRange rdfs:Datatype ] ,
29       [ rdf:type owl:Restriction ;
30         owl:onProperty ao:isVariableOf ;
31         owl:qualifiedCardinality "1"^^xsd:nonNegativeInteger ;
32         owl:onClass [ rdf:type owl:Class ;
33           owl:unionOf ( ao:ApplicationClass ao:ClassMethod ) ] ].
34
35    ao:codeElementDatatypeProperty rdf:type owl:DatatypeProperty.
36
37    ao:name rdf:type owl:DatatypeProperty ;
38       rdfs:subPropertyOf ao:codeElementDatatypeProperty ;
39       rdfs:domain [ rdf:type owl:Class ;
40         owl:unionOf ( ao:ApplicationClass ao:ClassMethod
            ao:Variable ) ] ;
41       rdfs:range xsd:string .
42
43    ao:datatype rdf:type owl:DatatypeProperty ;
44       rdfs:subPropertyOf ao:codeElementDatatypeProperty ;
45       rdfs:domain [ rdf:type owl:Class ;
46         owl:unionOf ( ao:ClassMethod ao:Variable ) ] ;
47       rdfs:range rdfs:Datatype .
48
49    ao:codeElementObjectProperty rdf:type rdf:Property ;
50       rdfs:domain ao:CodeElement .
51
52    ao:isVariableOf rdf:type owl:ObjectProperty ;
53       rdfs:subPropertyOf ao:codeElementObjectProperty ;
54       rdfs:domain ao:Variable ;
55       rdfs:range [ rdf:type owl:Class ;
56         owl:unionOf ( ao:ApplicationClass ao:ClassMethod ) ] .
57
58    ao:MethodParameter rdf:type owl:Class ;
59       rdfs:subClassOf ao:Variable .
60
61    ao:LocalVariable rdf:type owl:Class ;
62       rdfs:subClassOf ao:Variable .
```

```
63
64   ao:ClassVariable rdf:type owl:Class ;
65     rdfs:subClassOf ao:Variable .
66
67   ao:this rdf:type owl:NamedIndividual .
68
69   ao:ParameterList rdf:type owl:Class ;
70     rdfs:subClassOf ao:CodeElement , rdf:List .
71
72   ao:ClassMethod rdf:type owl:Class ;
73     rdfs:subClassOf ao:CodeElement ,
74       [ rdf:type owl:Restriction ;
75         owl:onProperty ao:name ;
76         owl:qualifiedCardinality "1"^^xsd:nonNegativeInteger ;
77         owl:onDataRange xsd:string ] ,
78       [ rdf:type owl:Restriction ;
79         owl:onProperty ao:datatype ;
80         owl:qualifiedCardinality "1"^^xsd:nonNegativeInteger ;
81         owl:onDataRange rdfs:Datatype ] ,
82       [ rdf:type owl:Restriction ;
83         owl:onProperty ao:isMethodOf ;
84         owl:onClass ao:ApplicationClass ;
85         owl:qualifiedCardinality "1"^^xsd:nonNegativeInteger ],
86       [ rdf:type owl:Restriction ;
87         owl:onProperty ao:hasParameters ;
88         owl:onClass ao:ParameterList ;
89         owl:qualifiedCardinality "1"^^xsd:nonNegativeInteger ].
90
91   ao:isMethodOf rdf:type rdf:Property ;
92     rdfs:subPropertyOf ao:codeElementObjectProperty .
93
94   ao:hasParameters rdf:type owl:ObjectProperty ;
95     rdfs:subPropertyOf ao:codeElementObjectProperty .
96
97   ##########Join Points##########
98
99   ao:AbstractJoinPoint rdf:type owl:Class ;
100    rdfs:subClassOf [ rdf:type owl:Restriction ;
101      owl:onProperty ao:hasSubject ;
102      owl:onClass ao:Variable ;
103      owl:qualifiedCardinality "1"^^xsd:nonNegativeInteger ] ,
104    [ rdf:type owl:Restriction ;
105      owl:onProperty ao:hasMethod ;
106      owl:onClass ao:ClassMethod ;
107      owl:qualifiedCardinality "1"^^xsd:nonNegativeInteger] .
108
109  ao:joinPointObjectProperty rdf:type owl:ObjectProperty ;
110    rdfs:domain ao:AbstractJoinPoint .
111
112  ao:hasSubject rdf:type owl:ObjectProperty ;
113    rdfs:subPropertyOf ao:joinPointObjectProperty ;
114    rdfs:range ao:Variable .
115
116  ao:hasMethod rdf:type owl:ObjectProperty ;
```

```
117      rdfs:subPropertyOf ao:joinPointObjectProperty ;
118      rdfs:range ao:ClassMethod .
119
120  ao:OnEnterPoint rdf:type owl:Class ;
121      rdfs:subClassOf ao:ActivityPoint .
122
123  ao:OnExitPoint rdf:type owl:Class ;
124      rdfs:subClassOf ao:AbstractJoinPoint ;
125      owl:disjointWith ao:OnEnterPoint .
126
127  ao:ActivityPoint rdf:type owl:Class ;
128      rdfs:subClassOf [ rdf:type owl:Restriction ;
129        owl:onProperty fo:hasTimePoint ;
130        owl:onClass fo:TimePoint ;
131        owl:maxQualifiedCardinality "1"^^xsd:nonNegativeInteger ] ;
132      rdfs:subClassOf ao:AbstractJoinPoint .
133
134  ao:FeaturePoint rdf:type owl:Class ;
135      rdfs:subClassOf ao:OnExitPoint ;
136      owl:disjointWith ao:ActivityPoint .
137
138  ao:ObjectPoint rdf:type owl:Class ;
139      rdfs:subClassOf ao:AbstractJoinPoint ;
140      owl:equivalentClass [ rdf:type owl:Restriction ;
141        owl:onProperty ao:hasObject ;
142        owl:onClass ao:Variable ;
143        owl:qualifiedCardinality "1"^^xsd:nonNegativeInteger ] .
144
145        ao:hasObject rdf:type owl:ObjectProperty ;
146      rdfs:subPropertyOf ao:joinPointObjectProperty ;
147      rdfs:domain ao:ObjectPoint ;
148      rdfs:range ao:Variable .
149
150  ao:LiteralValuePoint rdf:type owl:Class ;
151      rdfs:subClassOf ao:AbstractJoinPoint ;
152      owl:equivalentClass [ rdf:type owl:Restriction ;
153        owl:onProperty ao:literalValue ;
154        owl:qualifiedCardinality "1"^^xsd:nonNegativeInteger ;
155        owl:onDataRange rdfs:Datatype ] ;
156      owl:disjointWith ao:ObjectPoint .
157
158  ao:joinPointDatatypeProperty rdf:type owl:DatatypeProperty ;
159      rdfs:domain ao:AbstractJoinPoint .
160
161  ao:literalValue rdf:type owl:DatatypeProperty ;
162      rdfs:subPropertyOf ao:joinPointDatatypeProperty ;
163      rdfs:domain ao:LiteralValuePoint ;
164      rdf:range rdfs:Datatype .
165
166  ao:JoinPoint rdf:type owl:Class ;
167      rdfs:subClassOf ao:AbstractJoinPoint ,
168      [ rdf:type owl:Class ;
169        owl:unionOf ( ao:OnEnterPoint ao:OnExitPoint ) ] ,
170      [ rdf:type owl:Class ;
```

```
171       owl:unionOf ( ao:ActivityPoint ao:FeaturePoint ) ] ,
172    [ rdf:type owl:Class ;
173       owl:unionOf ( ao:LiteralValuePoint ao:ObjectPoint ) ] .
174
175    ##########Activities##########
176
177    ao:Activity rdf:type owl:Class .
178
179    ao:predicate rdf:type rdf:Property ;
180      rdfs:domain [ owl:unionOf ( ao:Activity ao:Feature ) ] ;
181      rdfs:range rdf:Property .
182
183    ##########Instant Activities##########
184
185    ao:InstantActivity rdf:type owl:Class ;
186      rdfs:subClassOf ao:Activity ,
187      [ rdf:type owl:Restriction ;
188        owl:onProperty ao:hasPoint ;
189        owl:onClass ao:OnExitPoint ;
190        owl:qualifiedCardinality "1"^^xsd:nonNegativeInteger ] .
191
192        ao:hasPoint rdf:type owl:ObjectProperty ;
193      rdfs:domain [ rdf:type owl:Class ;
194        owl:unionOf ( ao:Activity ao:Feature ) ] .
195
196    ##########Interval Activities##########
197
198    ao:IntervalActivity rdf:type owl:Class ;
199      rdfs:subClassOf ao:Activity ,
200      [ rdf:type owl:Restriction ;
201        owl:onProperty ao:hasEndPoint ;
202        owl:qualifiedCardinality "1"^^xsd:nonNegativeInteger ;
203        owl:onClass ao:OnExitPoint ] ;
204      owl:disjointWith ao:InstantActivity .
205
206    ao:hasPoint rdf:type owl:ObjectProperty ;
207      rdfs:domain [ rdf:type owl:Class ;
208        owl:unionOf ( ao:Activity ao:Feature )
209      rdfs:range ao:AbstractJoinPoint .
210
211    ao:hasEndPoint rdf:type owl:ObjectProperty ;
212      rdfs:subPropertyOf ao:hasPoint ;
213      rdfs:domain ao:IntervalActivity ;
214      rdfs:range ao:ActivityPoint .
215
216    ##########Single Method Activities##########
217
218    ao:SingleMethodActivity rdf:type owl:Class ;
219      rdfs:subClassOf ao:IntervalActivity .
220
221    ao:SingleInvocationActivity rdf:type owl:Class ;
222      rdfs:subClassOf ao:SingleMethodActivity ,
223      [ rdf:type owl:Restriction ;
224        owl:onProperty ao:hasStartPoint ;
```

```
225        owl:qualifiedCardinality "1"^^xsd:nonNegativeInteger ;
226        owl:onClass ao:OnEnterPoint ] .
227
228  ao:hasStartPoint rdf:type owl:ObjectProperty ;
229     rdfs:subPropertyOf ao:hasPoint ;
230     rdfs:domain ao:IntervalActivity ;
231     rdfs:range ao:ActivityPoint .
232
233  ao:DoubleInvocationActivity rdf:type owl:Class ;
234     rdfs:subClassOf ao:SingleMethodActivity ,
235     [ rdf:type owl:Restriction ;
236        owl:onProperty ao:hasStartPoint ;
237        owl:qualifiedCardinality "1"^^xsd:nonNegativeInteger ;
238        owl:onClass ao:OnExitPoint ] ;
239     owl:disjointWith ao:SingleInvocationActivity .
240
241  ##########Double Method Activities##########
242
243  ao:DoubleMethodActivity rdf:type owl:Class ;
244     rdfs:subClassOf ao:IntervalActivity ,
245     [ rdf:type owl:Restriction ;
246        owl:onProperty ao:hasStartPoint ;
247        owl:qualifiedCardinality "1"^^xsd:nonNegativeInteger ;
248        owl:onClass ao:OnExitPoint ] ;
249     owl:disjointWith ao:SingleMethodActivity .
250
251  ##########Features##########
252
253  ao:Feature rdf:type owl:Class ;
254     rdfs:subClassOf [ rdf:type owl:Restriction ;
255        owl:onProperty ao:hasPoint ;
256        owl:qualifiedCardinality "1"^^xsd:nonNegativeInteger ;
257        owl:onClass ao:FeaturePoint ] .
```

7.1.2 Join Points

Join points are places in implementations of XR components that are used by *activities* (described in Section 7.1.3) and features (described in Section 7.1.4) to specify the semantics of the implementations using domain knowledge described by the behavior model. The following specifications of classes and properties related to join points are included in the activity ontology.

AbstractJoinPoint (lines 99–107) is the class of all abstract join points. An abstract join point specifies a subset of all properties required for a join point used in a practical application of E-XR. The following obligatory properties describe every abstract join point:

1. Exactly one *hasSubject* (lines 112–114), which indicates the XR user or XR object that performs an activity or has a feature. The user or object is represented by a variable. The user or object is referred to as a *subject* in the property name to keep consistency with the notation of RDF statements (cf. Definition 3.77).
2. Exactly one *hasMethod* (lines 116–118), which indicates the application class method associated with the abstract join point. As explained in Sects. 7.1.3 and 7.1.4, the execution of the method signifies an activity or a feature of the XR component.

Different subclasses of *AbstractJoinPoint* are distinguished depending on indicated fragments of class methods, which may be the beginning or the end of a method.

1. *OnEnterPoint* (lines 120–121) is the class of all join points that indicate invocations of class methods and a subclass of *AbstractJoinPoint*. Every on-enter join point is also an instance of the *ActivityPoint* class (described below), i.e., on-enter join points are used only to represent activities.
2. *OnExitPoint* (lines 123–125) is the class of all join points that indicate successful finalizations (*completions*) of class methods and a subclass of *AbstractJoinPoint*.

OnEnterPoint and *OnExitPoint* are disjoint classes. Moreover, different subclasses of *AbstractJoinPoint* are also distinguished depending on what the indicated method implements—an activity or a feature of the component.

1. *ActivityPoint* (lines 127–132) is a subclass of *AbstractJoinPoint* and a subclass of all join points with at most one *hasTimePoint* property, which is specified in the fluent ontology (cf. Sect. 6.1.3). Activity join points are used to indicate methods whose invocation or completion means the beginning or finish of an activity.
2. *FeaturePoint* (lines 134–136) is a subclass of *AbstractJoinPoint* and the class of all join points with no *hasTimePoint* property assigned. The lack of a time point means that the indicated method sets permanent (time-independent) properties of the XR environment. Every feature join point is also an instance of the *OnExitPoint* class, i.e., only on-exit join points are used to represent features.

ActivityPoint and *FeaturePoint* are disjoint classes. Finally, different subclasses of *AbstractJoinPoint* are also distinguished depending on whether objects or literal values are linked.

1. *ObjectPoint* (lines 138–143) is the class of all join points that indicate objects and a subclass of *AbstractJoinPoint*. Every object join point is described

by exactly one *hasObject* property (lines 145–148), which indicates an object describing an activity or a feature. An object is represented by a variable.

2. *LiteralValuePoint* (lines 150–156) is the class of all join points that indicate literal values and a subclass of *AbstractJoinPoint*. Every literal value join point is described by exactly one *literalValue* property (lines 161–164), which indicates a literal value describing an activity or a feature.

ObjectPoint and *LiteralValuePoint* are disjoint classes. Join points used in practical applications of E-XR are instances of the *JoinPoint* class.
JoinPoint (lines 166–173) is a subclass of *AbstractJoinPoint* and a subclass of:

1. The union of *OnEnterPoint* and *OnExitPoint*.
2. The union of *ActivityPoint* and *FeaturePoint*.
3. The union of *ObjectPoint* and *LiteralValuePoint*.

7.1.3 Structure of Activities

Activities are the main entities specified in the activity ontology. Activities are states of XR components that change over time, particularly—animations and modifications of variables. An activity links fragments of the implementation of an XR component with the behavior model, thereby specifying the code semantics using domain knowledge. Activities link class methods to elements of *temporal statements* (subjects, predicates, and objects—cf. Definition 6.10). It permits creation and exploration of behavior logs, which represent users' and objects' activities with regard to their domain semantics. Furthermore, activities are used to compose explorable environments and explore potential users' and objects' behavior. Different activities use different types of join points, which is summarized in Fig. 7.4. The following specification of *Activity* is the basis for all other activities in the activity ontology.

Activity (line 177) is the class of all activities and a subclass of *State*. Every activity is described by exactly one *predicate* property (lines 179–181), which designates a predicate that specifies the activity's semantics using the behavior model. An activity predicate is a domain property specified in a domain ontology of the behavior model (cf. Sect. 6.1.1). A predicate represents an action or interaction, e.g., *assembles*, *watches*, and *selects*. Different subclasses of *Activity* are distinguished depending on whether they occur at a time point or a within time interval. They are described in the following subsections.

Instant Activities

InstantActivity (lines 185–190) is the class of all activities that occur at the time point when a class method is completed and a subclass of *Activity*. The *duration* of an instant activity is equal to 0. Every instant activity has exactly one *hasPoint* property (lines 192–194), which indicates an on-exit join point. Thereby, an instant activity is considered completed as the associated method is completed.

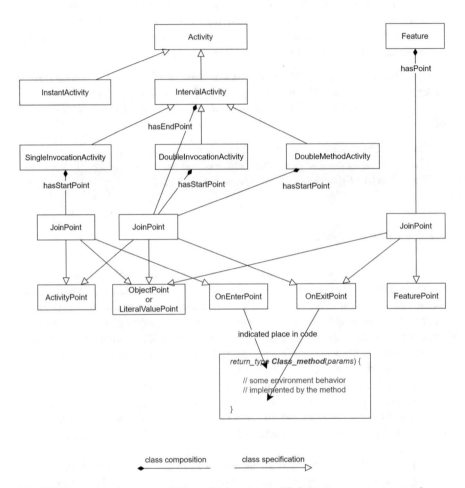

Fig. 7.4 Connections between activities and join points and their impact on component code

An example *instant activity* links the following domain knowledge to the completion of the `detachTransformer` method: an *electrician* (subject) for whom the method was invoked *detaches* (predicate) a *transformer* (object) passed as a method parameter, at a specific time point.

Interval Activities

IntervalActivity (lines 198–204) is the class of all activities that occur within an interval of time started by an invocation or completion of a class method and finished by a completion of a method and a subclass of *Activity*. The *duration* of an interval activity is larger than 0. Every *interval activity* is described by exactly one *hasEndPoint* property (lines 211–214), a subproperty of *hasPoint* (lines 206–209), that indicates an *on-exit join point* determining the end of the activity's time interval. Different subclasses of *IntervalActivity* are distinguished depending on their implementation based on methods, which is reflected by the used join points. The subclasses are described in the following subsections.

SingleMethodActivity (lines 218–219) is the class of all activities that occur within a time interval started by an invocation or completion of a class method and finished by a completion of the same method and a subclass of *IntervalActivity*. Hence, the join points of a single method activity indicated by the *hasStartPoint* and *hasEndPoint* properties indicate the same method, which is expressed by the same value of the *hasMethod* property of both join points. Different subclasses of *SingleMethodActivity* are distinguished.

1. *SingleInvocationActivity* (lines 221–226) is the class of all activities that occur within a time interval started by an invocation of a class method and finished by the completion of the method that follows the invocation, and a subclass of *SingleMethodActivity*. Every *single invocation activity* is described by exactly one *hasStartPoint* property (lines 228–231), a subproperty of *hasPoint*, that indicates an *on-enter join point* determining the start of the activity's time interval.

   An example *single invocation activity* links the following domain knowledge to the execution of the `movesAround` method: a *satellite* (subject) for which the method was invoked *moves around* (predicate) a *planet* (object), passed as a method parameter, since the invocation (on-enter join point) until the completion (on-exit join point) of the method.

2. *DoubleInvocationActivity* (lines 233–239) is the class of all activities that occur within a time interval started by a completion of a class method and finished by another completion of the method and a subclass of *SingleMethodActivity*. Every *double invocation activity* is described by exactly one *hasStartPoint* property that indicates an *on-exit join point* determining the start of the activity's time interval. The *hasEndPoint* property of the activity indicates the same join point. *DoubleInvocationActivity* is disjoint with *SingleInvocationActivity*.

   An example *double invocation activity* links the following domain knowledge to the time interval determined by two executions of the `paint` method for the same subject but different objects: a *room* (subject) for which the method was invoked *is painted* (predicate) by a specific *color* (object), passed as a method parameter, since the completion (on-exit join point) until another completion (on-exit join point) of the method for the same subject yet another object.

DoubleMethodActivity (lines 243–249) is the class of all activities that occur within a time interval started by a completion of a class method and finished by a completion of another method and a subclass of *IntervalActivity*. Every *double method activity* is described by exactly one *hasStartPoint* property that indicates an *on-exit join point* determining the start of the activity's time interval. A double method activity is also described by exactly one *has End Point* property that indicates an *on-exit join point* with another method than the method indicated by the start join point. *Double Method Activity* is disjoint with *Single Method Activity*. An example *double method activity* links the following domain knowledge to the time interval determined by executions of two different methods: a *customer* (subject) for whom the `startShopping` method was invoked *is shopping* (predicate) since the completion (on-exit join point) of the method until the completion (on-exit join point) of the `stopShopping` method.

7.1.4   Structure of Features

Apart from activities, the second main group of elements of the activity ontology are *features*. Features are states of XR components that do not change over time—represent time-independent properties. Like activities, features link fragments of the implementation (class methods) of XR components with the behavior model using join points (Fig. 7.4). Thereby, they also specify the semantics of methods using domain knowledge. However, as opposed to activities, methods linked by features implement immutable (time-independent) properties of users and objects, which do not change over time, e.g., landscape elements and buildings in a virtual town. The possible use of features is likewise the use of activities—for composition and exploration of XR environments, which is explained in detail in Chap. 8. Since a feature represents time-independent properties, it is related neither to a time point nor to a time interval. Thus, it has exactly one join point assigned. A feature is considered as set upon the completion of its associated class methods.

Feature (lines 253–257) is the class of all features and a subclass of *State*. The following obligatory properties describe every feature:

1. Exactly one *predicate* (lines 179–181), which designates a predicate that specifies the semantics of the feature using the behavior model.
2. Exactly one *has Point* (lines 192–194), which indicates a *feature join point*, which determines a point in a class method whose achievement means the satisfaction of the predicate.

An example *feature* links the following domain knowledge to the completion of a constructor of the *building* class: the created *building* (subject) *is located* (predicate) in a *specific position* in the scene (object), passed as a method parameter, throughout the whole life cycle of the scene.

Activities and features specified for an XR component form an *activity knowledge base*.

Definition 7.1 An ***activity knowledge base*** is an ABox that consists of statements describing activities and features.

7.2 Workflow Representation

The workflow representation adapts the behavior model to the description of states, events, and time related to the execution of class methods. Hence, it enables the specification of XR components' behavior upon their underlying imperative implementation. The workflow representation is based on the representation of activities and features provided by the link model as well as the fluent rule set of the behavior model (Fig. 5.2).

In the description of the workflow representation, we refer to methods using their identifiers. We assume that a method ID is globally unique. It can be the concatenation of the method name, list of parameters, class name, namespace or package name, and component name. Such a method ID is an *atom* according to the behavior model terminology (cf. Definition 3.1). However, to simplify the presentation, we use the method name (called *method*) as its ID.

7.2.1 Events and States for Methods

We formally represent different states and events of method processing such as *invocation*, *execution*, *finalization*, and *completion*.

Definition 7.2 A *method execution state* is a *state* that is specified for a triple: a *method*, a *parameter list*, and an *execution ID*, where the *parameter list* is a sequence of terms for which the *method* is executed, and the *execution ID* is a unique atom.

It is denoted as $executed(method(p_1, p_2, \ldots, p_n), executionID)$, where $(p_1, p_2, \ldots, p_n)$ is a parameter list. For example, state $executed(driveCar(50mph, 0.5h), 1)$ denotes an execution of the *driveCar* method with speed 50mph for half an hour. In the following rules in which we refer to methods, we use only the method ID and skip the list of parameters if it does not influence the conclusion—is not used in the rule head.

In addition, a method execution is marked by an execution ID. Every execution ID is unique for a particular method. Thus the pair $(method, executionID)$ is globally unique. Execution IDs can be generated by the system every time a method starts to be executed. In the following rules in this chapter, execution IDs could be generated in the rule bodies.

Definition 7.3 *MethodExecutionState* is the set of all *method execution states*.

As a non-empty method, which performs some operations, always takes time (has *duration* longer than zero—cf. Definition 6.19 and Theorem 6.7), we can conclude that:

Theorem 7.1 *A method execution state is an interval state:*

$$Method Execution State \subset Interval State. \tag{7.1}$$

Every method execution state is begun by a method invocation and finished by a method finalization that follows the invocation. Both invocations and finalizations are represented by events. An execution ID associated with a method execution state is also associated with the invocation and finalization events, thereby linking the consecutive method invocation, execution, and finalization.

Definition 7.4 A **method invocation event** is an *event* that begins a *method execution state*.

Like a method execution state, every method invocation event is determined by a pair $(method, executionID)$. Also, a parameter list can be specified for a method execution state. Hence, a method invocation event is denoted as $invoked(method(p_1, p_2, \ldots, p_n), executionID)$. For example, event $invoked(driveCar(50mph, 0.5h), 1)$ denotes the invocation of the *driveCar* method with the parameters, which is associated with execution ID equal to 1. Taking into account Definition 6.15, we can express the following relation between *method invocation event* and *method execution state*:

Theorem 7.2 *Every method execution state is begun by a method invocation event:*

$$\forall executed(method, executionID) \in MethodExecutionState:$$
$$\exists invoked(method, executionID) \in Event:$$
$$invoked(method, executionID)$$
$$= begin(executed(method, executionID)).$$

(7.2)

We have skipped parameter lists in the formulas because the pair *(method, executionID)* suffices to identify method execution states and method invocation events.

Definition 7.5 A **method finalization event** is an *event* that finishes a *method execution state*.

Like a method execution state and a method invocation event, every method finalization event is determined by a pair $(method, executionID)$. It is denoted as $finished(method(p_1, p_2, \ldots, p_n), executionID)$. For example, event $finished(driveCar(50mph, 0.5h), 1)$ denotes the finalization of the *driveCar* method with the parameters, which is associated with execution ID equal to 1. In other words, it finishes state $executed(driveCar(50mph, 0.5h), 1)$, which has been begun by event $invoked(driveCar(50mph, 0.5h), 1)$. Taking into account Definition 6.16, we can express the following relation between *method finalization event* and *method execution state*:

Theorem 7.3 *Every method execution state is finished by a method finalization event:*

$$\forall executed(method, executionID) \in Method\,Execution\,State:$$

$$\exists finished(method, executionID) \in Event:$$

$$finished(method, executionID) \tag{7.3}$$

$$= finish(executed(method, executionID)).$$

During a method execution, exceptions may be thrown.

Definition 7.6 The *exception* predicate is a predicate that is true for a given *method execution state* and an *exception* if and only if the *exception* is thrown during the *method execution state*.

It is denoted as $exception(executed(method, executionID), exc)$. For example, $exception(executed(driveCar, 1), runtimeException)$ evaluates whether *runtimeException* is thrown while executing the *driveCar* method.

A method is completed if no exceptions have been thrown during its execution, i.e., it has been successfully finished.

Definition 7.7 A *method completion event* is an *event* that finishes a *method execution state* during which no *exceptions* have been thrown. Throwing no exceptions is denoted by the *null* atom, which is a possible argument of the *exception* predicate:

$$\forall executed(method, executionID) \in Method\,Execution\,State:$$

$$(\exists completed(method, executionID) \in Event:$$

$$completed(method, executionID) = finished(method, executionID))$$

$$\Leftarrow exception(executed(method, executionID), null). \tag{7.4}$$

For the sake of simplification, we often refer to *method execution states* as *method executions* and to *method invocation, finalization*, and *completion* events as *method invocations, finalizations*, and *completions*, respectively.

7.2.2   Linking Method States and Events with Time

Using the *time, holdsAt*, and *holds* predicates (cf. Definitions 3.28, 3.34 and 3.35), we can link the states and events related to methods with temporal entities in which the states and events occur. Based on Theorem 7.1 and Definitions 7.4 and 7.5, we can state that a method finalization occurs later than the corresponding method invocation.

Theorem 7.4 *The method finalization event that finishes a method execution state occurs later than the method invocation event that begins the method execution state:*

$\forall executed(method, executionID) \in MethodExecutionState$:

$\exists tp_{fin}, tp_{inv} \in TimePoint$:

$tp_{fin} > tp_{inv} \Leftarrow time(finished(method, executionID), tp_{fin})$

$\qquad \land time(invoked(method, executionID), tp_{inv})$,

$$(7.5)$$

where tp_{fin} and tp_{inv} are time points when method finalization event and method invocation event occur.

Theorem 7.5 *A method invocation event that occurs at a time point begins a method execution state that occurs within a time interval starting from the time point:*

$\forall invoked(method, executionID) \in Event$:

$\quad \exists executed(method, executionID) \in MethodExecutionState,$

$\qquad ti \in TimeInterval, tp_{inv} \in TimePoint$:

$\qquad\quad holds(executed(method, executionID), ti) \land start(ti, tp_{inv})$

$\qquad\qquad \Leftarrow time(invoked(method, executionID), tp_{inv}).$

$$(7.6)$$

Theorem 7.6 *The time interval within which a method execution state occurs ends at the time point when the method finalization event that finishes the method execution state occurs:*

$\forall executed(method, executionID) \in MethodExecutionState$:

$\quad \exists finished(method, executionID) \in Event, ti \in TimeInterval,$

$\qquad tp_{fin} \in TimePoint$:

$\qquad\quad holds(executed(method, executionID), ti) \land end(ti, tp_{fin})$

$\qquad\qquad \Leftarrow time(finished(method, executionID), tp_{fin}).$

$$(7.7)$$

7.2.3   Generating Transitions

The elements of the link model presented in the previous sections: the *representation of activities and features* and the *workflow representation* are used together to generate *component transition sets* representing the semantics of *invocation*, *execution*, *finalization*, and *completion* of the class methods of an XR component. A *component transition set* associates invocations, executions, finalizations, and completions of the class methods, thereby describing the overall behavior of an XR component. A *component transition set* is generated for an XR component by the *transition generation algorithm*. We introduce the following definitions to facilitate the description of the algorithm.

Definition 7.8 An *instant activity method* is the class method indicated by the *hasMethod* property of the *join point* indicated by the *hasPoint* property of an *instant activity*.

Definition 7.9 An *activity start method* is the class method indicated by the *hasMethod* property of the *join point* indicated by the *hasStartPoint* property of an *interval activity*.

Definition 7.10 An *activity end method* is the class method indicated by the *hasMethod* property of the *join point* indicated by the *hasEndPoint* property of an *interval activity*.

Definition 7.11 An *instant activity join point* is the *join point* indicated by the *hasPoint* property of an *activity*.

Definition 7.12 An *activity start join point* is the *join point* indicated by the *hasStartPoint* property of an *activity*.

Definition 7.13 An *activity end join point* is the *join point* indicated by the *hasEndPoint* property of an *activity*.

Definition 7.14 An *activity fluent* is the *fluent* indicated by the *predicate* property of an *activity*.

Definition 7.15 A *feature join point* is the *join point* indicated by the *hasPoint* property of a *feature*.

Definition 7.16 A *feature method* is the class method indicated by the *hasMethod* property of a *feature join point*.

Definition 7.17 A *feature predicate* is the *predicate* indicated by the *predicate* property of a *feature*.

To specify transitions for component transition sets, we introduce the *occurred* predicate, which states that an event occurred at a past time point, which is always true since the occurrence of the event.

Definition 7.18 The *occurred* predicate is a fluent that is true for a given *event* within the *time interval* started by the *time point* of the *event* occurrence and finished by the *time point* of terminating the environment:

$\forall event \in Event: \exists tp \in TimePoint, ti \in TimeInterval:$

$$holds(occurred(event, tp), ti) \Leftrightarrow time(event, tp) \wedge start(ti, tp) \qquad (7.8)$$

$$\wedge\, end(ti, tp_{stopEnv}).$$

In addition, we also introduce a predicate designated to generate unique atoms that are used as IDs for various entities, such as objects, time points, time intervals, and method executions.

Definition 7.19 The **generated** predicate is a predicate that is true for a given *variable* if and only if a unique atom has been generated and set as the *variable's* value.

It is denoted as $generated(X)$. The predicate is intended for variables that have no value yet. For instance, $generated(ExecutionID)$ is satisfied if a unique ID has been generated and set for the $ExecutionID$ variable. For unset variables, we can assume that $generated$ is always satisfied in a properly working system. An example simplified implementation of the $generated$ predicate in Prolog is based on random numbers:

$$generated(X) \Leftarrow random(X), \qquad (7.9)$$

where $random$ is a Prolog built-in function and X is a generated random number. The *transition generation algorithm* performs the following steps:

1. Create an empty *component transition set*.
2. Add the pointing to the left implication from the equivalence in Definition 7.18, which specifies the necessary and sufficient condition for the *occurred* state, to the *component transition set*.
3. Add the implementation of the *generated* predicate (e.g., Formula 7.9) to the *component transition set*.
4. For every *method* that is an *instant activity method*, *activity start method*, *activity end method*, or *feature method*, add the following transitions to the *component transition set*:

   a. The transition that states a *method finalization* after the corresponding *method invocation*, which is entailed by Theorems 7.2, 7.3 and 7.4 as well as Definition 6.26:

   $$time(finished(Method, ExecutionID), TP_{fin})$$

   $$\Leftarrow time(invoked(Method, ExecutionID), TP_{inv}) \wedge generated(TP_{fin})$$

   $$\wedge\, assert(TP_{fin} > TP_{inv}),$$

   $$(7.10)$$

   where TP_{fin} is the time point of finishing *method execution*, which is generated by the system.

Comment: *Every method invoked is finally finished—not later than at the termination of the XR environment (cf. Definition 6.18). As the transition applies to any method, the Method variable is used. The method finalization is associated with its invocation by a common executionID. The exact time of the method finalization cannot be determined in advance. Therefore, it is only asserted that the finalization is after the invocation.*

b. The transition that states a *method completion* depending on its finalization, which is entailed by Definition 7.7:

$$time(completed(Method, ExecutionID), TP)$$

$$\Leftarrow time(finished(Method, ExecutionID), TP) \tag{7.11}$$

$$\wedge\ exception(executed(Method, ExecutionID), null).$$

Comment: *A method is completed at the time point when it is finished if no exceptions have been thrown during its execution.*

c. The transition that states the occurrence of events, which is entailed by Definition 7.18:

$$holds(occurred(Event, TP), TI)$$

$$\Leftarrow time(Event, TP) \wedge generated(TI) \wedge assert(start(TI, TP))$$

$$\wedge\ assert(end(TI, tp_{stopEnv})).$$

$$\tag{7.12}$$

Comment: *Due to the transition, the occurrence of an event is known until the termination of the environment.*

5. For every *instant activity*, add the transition that states the activity as completed at the time point as the instant activity method is completed (Sect. 7.1.3):

$$holdsAt(predicate(Subject, Object), TP)$$

$$\Leftarrow time(completed(method(Subject, Object), ExecutionID), TP), \tag{7.13}$$

where *method* is the *instant activity method*, *Subject* and *Object* are the subject and object or literal value of the *instant activity join point*, and *predicate* is the *activity fluent*.

Comment: *In the method parameter list, only Subject and Object are relevant. Other parameters in the list, even if used for the invocation, have been skipped in the transition because they do not influence the activity—do not appear in the transition head. As this transition is generated individually for particular activities, the method is represented by an atom rather than a variable, in contrast to the previous transitions that are common to different methods. Furthermore, the instant activity does not depend on ExecutionID, which may be set to any value. Similar notation is also used in the following transitions.*

6. For every *single invocation activity*, add the transition that states the activity as occurred within the time interval determined by the events of an invocation and completion of the *activity start method*, which is also the *activity end method* (cf. Sect. 7.1.3):

$$holds(predicate(Subject, Object), TI)$$

$$\Leftarrow holdsAt(occurred(completed(method(Subject, Object),$$

$$ExecutionID), TP_{comp}), TP_{comp})$$

$$\wedge holdsAt(occurred(invoked(method(Subject, Object),$$

$$ExecutionID), TP_{inv}), TP_{comp})$$

$$\wedge generated(TI) \wedge assert(start(TI, TP_{inv})) \wedge assert(end(TI, TP_{comp})),$$
$$(7.14)$$

where *method* is the *activity start method* and *activity end method*, *Subject* and *Object* are the subject and object or literal value of the *activity join points*, *predicate* is the *activity fluent*, and *TI* is a time interval with an ID generated by the system.

Comment: As a single invocation activity lasts from a method invocation to the method completion, its occurrence can be asserted a posteriori. As long as the method is being executed, we cannot be sure whether it will be completed. Therefore, the activity's time interval is asserted in the transition body if the invocation and completion events occurred. A common ExecutionID links the invocation and completion, i.e., it designates the completion that follows the invocation.

7. For every *double invocation activity*, add the transitions that state the activity as occurred within the time interval determined by the events of completing the *activity start method*, which is also the *activity end method* (cf. Sect. 7.1.3):

$$holds(predicate(Subject, Object_1), TI)$$

$$\Leftarrow time(completed(method(Subject, Object_1), ExecutionID), TP)$$

$$\wedge generated(TI) \wedge assert(start(TI, TP)).$$

$$holds(predicate(Subject, Object_1), TI)$$

$$\Leftarrow holdsAt(occurred(completed(method(Subject, Object_2),$$

$$ExecutionID), TP), TP)$$

$$\wedge holdsAt(predicate(Subject, Object_1), TP)$$

$$\wedge holds(predicate(Subject, Object_1), TI) \wedge in(TP, TI)$$

$$\wedge assert(end(TI, TP)),$$

$$(7.15)$$

where *method* is the activity start and activity end method, $Subject$, $Object_1$, and $Object_2$ are the subject and objects or literal values of the *activity join points*, and *predicate* is the *activity fluent*.

Comment: *As two different completions of a method are responsible for beginning and finishing a double invocation activity, the activity's occurrence can be asserted once it is started. Also, ExecutionIDs related to the invocation and completion of the method are independent. The time interval of a double invocation activity is asserted in the body of the first transition. The holds predicate in the second transition body is used to find the open time interval in which the activity is lasting to finish the activity.*

8. For every *double method activity*, add the transitions that state the activity as occurred within the time interval determined by the events of completing the *activity start method* and the *activity end method* (cf. Sect. 7.1.3):

$$holds(predicate(Subject, Object), TI)$$

$$\Leftarrow time(completed(method_1(Subject, Object), ExecutionID), TP)$$

$$\wedge generated(TI) \wedge assert(start(TI, TP)).$$

$$holds(predicate(Subject, Object), TI)$$

$$\Leftarrow holdsAt(occurred(completed(method_2(Subject, Object)), \qquad (7.16)$$

$$ExecutionID), TP), TP)$$

$$\wedge holdsAt(predicate(Subject, Object), TP)$$

$$\wedge holds(predicate(Subject, Object), TI) \wedge in(TP, TI)$$

$$\wedge assert(end(TI, TP)).$$

where $method_1$ and $method_2$ are activity start and activity end methods, respectively, $Subject$ and $Object$ are the subject and object or literal value of the *activity join points*, *predicate* is the *activity fluent*, and *TI* is a time interval with an ID generated by the system.

Comment: *As two completions of different methods are responsible for beginning and finishing a double method activity, the activity's occurrence can be asserted once it is started. Also, ExecutionIDs related to the invocation and completion of the methods are independent. The time interval of a double method activity is asserted in the body of the first transition. The holds predicate in the second transition body is used to find the open time interval in which the activity is lasting to finish the activity.*

9. For every *feature*, add the transition that sets the feature if the *feature method* is completed (cf. Sect. 7.1.4):

$$predicate(Subject, Object)$$

$$\Leftarrow time(completed(method(Subject, Object), ExecutionID), TP),$$

$$(7.17)$$

where *method* is the *feature method*, *Subject* and *Object* are the subject and object or literal value of the *feature join point*, and *predicate* is the *feature predicate*.

Comment: *The feature is set if the method is completed, independently of completion time point TP and ExecutionID.*

A component transition set created by the transition generation algorithm represents the behavior of an XR component. According to Definition 6.27, it includes:

1. *Events* that represent invocation, finalization, and completion of methods (cf. Definitions 7.4, 7.5, and 7.7).
2. *States* that represent execution and occurrence of methods (cf. Definitions 7.2 and 7.18) as well as *activities* and *features* (cf. Sects. 7.1.3 and 7.1.4).
3. *Transitions* that link events and states.

In Listing 7.2, we present an example of a component transition set generated for an XR component of an explorable service guide for home appliances. The transitions in lines 1–3 and 5–7 link method invocations, finalizations, and completions. They have been added by Steps 4a and 4b of the transition generation algorithm. The transitions in lines 9–12 and 14–17 associate states with method invocations and completions and have been added by Step 4c of the algorithm. The next transition (19–26) specifies a *double method activity* of including elements by a serviced hob. It is started upon a completion of the *assembles* method and finished upon the corresponding completion of the *disassembles* method.

Listing 7.2 Example of component transition set for an XR hob used to compose immersive service guide

```
1    time(finished(Method, ExecutionID), TP_fin)
2       ⇐ time(invoked(Method, ExecutionID), TP_inv)
3          ∧generated(TP_fin) ∧ assert(TP_fin > TP_inv).
4
5    time(completed(Method, ExecutionID), TP)
6       ⇐ time(finished(Method, ExecutionID), TP)
7          ∧exception(executed(Method, ExecutionID), null).
8
9    holds(occurred(invoked(Method, ExecutionID), TP), TI)
10      ⇐ time(invoked(Method, ExecutionID), TP)
11         ∧generated(TI) ∧ assert(start(TI, TP))
12         ∧assert(end(TI, tp_stopEnv)).
13
14   holds(occurred(completed(Method, ExecutionID), TP), TI)
15      ⇐ time(completed(Method, ExecutionID), TP)
16         ∧generated(TI) ∧ assert(start(TI, TP))
17         ∧assert(end(TI, tp_stopEnv)).
18
```

19 $holds(includes(hob, Element), TI)$
20 $\Leftarrow time(completed(assembles(User, Element), ExecutionID), TP).$
21
22 $holds(includes(hob, Element), TI)$
23 $\Leftarrow holdsAt(occurred(completed(disassembles(User, Element),$
24 $ExecutionID), TP), TP) \wedge holdsAt(includes(hob, Element), TP)$
25 $\wedge holds(includes(hob, Element), TI) \wedge in(TP, TI)$
26 $\wedge assert(end(TI, TP)).$

7.3 Mapping

Mapping is a connection between the implementation of an XR component and domain ontologies of the behavior model, which are understandable to domain experts who use the E-XR approach. Therefore, the creation of mappings requires domain knowledge. We introduce two types of mappings: class mappings, which connect application classes to domain classes, and event mappings, which connect invocations, finalizations, and completions of methods to domain events. Hence, mappings are based on domain ontologies of the behavior model and the workflow representation of the link model (Fig. 5.2). Mappings enable the satisfaction of functional requirement 1 for the E-XR approach (cf. Sect. 5.2.1).

7.3.1 Mapping Classes

Formalism

We introduce *class mappings*, which enable knowledge-based representation of *application classes* specified in implementations of XR components, using *domain classes* specified in a *domain ontology*.

Definition 7.20 A *class mapping* is an RDF statement
(application class, rdfs:subClassOf, domain class), where:

- the *application class* is a class specified in the implementation of an XR component,
- the *domain class* is a domain class specified in a domain ontology.

A class mapping states that every object that belongs to an *application class* also belongs to an associated *domain class*. An example of a mapping is *(imp:Fan, rdfs:subClassOf, do:Fan)*, which refers to two classes describing fans—the application class specified in an XR component and the domain class specified in a domain ontology.

Definition 7.21 A *mapping knowledge base* is a set of *class mappings*.

An example of a mapping knowledge base with three class mappings is presented in Listing 7.3. The link between an object-oriented data model and an ontology-based data model provided by class mappings permits composition and exploration of XR environments. The mappings permit reasoning and queries about users and objects represented by application classes, which also become represented by domain classes.

Listing 7.3 Example of a mapping knowledge base with class mappings between application classes and domain classes (RDF Turtle format)

```
1  @prefix do: <http://semantic3d.org/e-xr/household-ontology#>.
2  @prefix imp: <http://semantic3d.org/e-xr/service-guide/
      implementation#> .
3  @prefix rdf: <http://www.w3.org/1999/02/22-rdf-syntax-ns#> .
4
5  imp:Appliance  rdfs:subClassOf  do:Appliance .
6  imp:Fan  rdfs:subClassOf  do:Fan .
7  imp:Display  rdfs:subClassOf  do:Display .
```

Classification of Application Objects

Definition 7.22 An ***application object*** is an instance of an *application class* (cf. Sect. 7.1.1).

Application objects can be contextually assigned to application classes using the component rule set, *method invocation events* and the associated method declarations in the XR component's implementation. Thus, taking into account class mappings associated with the application class of an application object, we conclude that:

Theorem 7.7 *Every parameter in the parameter list of a method belongs to the application class determined by the method's declaration in the XR component's implementation. Thus, it also belongs to all domain classes that are mapped to the application class.*

Classification of application objects is the job of the *object classification algorithm*, which performs the following steps for the *component transition set* of an XR component.

- For every *event-based transition* (cf. Definition 6.23) whose body includes a statement based on the *time* predicate and a *method invocation event*:

  - For every parameter included in the *method parameter list*:

    . Add the following statement based on the *assert* predicate: *assert(applicationClass(parameter))*, where *applicationClass* is determined by the method declaration in the implementation of the XR component for which the *transition* is specified.

The result of the algorithm is the *component transition set* extended with information about assignments of application objects to application classes. Therefore, using a *mapping knowledge base*, the objects can also be associated with domain classes that are superclasses of the application classes.

7.3.2   Mapping Events

Formalism

In addition to class mappings, we introduce *event mappings*, which enable domain-specific knowledge-based representation of events related to class methods of XR components. It further allows for the exploration of events and the associated states using domain knowledge.

Definition 7.23   An *event mapping* is an *event-based transition* whose body evaluates the occurrence of an event (called *body event*), and the head consists of an ISEP predicate that states the occurrence of an event (called *head event*). The events satisfy one of the following conditions:

1. The *body event* is an event that *begins* an activity, and the *head event* is a method invocation event.
2. The *body event* is a method completion event, and the *head event* is an event that *begins* or *finishes* an activity.

An event mapping states that the beginning of an activity is a method invocation or that a method completion is the finish of an activity. Hence, event mappings enclose states of method executions using domain events (Fig. 7.5). It permits XR designers to hide events and states on methods behind domain terminology. It is crucial to domain experts who are not familiar with procedural terminology. Due to event mappings, domain experts can use domain events to invoke methods and monitor the methods' finalization.

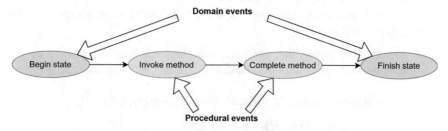

Fig. 7.5 Enclosing procedural events using domain events in event mapping

The event mappings presented in Listing 7.4 determine that the initialization of the *watches* state, in which a user is watching an artifact, is the invocation of the *watch* method. In turn, the completion of the method is the finalization of the state.

Listing 7.4 Example of event mappings

```
1   time(invoked(watch(User, Artifact), ExecutionID), TP)
2       ⇐ time(watchesInitialization(User, Artifact), TP)
3           ∧generated(ExecutionID).
4
5   time(watchesFinalization(User, Artifact), TP)
6       ⇐ time(completed(watch(User, Artifact), ExecutionID), TP).
```

Event mappings can be used to designate domain events that begin *single method activities*, because invocations of methods start such activities. It can be done according to point 1 of Definition 7.23. If an event mapping is used to begin a single invocation activity with a domain event, the domain event *indirectly determines* the invocation of the method that implements the activity. Furthermore, event mappings enable us to designate method completions that finish *single invocation activities* as well as method completions that begin or finish *instant activities*, *double invocation activities*, and *double method activities*, because such activities are begun and finished by method completions. It can be done according to point 2 of Definition 7.23. Event mappings are specified within *mapping transition sets*.

Definition 7.24 A *mapping transition set* is a set of *event mappings*.

Generating Event Mappings

Event mappings can be derived from an *activity knowledge base* using the *event mapping generation algorithm*. In the description of the algorithm, we use Definitions 7.8–7.13. The algorithm executes the following steps for an *activity knowledge base* of an XR component:

1. Create an empty *mapping transition set*.
2. For every *single invocation activity*, add the following *event mapping* to the *mapping transition set*:

   a. The event mapping that designates the beginning of the *activity* as the invocation of the *activity start method* (cf. point 1 of Definition 7.23):

$$time(invoked(activityStartMethod(Subject, Object),$$
$$ExecutionID), TP)$$
$$\Leftarrow time(initializationEvent(Subject, Object), TP)$$
$$\wedge generated(ExecutionID), \tag{7.18}$$

where *Subject* and *Object* are the subject and object or literal value of the *activity start join point*, and *initializationEvent* is a domain event that begins the *activity*.

Comment: *Single invocation activities are the only activities that can be initiated by domain events because they start upon method invocations. Unlike single invocation activities, other activities are begun by method completions, which cannot be assumed in advance without stating the method invocations before.*

b. Execute Step 3b.

3. For every *instant activity, double invocation activity,* and *double method activity,* add the following *event mappings* to the *mapping transition set:*

a. The event mapping that designates the completion of the *activity method* as the *beginning* of the *activity* (cf. point 2 of Definition 7.23):

$$time(initializationEvent(Subject, Object), TP)$$

$$\Leftarrow time(completed(activityMethod(Subject, Object), \qquad (7.19)$$

$$ExecutionID), TP),$$

where *activityMethod* is the *instant activity method* or *activity start method* (depending on the activity type), *Subject* and *Object* are the subject and object or literal value of the *instant activity join point* or *activity start join point*, and *initializationEvent* is a domain event that signalizes the beginning of the *activity*.

b. The event mapping that designates the completion of the *activity method* as the *finish* of the *activity* (cf. point 2 of Definition 7.23):

$$time(finalizationEvent(Subject, Object), TP)$$

$$\Leftarrow time(completed(activityMethod(Subject, Object), \qquad (7.20)$$

$$ExecutionID), TP),$$

where *activityMethod* is the *instant activity method* or *activity end method* (depending on the activity type), *Subject* and *Object* are the subject and object or literal value of the *instant activity join point* or *activity end join point*, and *finalizationEvent* is a domain event that signalizes the finish of the *activity*.

Comment: *Both event mappings determine domain events that initialize and finalize activities based on appropriate method completions.*

7.4   Code Templates

Transformation of component transition sets to imperative object-oriented or procedural implementations is necessary to enable query-based composition of explorable XR environments. Since a workflow composition set represents the behavior of an XR component with its states, events, facts, and transitions, we associate them with code templates, which can be further composed. Code templates are based on the fluent ontology of the behavior model and the workflow representation of the link model (Fig. 5.2). We present an exemplary implementation of the templates in C#, which is one of widely used languages for XR development, e.g., in the Unity game engine. However, the templates can be analogously implemented using other languages, such as C++, Java, and Python.

According to Definitions 6.23 and 6.24, every transition leads either to an event or to a state. In the following subsections, we discuss how events and states are represented and processed using code templates. Moreover, processing events and states requires variables, whose representation is discussed in the last subsection.

7.4.1   Processing Events

Method Wrappers

Method wrappers are methods that enable the management of knowledge related to the occurrence of events—methods' *invocations, finalizations*, and *completions*, which are used in the bodies of transitions in component transition sets.

Definition 7.25 A *method invocation wrapper* is a *method* that executes some additional code prior to invoking a *method* (called a *wrapped method*). A method invocation wrapper has the same parameter list and returns the same values as the *wrapped method*.

The generic template of a *method invocation wrapper* is presented in Listing 7.5.

Listing 7.5 Generic template of method invocation wrapper
```
1   returnType wrapper(parameterList) {
2     // insert a wrapper code block here
3     return wrappedMethod(parameterList);
4   }
```

A possible object-oriented implementation of the template in C# is presented in Listing 7.6. The `wrapper` is a method of a subclass of the class implementing the `wrappedMethod` (line 1). The *wrapper code block* is a sequence of instructions that manage the knowledge related to the invocation of the `wrapped method` (2). This code block is created by the environment composition algorithm discussed in Sect. 8.3. The wrapper code block is executed before the `wrappedMethod` is invoked (3). Hence, the template respects Definition 7.4. The `wrappedMethod` is invoked with the same parameters as the `wrapper` has been invoked with. Finally, the value returned by the `wrappedMethod` is also returned by the `wrapper`.

Listing 7.6 Template of method invocation wrapper encoded in C#

```
1   public override returnType wrapper(parameterList) {
2      // insert a wrapper code block here
3      return base.wrappedMethod(parameterList);
4   }
```

Although the implementation of templates in our approach is based on an object-oriented language, the templates can also be implemented using procedural languages, e.g., as separate wrapping procedures instead of overriding methods.

Definition 7.26 A ***method finalization wrapper*** is a *method* that executes some additional code once a *method* (called a *wrapped method*) is finished. A method finalization wrapper has the same parameter list and returns the same values as the *wrapped method*.

The template of a *method finalization wrapper* encoded in C# is presented in Listing 7.7. The *wrapper code block* is executed once the `wrappedMethod` is finished (line 12). The code is enclosed within the `finally` clause to make its execution independent of any exception that may be thrown. If an exception has been thrown by the `wrappedMethod`, it is caught (9) and finally thrown also by the `wrapper` (14). If no exception has been thrown, the `wrapper` returns the value returned by the `wrappedMethod` (16).

Listing 7.7 Template of method finalization wrapper encoded in C#

```
1   public override returnType wrapper(parameterList) {
2      returnType result = null;
3      Exception exception = null;
4
5      try {
6         result = base.wrappedMethod(parameterList);
7      }
8      catch (Exception exc) {
9         exception = exc;
10     }
11     finally {
12        // insert a wrapper code block here
13        if (exception != null)
14           throw exception;
15     }
16     return result;
17  }
```

Definition 7.27 A ***method completion wrapper*** is a *method* that executes some additional code once a *method* (called a *wrapped method*) is completed. A method completion wrapper has the same parameter list and returns the same values as the *wrapped method*.

The template of a *method completion wrapper* encoded in C# is presented in
Listing 7.8. The *wrapper code block* is executed once the wrappedMethod is
finished without exceptions (line 13). In such a case, the wrapper returns the
result of the wrappedMethod (17). If the wrappedMethod threw an exception,
the *wrapper code block* is not executed and the exception is further thrown by the
wrapper (15).

Listing 7.8 Template of method completion wrapper encoded in C#

```
1   public override returnType wrapper(parameterList) {
2     returnType result = null;
3     Exception exception = null;
4
5     try {
6       result = base.wrappedMethod(parameterList);
7     }
8     catch (Exception exc) {
9       exception = exc;
10    }
11    finally {
12      if (exception == null)
13        // insert a wrapper code block here
14      else
15        throw exception;
16    }
17    return result;
18  }
```

All three types of wrappers can be combined into one wrapper that manages
knowledge related to method invocation, finalization, and completion. The template
of such a wrapper is presented in Listing 7.9. The appropriate wrapper code blocks
appear in lines 7, 15, and 18.

Listing 7.9 Template of combined method invocation, finalization, and completion wrapper
encoded in C#

```
1   public override returnType wrapper(parameterList) {
2     returnType result = null;
3     Exception exception = null;
4
5     try {
6       // insert a wrapper code block for method invocation
7       // here
8       result = base.wrappedMethod(parameterList);
9     }
10    catch (Exception exc) {
11      exception = exc;
12    }
13    finally {
14      // insert a wrapper code block for method finalization
15      // here
16      if (exception == null)
17        // insert a wrapper code block for method completion
18        // here
```

```
19        else
20           throw exception;
21     }
22     return result;
23  }
```

Data Structures

In addition to method wrappers, we also introduce data structures to represent events in the implementations of explorable XR environments.

Definition 7.28   An *event item* is a compound term that represents an *event* and the *time point* when the *event* occurs.

It is denoted as *time*(*event*, *tp*). An example of an event item is *time*(*begin*(*assembles*(*serviceman*, *coil*)), 10*sec*), which means that *serviceman* begins to assemble *coil* at the 10th second of an XR presentation.

In imperative implementations of explorable XR environments, event items are represented by the *EventItem* class with a constructor that gets two parameters: an *event* and a *time point* when the *event* occurs. In an environment, event items are stored in a common structure called *event item set*.

Definition 7.29   An *event item set* is a set of *event items*.

An event item set is associated with one explorable XR environment, and every environment has one event item set. An event item set represents all events that occurred, are occurring, and are scheduled to occur in the environment. An event item set is represented by the *EventSet* variable. Its *add* method inserts a new *event item* to the set.

7.4.2   Processing Variables

Processing variables that appear in transitions can be considered in two contexts: generating unique values of variables, e.g., execution IDs and time points, and inferring variable values from the available facts and transitions. In this section, we specify functions responsible for these tasks. In the following definition, UniqueValue denotes a class of unique values.

Generating Unique Variable Values

Definition 7.30   The *generate* function is a function that for a given *type* returns one of:

1. A unique value, if the *type* is UniqueValue.
2. A time point, if the *type* is TimePoint.

Its declaration is the following: `type generate(type t)`. For example, while invocation `generate(UniqueValue)` can return a unique atom (string), invocation `generate(TimePoint)` returns a time point, which may be, in particular, the current timestamp. Time points returned by `generate` depend on a particular implementation and use case of the environment. For instance, while returning the current timestamp may be appropriate to games, returning real past timestamps may be appropriate to XR presentations of historical events, and returning possible future timestamps may be appropriate to simulations. Finally, if an environment does not need to be linked to the real time, the returned time points may belong to the `UniqueValue` class.

Inferring Variable Values

Variables used in transitions may also represent values that can be inferred from the available facts and transitions. The `infer` function enables it.

Definition 7.31 The *infer* function is a function that for a given *variable*, a *transition set*, and a *statement set* returns the permitted values of the *variable*, which satisfy the conjunction of all the *statements* in the *statement set* evaluated against the *transition set*.

Its declaration is the following:
`type[] infer(variable, transitionSet, varStmtSet)`,
where `type[]` is an array of values of `type`. The type of a variable can be contextually inferred on the basis of the methods in which invocations, finalizations, and completions the variable appears, as it is done for *application objects* (cf. Sect. 7.3.1). The `infer` function is implemented using well-recognized reasoning algorithms for first-order logic and the Semantic Web.

To create sets of statements that should be respected while inferring variable values, the *CreateVariableStmtSet* function is specified.

Definition 7.32 The *CreateVariableStmtSet* function is a function that for a given *variable* and a *transition* returns all statements that are included in the *transition* body and include the *variable*.

Chapter 8
E-XR Development Pipeline of Explorable Environments

The *pipeline of developing explorable XR environments* enables creation of new environments as well as transformation of existing environments into their explorable counterparts. The pipeline employs the E-XR visual knowledge-based behavior model and the E-XR semantic link model. Hence, it combines imperative object-oriented and procedural programming with declarative logic programming and the Semantic Web. The pipeline can be implemented in widely used software development environments, including programming tools and game engines.

The pipeline consists of four main stages, which correspond to the knowledge engineering process (cf. Sect. 3.2.3). At the stages, different groups of users are involved in the preparation of different elements of XR environments. They use different tools, in particular—from the E-XR development toolkit presented in Chap. 10. The result of the pipeline—explorable XR environments—represents users' and objects' behavior with domain knowledge and visual descriptors. Such behavior can be subject to exploration and visualization based on reasoning and queries about states and events at different points and intervals of time, which is described in Chap. 9. The pipeline is depicted in Fig. 8.1. Its main stages are described below.

1. *Designing a domain ontology* provides a specification of domain terminology, including classes and properties as well as relations between them. The entities have formal semantics understandable to target groups of users of a particular E-XR application.
2. *Developing XR components* provides 2D and 3D shapes covering geometry, structure, spatial properties, presentation, animation, scripts as well as knowledge bases and transition sets describing the domain semantics of the components and their behavior.
3. *Composing an environment with queries* provides the implementation of an explorable XR environment composed of XR components using queries. As queries may express various requirements of target users, the generated environments are customized.

© The Author(s), under exclusive license to Springer Nature Switzerland AG 2020
J. Flotyński, *Knowledge-Based Explorable Extended Reality Environments*,
https://doi.org/10.1007/978-3-030-59965-2_8

4. *Compiling the environment* provides an explorable XR environment, which allows for knowledge-based exploration of users' and objects' behavior, in addition to the primary environment's functionality.

The result of every stage is the input to the next stages. The stages are described in detail in the following subsections.

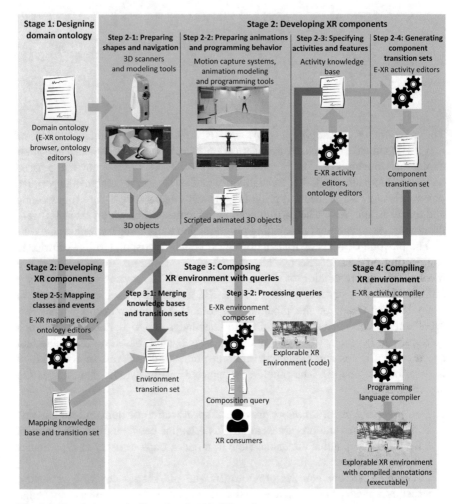

Fig. 8.1 Development pipeline of explorable XR environments

8.1   Stage 1: Designing Domain Ontology

This stage provides a domain ontology (cf. Sect. 6.1.1) encoded using the Semantic Web standards: RDF, RDFS, and OWL. Domain classes and properties (cf. Sect. 6.1.1) specified in a domain ontology are used in the pipeline to represent activities and features of users and objects of the XR environment being developed. Such representation is comprehensible to domain experts, who typically are the authors of the ontology and the main users of XR environments based on the ontology. Domain ontologies may be created using ontology engineering tools, such as Protégé (Stanford University 2020).

A fragment of a domain ontology for servicing home appliances is presented in Fig. 8.2 and Listing 8.1. It specifies entities that represent appliances and possible actions of users on the appliances while servicing. The nodes represent domain classes with the RDFS *subclass of* relation (W3C 2014b): *user* (line 11), *appliance* (with subclasses *electric cooker* and *induction hob*, lines 13–19), and *element* (with subclasses *fan*, *display*, *heating plate*, and *coil*, lines 21–33). The arcs in the graph present domain properties: the *includes* relation between *appliances* and their *elements* (lines 35–37) as well as activities executed on *elements* by *users* (*assembles*, *disassembles*, and *tests*, lines 39–49). For every property, a domain and range are specified.

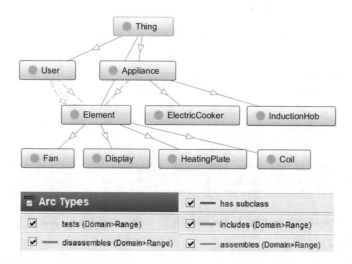

Fig. 8.2 Example of domain ontology for servicing home appliances. Visualization of OWL graph in Protégé OntoGraf

Listing 8.1 Example of domain ontology for servicing home appliances encoded in RDF, RDFS, and OWL (RDF Turtle format)

```
1   @prefix : <http://semantic3d.org/e-xr/household-ontology#> .
2   @prefix owl: <http://www.w3.org/2002/07/owl#> .
3   @prefix rdf: <http://www.w3.org/1999/02/22-rdf-syntax-ns#> .
4   @prefix xml: <http://www.w3.org/XML/1998/namespace> .
5   @prefix xsd: <http://www.w3.org/2001/XMLSchema#> .
6   @prefix rdfs: <http://www.w3.org/2000/01/rdf-schema#> .
7   @base <http://semantic3d.org/e-xr/household-ontology> .
```

```
8
9   <http://semantic3d.org/e-xr/household-ontology> rdf:type
        owl:Ontology .
10
11  :User rdf:type owl:Class .
12
13  :Appliance rdf:type owl:Class .
14
15  :ElectricCooker rdf:type owl:Class ;
16    rdfs:subClassOf :Appliance .
17
18  :InductionHob rdf:type owl:Class ;
19    rdfs:subClassOf :Appliance .
20
21  :Element rdf:type owl:Class .
22
23  :Fan rdf:type owl:Class ;
24    rdfs:subClassOf :Element .
25
26  :Display rdf:type owl:Class ;
27    rdfs:subClassOf :Element .
28
29  :HeatingPlate rdf:type owl:Class ;
30    rdfs:subClassOf :Element .
31
32  :Coil rdf:type owl:Class ;
33    rdfs:subClassOf :Element .
34
35  :includes rdf:type owl:ObjectProperty ;
36    rdfs:domain :Appliance ;
37    rdfs:range :Element .
38
39  :assembles rdf:type owl:ObjectProperty ;
40    rdfs:domain :User ;
41    rdfs:range :Element .
42
43  :disassembles rdf:type owl:ObjectProperty ;
44    rdfs:domain :User ;
45    rdfs:range :Element .
46
47  :tests rdf:type owl:ObjectProperty ;
48    rdfs:domain :User ;
49    rdfs:range :Element .
```

Domain ontologies should reflect anticipated use cases of XR environments that can potentially be developed and their knowledge-based exploration. Hence, individual domain ontologies are common to the composition and exploration of different XR environments in a particular application domain. Different domain ontologies are used to develop environments for different application domains, e.g., shopping in virtual stores, visiting virtual museums, and designing virtual cities. The detailed description of the ontology design process has been thoroughly addressed in the literature (Gayathri & Uma 2018; Baset & Stoffel 2018; Pouriyeh et al. 2018; Mkhinini, Labbani-Narsis, & Nicolle 2020), and it is out of the scope of this book.

8.2 Stage 2: Developing XR Components

At this stage, independent, reusable *XR components* are created. The particular elements of behavioral XR components are prepared in different steps of this stage, which are described in the following subsections. XR components are prepared with regard to the domain ontology designed at the previous stage.

8.2.1 Step 2-1: Preparing Shapes and Navigation

In this step, elements 1–4 of XR components (Definition 6.1): geometry, transformations, presentation, and navigation are created. First, 2D and 3D shapes are prepared, e.g., real artifacts are scanned and converted to 3D meshes. Second, they undergo appropriate geometrical and spatial transformations, e.g., scaling, rotating, and positioning. Next, they are enriched with presentational elements (e.g., materials). Finally, they are aggregated into hierarchies. In addition, navigational elements are prepared to enable viewing of hierarchies. This step is typically completed by graphic designers using 3D scanners (e.g., Artec 3D) and modeling tools (e.g., Blender and 3ds Max).

This step follows the design of a domain ontology because XR components should be prepared with regard to domain classes, which correspond to possible use cases of environments that can be composed of the components. The following *design guidelines* are specified for graphic designers who accomplish this step.

1. For every domain class that requires an individual representation in XR environments, an individual XR component is prepared, e.g., user, cooker, hob, fan, and display. This group also encompasses classes of objects that depend on other objects, e.g., materials and textures.
2. For every domain class that represents a complex object composed of other objects, a hierarchy of XR components (created in point 1) is formed, e.g., a hob includes a fan, display, and coil.
3. For every domain class that represents a navigational element in a 3D scene, an individual XR component is created, e.g., a viewpoint and a camera.

Examples of XR components representing domain classes designed in the previous step are depicted in Fig. 8.3.

Fig. 8.3 Examples of XR components representing domain classes shown in Fig. 8.2 and Listing 8.1: user, fan, heating plate, and coil (with materials) as well as hob, which is a complex object

8.2.2   Step 2-2: Preparing Animations and Programming Behavior

This step augments XR components prepared in the previous step with elements 4–5 in Definition 6.1: animations and scripts implementing the behavior of the XR components. Animations are prepared by graphic designers using motion capture systems (e.g., OpenStage) and animation modeling tools (e.g., MotionBuilder). Animations should correspond to the possible behavior of the XR components, which is determined by the domain ontology. For example, an animation may demonstrate a rotating fan if the domain ontology enables switching it on. Another animation can show various states of a display, which are permitted by domain properties of displays. Finally, if a heating plate may be assembled on a hob, the hob should be available in two versions—with and without the plate.

In addition to animations, XR components with more complex behavior are scripted by developers. Scripts are written in an object-oriented or procedural programming language, e.g., C#, Java, or C. Scripts should be developed as microservices. They contain classes representing objects, with methods representing possible activities of the objects. Methods can be parametrized.

The following *design guidelines* can be specified for developers who perform this step.

1. For every domain property that influences the presentation or behavior of objects of an application class that is mapped to a domain class, an individual method of the application class should be implemented. A method parameter should be used to represent possible values of the property.
2. Methods should be implemented in such a way that their successful execution can be regarded as the accomplishment of the methods' tasks. Any untypical situation that prevents the successful execution of a method should be evinced by a thrown exception so as to consider the method unsuccessfully finished.

Since XR components should be reusable to enable composition of various environments, their methods should be perceived as microservices, implementing activities that are maximally independent of other components. For instance, a user can assemble a coil on a virtual hob, which is accomplished by the *assemble* method of the *user* class. The method takes a *coil* and a *hob* as parameters. In turn, the *assemble* method may invoke the *attach* method of the *hob* class, which takes a *coil* as a parameter and places it in a proper position.

Although the E-XR approach allows XR components to be scripted in different ways, some *implementation guidelines* are recommenced to facilitate further steps of the pipeline. In the next steps, additional code is injected into XR components developed in this step. It requires variables used in methods of XR components to be accessible to the additional injected code. The following guidelines are intended for developers who create new XR environments that can potentially be made explorable or adjust existing environments before their transformation into explorable environments. The guidelines allow for the fulfillment of requirement 6 for the approach (cf. Sect. 5.2.1).

1. Local method variables should be declared in the main scope of the method, but not in narrower scopes, e.g., within conditional and loop instructions.
2. Local variables of methods whose single execution—from start to finish—reflects a *single invocation activity* (e.g., animation) should be initialized once declared.
3. A method should finalize with up-to-date values of variables, which should be equal to the values used in the method. The preparation of variable values should be done at the beginning of the method.

Although the guidelines introduce certain restrictions on how the E-XR approach is used, they may be applied by developers before transforming an environment by minor changes in the code. The following modifications should be accomplished if the guidelines are not met.

1. If a local method variable is not defined in the main scope of the method, the variable declaration is moved to the main scope.
2. After completing its main task, if the method is preparing new values of variables to be used by other methods later on, the preparation should be moved to those methods, while leaving the variables unchanged in the end of the primary method.

3. If a method, after completing its main task, is invoking other methods:

    a. Copies of the variables should be passed to the methods instead of references to the variables. It prevents modification of the variables by the other methods, which would lead to the exploration of invalid values, or

    b. The invocations of the methods should be moved before the primary method performs its main task.

    In particular, it is relevant to methods with tail recursion. Such recursion might be required to be exchanged with head recursion or a loop.

4. If it is necessary to explore behavior implemented by methods in external libraries that are available only as binaries, the methods should be wrapped by additional methods in the XR components. For instance, if a component invokes a web service to get a new 3D shape for a scene, which should be explored, the invocation is moved to an additional method, which will be subject to exploration.

The completion of this step enables the XR designers to perform the following steps, which are focused on knowledge-based representation of the XR components.

8.2.3   Step 2-3: Specifying Activities and Features

In this step, *activity knowledge bases* (cf. Definition 7.1), which are element 7 of XR components (cf. Definition 6.1), are created using the activity ontology of the E-XR semantic link model. The specification of activities and features is performed by domain experts with basic knowledge about the object-oriented and procedural workflow and data model. The following *specification guideline* for activities and features is formulated. Every class method that can potentially be used in at least one of:

1. Query-based environment composition at Stage 3,
2. Logging behavior of the environment, which enables its backward exploration (discussed in Sect. 9.4),

is subject to the specification of an activity or feature depending on the presence or lack of its temporal properties, as discussed in Sect. 7.1.

A fragment of an activity knowledge base that specifies an instant activity is presented in Fig. 8.4 and Listing 8.2. The activity is the assemblage of an appliance element by a user. The activity is completed upon the completion of the assemble method (lines 20, 23–26). Since the method belongs to the user class, the this keyword specified in the activity ontology indicates the subject as the user for whom the method is invoked (19). The activity predicate is assembles (14), and the object is the appliance element method parameter (21). Only one activity point is assigned to the activity as it is instant, thereby having no duration and occurring at a time point, which is denoted by the now keyword (15). The activity point (18–21) indicates the assemble method as well as the subject (this) and

the object (appliance element) involved in the activity. The activity links
the subject and object using the assembles predicate. Similarly, other activities
can be created, e.g., an activity associated with the assemble method imposing
that an appliance element starts to be included in an appliance
since it gets assembled. This activity is started on the completion of the assemble
method. Similar statements are created for the disassemblyActivity and
selectionActivity, which are based on the disassemble and select
methods as well as the disassembles and selects predicates.

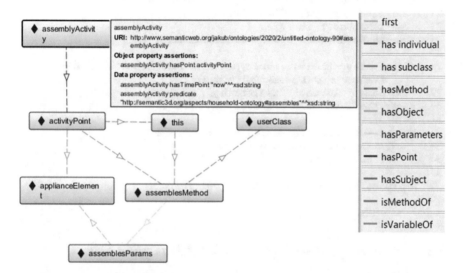

Fig. 8.4 Instant activity specification visualized as OWL graph in Protégé OntoGraf

Listing 8.2 Instant activity specification (RDF Turtle format)

```
 1   @base <http://semantic3d.org/e-xr/service-guide/akb> .
 2   @prefix akb: <http://semantic3d.org/e-xr/service-guide/akb#>.
 3   @prefix ao: <http://semantic3d.org/e-xr/activity-ontology#>.
 4   @prefix do: <http://semantic3d.org/e-xr/service-guide/
         household-ontology#> .
 5   @prefix fo: <http://semantic3d.org/e-xr/fluent-ontology#> .
 6   @prefix imp: <http://semantic3d.org/e-xr/service-guide/
         implementation#> .
 7   @prefix owl: <http://www.w3.org/2002/07/owl#> .
 8   @prefix rdf: <http://www.w3.org/1999/02/22-rdf-syntax-ns#> .
 9   @prefix xsd: <http://www.w3.org/2001/XMLSchema#> .
10
11   <http://semantic3d.org/e-xr/service-guide/akb> rdf:type owl:
         Ontology .
12
13   akb:assemblyActivity rdf:type ao:InstantActivity ;
```

```
14    ao:predicate do:assembles ;
15    fo:hasTimePoint "now"^^xsd:string ;
16    ao:hasPoint akb:activityPoint .
17
18  akb:activityPoint rdf:type ao:OnExitPoint , owl:
          NamedIndividual , owl:Thing ;
19    ao:hasSubject ao:this ;
20    ao:hasMethod akb:assemblesMethod ;
21    ao:hasObject akb:applianceElement .
22
23  akb:assemblesMethod rdf:type ao:ClassMethod ;
24    ao:name "assemble"^^xsd:string ;
25    ao:isMethodOf imp:User ;
26    ao:hasParameters akb:assemblesParams .
27
28  akb:applianceElement rdf:type ao:MethodParameter , imp:
          Element , owl:NamedIndividual ;
29    ao:name "element"^^xsd:string ;
30    ao:isVariableOf akb:assemblesMethod .
31
32  akb:assemblesParams rdf:type ao:ParameterList ;
33    ao:first akb:applianceElement ;
34    rdf:rest rdf:nil .
35
36  imp:User rdf:type owl:Class , owl:Thing .
```

8.2.4   Step 2-4: Generating Component Transition Sets

In this step, the *transition generation algorithm* (cf. Sect. 7.2.3) is used to generate *component transition sets* for all XR components prepared in the previous steps. An example of a component transition set describing an XR hob is presented in Listing 7.2. Another component transition set, which describes an XR user, is presented in Listing 8.3. The component is responsible for users' activities on a serviced hob—assembling, disassembling, and selecting its elements, which are instant activities represented by three different methods (lines 1–10). Moreover, it includes two features responsible for setting up the used XR devices and libraries (12–17), which will be explained in Sect. 8.3.

Listing 8.3 Example of component transition set of XR user

1   *holds At (assembles (User, Element), TP)*
2       $\Leftarrow$ *time(completed(assemble(User, Element), Execution I D), TP).*
3
4   *holds At (disassembles (User, Element), TP)*
5       $\Leftarrow$ *time(completed(disassemble(User, Element),*
6   *Execution I D), TP).*
7

```
 8   holdsAt(selects(UserFinger, Element), TP)
 9      ⇐ time(completed(select(UserFinger, Element),
10         ExecutionID), TP).
11
12   watcher(Watcher) ⇐ time(completed(setWatcher(Watcher),
13         ExecutionID), TP).
14
15   elementSelection(Selection)
16      ⇐ time(completed(setElementSelection(Selection),
17         ExecutionID), TP).
```

The transitions that are common to all component transition sets (Listing 7.2, lines 1–7 and 9–17) apply to any method of an XR component. They entail transitions for particular methods of XR components. The transitions entailed for the *assemble* method are presented in Listing 8.4, lines 1–8 and 10–20, respectively.

Listing 8.4 Transitions entailed by example component transition set

```
 1   time(finished(assemble(User, Element), ExecutionID), TP_{fin})
 2      ⇐ time(invoked(assemble(User, Element), ExecutionID), TP_{inv})
 3         ∧generated(TP_{fin}) ∧ assert(TP_{fin} > TP_{inv}).
 4
 5   time(completed(assemble(User, Element), ExecutionID), TP)
 6      ⇐ time(finished(assemble(User, Element), ExecutionID), TP)
 7         ∧exception(executed(assemble(User, Element),
 8            ExecutionID), null).
 9
10   holds(occurred(invoked(assemble(User, Element),
11         ExecutionID), TI))
12      ⇐ time(invoked(assemble(User, Element), ExecutionID), TP).
13         ∧generated(TI) ∧ assert(start(TI, TP))
14         ∧assert(end(TI, tp_{stopEnv})).
15
16   holds(occurred(completed(assemble(User, Element),
17         ExecutionID), TI))
18      ⇐ time(completed(assemble(User, Element), ExecutionID), TP).
19         ∧generated(TI) ∧ assert(start(TI, TP))
20         ∧assert(end(TI, tp_{stopEnv})).
```

8.2.5   Step 2-5: Mapping Classes and Events

In this step, application classes implementing XR components are linked to domain classes of the domain ontology by *class mappings* (cf. Definition 7.20), and events related to class methods are linked to activities by *event mappings*. Mappings are created by domain experts who have basic knowledge about the foundations of the object-oriented and procedural workflow and data model.

The following *mapping guideline* can be specified. Every domain class specified in the domain ontology designed at Stage 1 should be mapped to an application class of an XR component prepared at this stage of the pipeline. The created *mapping knowledge base* can be reused to compose various XR environments with the XR component.

Next, the *object classification algorithm* is used to extend transitions in *component transition sets* with assignments of objects to application classes, from which assignments to domain classes can be inferred by automated reasoning. Finally, the *event mapping generation algorithm* is executed for XR components to generate their *mapping transition sets*.

8.3   Stage 3: Composing XR Environment with Queries

This stage consists of two steps: merging knowledge bases and transition sets created at Stage 2 and processing queries to such generated specifications of XR environments. The steps are described in the following subsections.

8.3.1   Step 3-1: Merging Knowledge Bases and Transition Sets

In this step, all the knowledge bases and transition sets generated for XR components at Stage 2 are merged into a single *environment specification*.

Definition 8.1 An *environment specification* is the union of:

1. A domain ontology (cf. Sect. 6.1.1),
2. The fluent ontology (cf. Sect. 6.1.3),
3. The fluent rule set (cf. Sect. 6.2.4),
4. Activity knowledge bases (cf. Sect. 7.1),
5. Component transition sets (cf. Sect. 7.2.3),
6. Mapping knowledge bases (cf. Sect. 7.3.1),
7. Mapping transition sets (cf. Sect. 7.3.2).

While elements 1–3 in the definition are common to all XR components, elements 4–7 are unions of knowledge bases and transition sets prepared for individual components. An environment specification describes the behavior (cf. Definition 6.27) of all prepared XR components, which still remain independent, i.e., there are no interactions between them. An environment specification can serve as a foundation for determining such interactions and combining the components into an explorable XR environment.

Taking into account the implementation of *environment specifications*, which combine a number of ontologies, knowledge bases, and transition sets, syntactic conversion is used to unify the data format. For instance, RDF statements in ontologies and knowledge bases are converted to facts encoded in the syntax of rule sets, e.g., Prolog based. Furthermore, reasoning on *environment specifications* generated in such a way is performed by reasoning engines for Horn clauses and the Semantic Web standards.

8.3.2   Step 3-2: Processing Queries

In this step, XR components are composed using *composition queries* based on the domain ontology designed at Stage 1. Hence, this step enables the satisfaction of functional requirement 3 for the approach (cf. Sect. 5.2.1). First, we explain how queries are specified. Second, we describe how the query-based environment composition is performed.

Specifying Queries

Definition 8.2   A *composition query* is a set of *transitions* (cf. Definition 6.25) on *events* and *states* that describe the *behavior* (cf. Definition 6.27) of XR components.

A composition query complements an environment transition set with interactions between XR components, which are necessary to compose the components into an XR environment with a common dataflow and workflow. Since the representation of *features* is more straightforward than the representation of *activities* (cf. Sect. 7.1), our approach can also be used to compose static environments.

   In multiple practical applications, negation is necessary to specify complex conditions in transitions. Therefore, we introduce the *unsaid* predicate.

Definition 8.3   The *unsaid* predicate is a predicate that is true for a given *statement* and a *transition set* if and only if the *statement* is unspecified in the *transition set*. It is denoted as *unsaid*:

$\forall statement, transitionSet$:

$$unsaid(statement, transitionSet) = true \Leftrightarrow statement \notin transitionSet. \quad (8.1)$$

The predicate is used, in particular, to evaluate whether a state does not occur in a particular time point or time interval. For example, $unsaid(holdsAt(isWalking(avatar), tp))$ is satisfied if $avatar$ is not walking at time point tp. A possible implementation of the predicate in the Prolog language is based on negation as failure:

$$unsaid(S) \Leftarrow S \wedge ! \wedge fail.$$

$$unsaid(S). \quad (8.2)$$

where S is a statement, $fail$ is an atom that means *false*, and ! is the cut, which prevents from evaluating other clauses. Therefore, if S is true, $unsaid(S)$ is false. Otherwise, if S is false, the second clause, which is a fact, is evaluated and asserts that $unsaid(S)$ is true.

A fragment of an example query that composes an XR service guide for home appliances is presented in Listing 8.5. The query uses the domain ontology designed at Stage 1 to specify interactions between the XR components prepared at Stage 2. In lines 1–6, invocations of methods within the XR user component are managed. Upon starting the environment, the *OnEnable* method of the user component, which is inherited from the Unity game engine (Unity Technologies 2020b), is invoked. Upon the completion of the method, another Unity game engine method—*startCoroutine*—is invoked. It gets the *watcher* and *selection* methods of the Leap Motion device (Leap Motion 2020), which are represented by features. *ExecutionIDs* of the *OnEnable* and *startCoroutine* methods are unrelated. The latter is automatically generated by the system, likewise time point TP_2 of the *startCoroutine* invocation. TP_2 is later than time point TP_1 of the *OnEnable* completion, which conforms to Axiom 6.2.2. This transition enables capture of user's hands, which are the main interface of the environment. If the *selects* activity for the *indexFinger* pointing to an appliance element occurs while the element is not included in the hob, the *assemble* method is invoked (8–11). The invocation event occurs at the same time point as the evaluation of the states in the transition body, which complies with Axiom 6.2.5. *hob* and *user* are unique across the query, thus setting and getting them have been skipped to make the listing clearer. If the *selects* activity occurs while the element is included in the hob, the *disassemble* method is invoked (13–16).

Listing 8.5 Fragment of a query composing XR service guide for home appliances from user and hob components

```
 1   time(invoked(startCoroutine(Watcher, Selection),
 2          ExecutionID₂), TP₂)
 3      ⇐ time(completed(OnEnable, ExecutionID₁), TP₁)
 4          ∧watcher(Watcher) ∧ elementSelection(Selection)
 5          ∧generated(ExecutionID₂) ∧ generated(TP₂)
 6          ∧assert(TP₂ > TP₁).
 7
 8   time(invoked(assemble(user, Element), ExecutionID), TP)
 9      ⇐ holdsAt(selects(indexFinger, Element), TP)
10          ∧unsaid(holdsAt(includes(hob, Element), TP))
11          ∧generated(ExecutionID).
12
13   time(invoked(disassemble(user, Element), ExecutionID), TP)
14      ⇐ holdsAt(selects(indexFinger, Element), TP)
15          ∧unsaid(holdsAt(includes(hob, Element), TP))
16          ∧generated(ExecutionID).
```

Environment Composition Algorithm

A *workflow specification* fully specifies the workflow of an XR environment.

Definition 8.4   A *workflow specification* is the union of:

1. An environment specification (cf. Definition 8.1),
2. A composition query (cf. Definition 8.2).

The composition of an explorable XR environment is the processing of a composition query against an environment specification, which leads to the creation of the environment. An environment specification can be used multiple times to compose various environments using different composition queries.

Taking into account the implementation of *workflow specifications*, which combine several ontologies, knowledge bases, and rule sets, syntactic transformation can be used to convert all data to a common format. The transformation between description logic statements and Horn clauses has been discussed in Grosof, Horrocks, Volz, & Decker (2003). Reasoning on *workflow specifications* generated in such a way can be performed by reasoners for first-order logic (cf. Sect. 3.1.2).

We propose an *environment composition algorithm* to enable query-based composition of XR environments from the components prepared at Stage 2. The algorithm processes a workflow specification and produces supplementary application classes with methods that implement interactions between XR components, thereby enabling workflow in the composed environment. The algorithm executes the following steps for a *workflow specification*:

1. For every *event-based transition* (cf. Definition 6.23) such that its body includes an ISEP statement based on the *time* predicate for an *event* on a method $method_1$ that belongs to an application class $class_1$:
   Comment: Only event-based transitions whose bodies include invocations, finalizations, or completions of methods require generating new application classes responsible for interactions between XR components.

   a. Designate $method_1$ as a virtual method.
      Comment: Virtual methods can be overridden in subclasses, which will be done in the next steps.
   b. Create a new class $class_2$ that is a subclass of $class_1$, if it has not been created yet.
      Comment: The new class is created to wrap the original class and augment it with new functions responsible for interactions between XR components, which will be implemented using code templates (cf. Sect. 7.4).
   c. Create a new method $method_2$ of $class_2$ that overrides $method_1$.
   d. Determine the appropriate type of *wrapper* to be applied to $method_2$ according to the following rules:
      Comment: Different wrappers are created depending on the type of the managed events related to methods, as described in Sect. 7.4.

    i. If the *event* is a *method invocation event*, *method₂* is a *method invocation wrapper*, else

    ii. If the *event* is a *method finalization event*, *method₂* is a *method finalization wrapper*, else

    iii. If the *event* is a *method completion event*, *method₂* is a *method completion wrapper*.

e. Set the invocation of the *wrapped method* in *method₂* to *method₁*, which is overridden by *method₂*.
   Comment: This affects lines 3, 6, and 6 in Listings 7.6, 7.7, and 7.8, respectively, for method invocation, finalization, and completion events. It enables method₂ to maintain the original functionality of the overridden method₁ while augmenting it with interactions between XR components.

f. For every *variable* used in the *head* of the *transition* or in a statement based on the *assert* predicate in the *body* of the *transition*:

    i. If the *variable* appears within the *generated* predicate in the *transition body*:

        A. If the *variable* denotes a *time point*, append the following instruction to the *wrapper code block*: `TimePoint variable = generate(TimePoint)`.
   Comment: This instruction generates a time point, which will be used in the method invocation (cf. Sect. 7.4.2). It can be, e.g., the current timestamp.

        B. Else, append the following instruction to the *wrapper code block*: `UniqueValue variable = generate(UniqueValue)`.
   Comment: This instruction generates a unique value for the variable, which will be used in the method invocation. It can be, in particular, an execution ID.

    ii. Else:

        A. Append the following instruction to the *wrapper code block*: `Set<Statement> varStmtSet = CreateVariableStmtSet(variable, transition)`.
   Comment: It creates the set of all statements from the transition body that include the variable (cf. Sect. 7.4.2).

        B. Append the following instruction to the *wrapper code block*: `type[] values = infer(variable, workflowSpecification, varStmtSet)`.
   Comment: This instruction runs a reasoning algorithm on the workflow specification to infer permitted variable values. The entailment is also added to the workflowSpecification to be used for further inferences. The type of the variable can be inferred from the context in which it appears in the transition head.

g. For every *statement* such that *assert(statement)* appears in the *body* of the *transition*, add the *statement* to *workflowSpecification*.

h. If the *head* of the *transition* determines (cf. Sect. 7.3.2) the occurrence of a *method invocation event* called *event$_2$*, append the following instruction to the *wrapper code block*: `event2_method(parameterList)`, where `event2_method` is the method for which *event$_2$* is specified, and `parameterList` includes all the method parameters with values determined in Steps 1(f)i and 1(f)ii.

   Comment: *This invokes the method for which event$_2$ is specified with all the method parameters such that each of them may be either an atom or a value passed by a variable.*

i. Else, if the *head* of the *transition* determines the occurrence of a *state*:

   i. Append the following instructions to the *wrapper code block*:
   ```
   EventItem eventItem1 = new eventItem(begin(state),
   tp1);
   EventItem eventItem2 = new eventItem(finish(state),
   tp2),
   ```
   where *tp* denotes time points when the events that begin and finish the *state* occur. *tp* values are taken directly from the *transition head* or inferred in Step 1(f)iiB.

   Comment: *This creates new event items.*

   ii. Append the following instructions to the *wrapper code block*:
   `EventSet.Add(eventItem1); EventSet.Add(eventItem2)`,
   which add event items to the *event item set* of the environment.

j. Add *class$_2$* to the code project of the environment.

2. Create a new class that implements the *workflow execution algorithm* (explained in Sect. 9.2) and set it up to be launched upon starting the environment.

8.4 Stage 4: Compiling XR Environment

In this step, the entire code project of the XR environment is processed by a software module referred to as the *activity compiler*, which completes the following actions.

1. It attaches a software library (called the *log library*) to the project. The library implements the *log generation algorithm*, which produces behavior logs while the explorable environment is running. The algorithm is explained in detail in Sect. 9.3. It generates temporal statements (cf. Definition 6.10) based on activities and features and loads the statements to a triplestore. The library is presented in more detail in Sect. 10.6.

2. It injects instructions that are capturing the screen while the environment is running. The captured data is represented by *visual descriptors* (cf. Definition 6.1.3),

e.g., images and movies, which are elements of temporal statements of behavior logs.

3. It extends the class methods for which activities and features have been specified at Stage 2 by capturing the invocations, finalizations, and completions of the methods according to the aspect-oriented approach. It is done by injecting invocations of log library functions into the bodies of the methods. An invocation is injected at the beginning or the end of a class method, depending on the activity or feature type. The scheme of a class method with injected code is presented in Fig. 7.4 (blue code). The injected instructions are responsible for extracting information about the classes of the variables used by the activities and features, creating timestamps, setting identifiers of the semantic individuals to be inserted to the log, and invoking functions of the log library that build temporal statements and store them in a triplestore. The input parameters of the log library functions are variables and literal values specified in the activities and features, the extracted classes of variables, and created timestamps.

4. It injects additional common classes and methods responsible for setting values of temporary variables used by the instructions inserted in the previous actions.

Finally, a native compiler specific to a particular hardware and software platform (e.g., the VS C# compiler) is used to generate the explorable XR environment in its executable form, which is the result of the development pipeline. The explorable XR environment comprises all the classes included in the prototype environment and, additionally, the log library and the instructions injected at this stage. Hence, its objects appear and behave like their prototypes. However, in addition to the original functionality, class methods used by activities and features generate behavior logs while the environment is running. Behavior logs conform to the *behavior model* and *link model* explained in Chaps. 6 and 7.

Chapter 9
E-XR Exploration Methods

In this chapter, we present possible types of knowledge exploration and visualization in explorable XR environments composed using the models proposed in Chaps. 6 and 7 and the development pipeline proposed in Chap. 8. In terms of the target periods, we distinguish two types of exploration: *simulation with forward exploration* and *backward exploration*, which fulfill functional requirement 5 for the approach (cf. Sect. 5.2.1). *Simulation and forward exploration* enables reasoning on and queries about possible events and states. Such events and states can be undetermined—if they depend on other events and states that may, but do not have to, occur in the environment. Simulation and forward exploration need a composed XR environment, which does not have to be compiled and running. Hence, simulation and forward exploration can be accomplished directly after composing the environment at Stage 3 and before compiling it at Stage 4. Simulation and forward exploration are presented in Sect. 9.1. *Backward exploration* enables reasoning on and queries about as well as visualization of past and current events and states that have been registered in behavior logs. Therefore, backward exploration must be preceded by the execution of the environment and generating behavior logs, which is possible after completing the overall development pipeline. Hence, we present algorithms responsible for both activities in Sects. 9.2 and 9.3, prior to describing backward exploration itself in Sect. 9.4.

In this chapter, we consider queries as a way to acquire knowledge about explorable XR environments. We do not focus on operations that are specific to the form of presenting query results such as limiting their number, sorting, and aggregating data, even if they are permitted by the used query languages, e.g., SPARQL.

J. Flotyński, *Knowledge-Based Explorable Extended Reality Environments*,
https://doi.org/10.1007/978-3-030-59965-2_9

9.1   Simulation and Forward Exploration

Forward exploration enables reasoning on and queries about the potential behavior of users and objects, which may occur in explorable XR environments. It encompasses arbitrary states and events related to features and activities, including autonomous actions and interactions between different users, objects, as well as between users and objects. It is inextricably connected to the simulation of the environment behavior whose goal is to satisfy conditions necessary to permit the events and states. Thereby, simulation precedes forward exploration. Nonetheless, they are specified in common queries called *simulation queries*. A ***simulation query*** is a query (cf. Definition 3.23). Since simulation and forward exploration are related to potential events and states, they require a *workflow specification* but do not require the XR environment to be running. Hence, they may be performed once Stage 3 of the pipeline (cf. Sect. 8.3) is completed.

We use an explorable *XR fitness guide* (Flotyński et al. 2017; Flotyński, Krzyszkowski, & Walczak 2018; Flotyński, Walczak, & Krzyszkowski 2020) to illustrate a simulation and a forward exploration. Exploring the guide can help acquire knowledge about different exercises, which can be useful in setting up a training program. The fitness guide has been composed using an environment specification (cf. Definition 8.1), including a domain ontology, the fluent ontology, the fluent rule set, activity knowledge bases, component transition sets, mapping knowledge bases, and mapping transition sets, as well as a composition query, which form a *workflow specification* (cf. Definition 8.4). The fluent ontology and fluent rule set, which are common to all explorable XR environments, have been presented in Sects. 6.1.3 and 6.2.4. The other datasets, specific to this example, are presented and discussed in the following subsections.

Domain Ontology
The domain ontology for the fitness guide (Listing 9.1) specifies classes of avatars (line 10) and exercises (12–27). Avatars can train different exercises, which is expressed by the `trains` property (29–31).

Listing 9.1   Domain ontology for explorable XR fitness guide

```
 1  @prefix do: <http://semantic3d.org/e-xr/fitness-ontology#> .
 2  @prefix owl: <http://www.w3.org/2002/07/owl#> .
 3  @prefix rdf: <http://www.w3.org/1999/02/22-rdf-syntax-ns#> .
 4  @prefix rdfs: <http://www.w3.org/2000/01/rdf-schema#> .
 5  @base <http://semantic3d.org/e-xr/fitness-ontology> .
 6
 7  <http://semantic3d.org/e-xr/fitness-ontology> rdf:type
 8    owl:Ontology .
 9
10  do:Avatar rdf:type owl:Class .
11
12  do:Exercise rdf:type owl:Class .
13
14  do:BearCrawl rdf:type owl:Class ;
```

```
15      rdfs:subClassOf do:Exercise .
16
17  do:Burpees rdf:type owl:Class ;
18      rdfs:subClassOf do:Exercise .
19
20  do:PushUps rdf:type owl:Class ;
21      rdfs:subClassOf do:Exercise .
22
23  do:SideLunges rdf:type owl:Class ;
24      rdfs:subClassOf do:Exercise .
25
26  do:SquatJump rdf:type owl:Class ;
27      rdfs:subClassOf do:Exercise .
28
29  do:trains rdf:type owl:ObjectProperty ;
30      rdfs:domain do:Avatar ;
31      rdfs:range do:Exercise .
```

Activity Knowledge Base

Listing 9.2 presents a fragment of the activity knowledge base of the XR avatar component, which is employed to build the fitness guide. It specifies the `trainsActivity` (11–15). It is a single invocation activity with two join points: the point that starts the activity (17–20) and the point that ends the activity (22–25). Both join points indicate the same method (`trainMethod`, 27–30), which gets an `exercise` as the only parameter (32–38). It is also the object of temporal statements that represent the activity (20, 25). The subject of the temporal statements is the entity for which the method has been invoked, designated by the `this` individual (18, 23).

Listing 9.2 Activity knowledge base of XR avatar used in explorable fitness guide

```
1   @prefix akb: <http://semantic3d.org/e-xr/fitness-guide/akb#>.
2   @prefix ao: <http://semantic3d.org/e-xr/activity-ontology#>.
3   @prefix do: <http://semantic3d.org/e-xr/fitness-ontology>.
4   @prefix fo: <http://semantic3d.org/e-xr/fluent-ontology#>.
5   @prefix imp: <http://semantic3d.org/e-xr/fitness-guide/
            implementation#>.
6   @prefix owl: <http://www.w3.org/2002/07/owl#>.
7   @prefix rdf: <http://www.w3.org/1999/02/22-rdf-syntax-ns#>.
8   @prefix xsd: <http://www.w3.org/2001/XMLSchema#>.
9   @base <http://semantic3d.org/e-xr/fitness-guide/akb>.
10
11  akb:trainsActivity rdf:type ao:SingleInvocationActivity ;
12      ao:predicate do:trains ;
13      fo:hasTimeInterval akb:trainTimeInterval ;
14      ao:hasStartPoint akb:trainStartPoint ;
15      ao:hasEndPoint akb:trainEndPoint .
16
17  akb:trainStartPoint rdf:type ao:OnEnterPoint ,
            owl:NamedIndividual , owl:Thing ;
```

```
18    ao:hasSubject ao:this ;
19    ao:hasMethod akb:trainMethod ;
20    ao:hasObject akb:exercise .
21
22  akb:trainEndPoint rdf:type ao:OnExitPoint ,
        owl:NamedIndividual , owl:Thing ;
23    ao:hasSubject ao:this ;
24    ao:hasMethod akb:trainMethod ;
25    ao:hasObject akb:exercise .
26
27  akb:trainMethod rdf:type ao:ClassMethod ;
28    ao:name "train"^^xsd:string ;
29    ao:isMethodOf imp:Avatar ;
30    ao:hasParameters akb:trainParams .
31
32  akb:trainParams rdf:type ao:ParameterList ;
33    ao:first akb:exercise ;
34    rdf:rest rdf:nil .
35
36  akb:exercise rdf:type ao:MethodParameter , imp:Exercise ,
        owl:NamedIndividual ;
37    ao:name "exercise"^^xsd:string ;
38    ao:isVariableOf akb:trainMethod .
39
40  imp:Exercise rdf:type owl:Class , owl:Thing .
```

Component Transition Set

The component transition set of the XR avatar (Listing 9.3) includes two transitions.
The first transition (1–4) overrides transition 7.10 of the transition generation
algorithm (cf. Sect. 7.2.3) specifically to the train method parameters and task.
The method gets an Avatar, Exercise, and Length of the Exercise. Thus,
the time point of finishing the method execution may be calculated based on the time
point of invoking the method and the exercise length. The second transition (6–12) is
transition (7.14) of the algorithm generated for the *trains* single invocation activity.
The activity is started by the time point of invoking the train method and finished
at the time point of completing the method.

Listing 9.3 Component transition set of XR avatar used in explorable fitness guide

```
1   time(finished(train(Avatar, Exercise, Length), ExecutionID), TP₂)
```
$$1 \quad time(finished(train(Avatar, Exercise, Length), ExecutionID), TP_2)$$
$$2 \quad \Leftarrow time(invoked(train(Avatar, Exercise, Length),$$
$$3 \quad \quad ExecutionID), TP_1)$$
$$4 \quad \quad \wedge generated(TP_2) \wedge assert(TP_2 = TP_1 + Length).$$
$$5$$
$$6 \quad holds(train(Avatar, Exercise, Length), TI)$$
$$7 \quad \Leftarrow holdsAt(occurred(completed(train(Avatar, Exercise, Length),$$
$$8 \quad \quad ExecutionID), TP_{comp}), TP)$$
$$9 \quad \quad \wedge holdsAt(occurred(invoked(train(Avatar, Exercise, Length),$$

```
10          ExecutionID), TP_{inv}), TP)
11          ∧generated(TI) ∧ assert(start(TI, TP_{inv}))
12          ∧assert(end(TI, TP_{comp})).
```

Mapping Knowledge Base
The mapping knowledge base of the XR avatar (Listing 9.4) specifies domain classes as superclasses of the corresponding application classes. Hence, every object that belongs to an application class also belongs to the proper domain class, which will enable reasoning on and queries about the object in the domain.

Listing 9.4 Mapping knowledge base of XR avatar used in explorable fitness guide

```
 1  @prefix imp: <http://semantic3d.org/e-xr/fitness-guide#> .
 2  @prefix do:  <http://semantic3d.org/e-xr/fitness-ontology#> .
 3  @prefix rdf: <http://www.w3.org/1999/02/22-rdf-syntax-ns#> .
 4
 5  imp:Avatar     rdfs:subClassOf  do:Avatar  .
 6  imp:Exercise   rdfs:subClassOf  do:Exercise .
 7  imp:BearCrawl  rdfs:subClassOf  do:BearCrawl .
 8  imp:Burpees    rdfs:subClassOf  do:Burpees  .
 9  imp:PushUps    rdfs:subClassOf  do:PushUps  .
10  imp:SideLunges rdfs:subClassOf  do:SideLunges .
11  imp:SquatJump  rdfs:subClassOf  do:SquatJump  .
```

Mapping Transition Set
The mapping transition set of the XR avatar (Listing 9.5) includes two transitions that link invocation and completion events for the `train` method with domain events that denote, respectively, the initialization and the finalization of an exercise. The domain events have been created by the *mapping generation algorithm* (cf. Sect. 7.3.2). They are regarded as more understandable to non-IT professionals than events directly related to methods. The domain events appear in the body or head of a transition in line with Definition 7.23 of event mapping. The *trainsInitialization* event implies the invocation of the *train* method (1–3). The *trainsFinalization* event is implied by the completion of the *train* method (5–7). Since *trains* is a single method activity, both domain events may be specified. Thus, the events embrace the transitions from the method invocation to method completion (Formulas 7.10 and 7.11).

Listing 9.5 Mapping transition set of XR avatar used in explorable fitness guide

```
 1  time(invoked(train(Avatar, Exercise, Length), ExecutionID), TP)
 2     ⇐ time(trainsInitialization(Avatar, Exercise, Length), TP)
 3         ∧generated(ExecutionID).
 4
 5  time(trainsFinalization(Avatar, Exercise, Length), TP)
 6     ⇐ time(completed(train(Avatar, Exercise, Length),
 7         ExecutionID), TP).
```

Composition Query

The composition query (Listing 9.6) composes the explorable XR fitness guide, putting stress on its behavior. The guide arranges exercises performed by three avatars: Joe, Alice, and Katy. The transitions describe the exercises on domain events—*trainsInitialization* and *trainsFinalization*—for the *trains* activity, as specified in the mapping transition set. The exercises start at the fifth minute of the XR presentation (1). First, Joe starts the *squatJump* exercise, which lasts for 2 min (3–4). The next Joe's exercise are *pushUps*, which last for 1 min (6–9). Once the exercise is finished, two other exercises are begun—Joe's *sideLunges* lasting for 3 min (11–14) and Alice's *burpees* lasting for 4 min (16–19). Finally, once both exercises are finished, Katy begins *bearCrawl* lasting for 1.5 min (21–26). All exercises are delayed relative to the finish of the preceding exercises, which is represented by the *Delay* variable.

Listing 9.6 Query composing explorable XR fitness guide

```
1    time(startTraining, 5).
2
3    time(trainsInitialization(joe, squatJump, Length), TP₁)
4        ⇐ time(startTraining, TP₁) ∧ Length = 2.
5
6    time(trainsInitialization(joe, pushUps, Length₂), TP₂)
7        ⇐ time(trainsFinalization(joe, squatJump, Length₁), TP₁)
8            ∧Length₂ = 1 ∧ generated(TP₂)
9            ∧assert(TP₂ = TP₁ + Delay).
10
11   time(trainsInitialization(joe, sideLunges, Length₂), TP₂)
12       ⇐ time(trainsFinalization(joe, pushUps, Length₁), TP₁)
13           ∧Length₂ = 3 ∧ generated(TP₂)
14           ∧assert(TP₂ = TP₁ + Delay).
15
16   time(trainsInitialization(alice, burpees, Length₂), TP₂)
17       ⇐ time(trainsFinalization(joe, pushUps, OldLen), TP₁)
18           ∧Length₂ = 4 ∧ generated(TP₂)
19           ∧assert(TP₂ = TP₁ + Delay).
20
21   time(trainsInitialization(katy, bearCrawl, Length), TP₃)
22       ⇐ holdsAt(occurred(trainsFinalization(alice, burpees, Length₁),
23               TP₁), TP)
24           ∧holdsAt(occurred(trainsFinalization(joe, sideLunges,
25               Length₂), TP₂), TP) ∧ Length = 1.5 ∧ TP = max(TP₁, TP₂)
26           ∧generated(TP₃) ∧ assert(TP₃ = TP + Delay).
```

Simulation Queries

Simulation queries to an *environment specification* enable forward exploration of the environment without running it. Therefore, they must specify conditions for which the exploration is accomplished. The illustrative simulation queries presented in this section assume that the delay between an event and another following event is equal to 0.001, and no exceptions are thrown during the execution of methods:

$$Delay = 0.001 \wedge exception(executed(Method, ExecutionID), null).$$

Thus, every invoked method is finally completed. Examples of possible cases of simulation and forward exploration are the following:

1. How long will the consecutive Joe's exercises last, and what time do they begin and finish? The following conjunction can express the query:

$$holds(trains(joe, Exercise, Length), TI) \wedge start(TI, TP_{start})$$
$$\wedge end(TI, TP_{end}).$$

   It associates Joe's exercises with time intervals and their time points. The query result consists of the following three tuples (answers), which include permitted values of the variables used in the query:

```
 1  % answer 1
 2  Exercise = squatJump,
 3  Length = 2,
 4  TI =' ti − joe − squatJump',
 5  TP_start = 5,
 6  TP_end = 7.
 7
 8  % answer 2
 9  Exercise = pushUps,
10  Length = 1,
11  TI =' ti − joe − pushUps,
12  TP_start = 7.001,
13  TP_end = 8.001.
14
15  % answer 3
16  Exercise = sideLunges,
17  Length = 3,
18  TI =' ti − joe − sideLunges,
19  TP_start = 8.002,
20  TP_end = 11.002.
```

   where time intervals (*TI*) have unique IDs generated by the system, and time points (*TP*) start and end time intervals.

2. How long will the overall training of the avatars last? The query can be expressed by the following conjunction:

$$time(startTraining, TP_{start}) \wedge time(trainsFinalization(katy, bearCrawl,$$

$$Len), TP_{end}) \wedge Length = TP_{end} - TP_{start}.$$

It determines the time points of starting and finishing the training and calculates the length of the training. The query result is the following:

1   $Len = 1.5$,
2   $TP_{start} = 5$,
3   $TP_{end} = 13.503$,
4   $Length = 8.503$.

3. Which exercise will Joe start after the third minute since the beginning of the training? The query can be expressed by the following conjunction:

$$holds(trains(joe, Exercise, Len), TI) \wedge start(TI, TP_{start})$$

$$\wedge time(startTraining, TP_{startTraining}) \wedge Time = TP_{start} - TP_{startTraining}$$

$$\wedge Time > 3.$$

It searches for an exercise whose time point satisfies the condition relative to the start of the training. The query result is the following:

1   $Exercise = sideLunges$,
2   $Len = 3$,
3   $TI =' ti - joe - sideLunges'$,
4   $TP_{start} = 8.002$,
5   $TP_{startTraining} = 5$,
6   $Time = 3.002$.

4. Will be there a time point when any two avatars start new exercises? The query can be expressed by the following conjunction:

$$holds(trains(Avatar_1, Exercise_1, Len_1), TI_1) \wedge start(TI_1, TP)$$

$$\wedge holds(trains(Avatar_2, Exercise_2, Len_2), TI_2) \wedge start(TI_2, TP)$$

$$\wedge Avatar_1 \neq Avatar_2.$$

It searches for exercises with time intervals that start at the same time point. The query result is the following:

1   $Avatar_1 = joe$,
2   $Exercise_1 = sideLunges$,
3   $Len_1 = 3$,
4   $TI_1 =' ti - joe - sideLunges'$,

5   $TP_1 = TP_2 = 8.002,$
6   $Avatar_2 = alice,$
7   $Exercise_2 = burpees,$
8   $Len_2 = 4,$
9   $TI_2 =' ti - alice - burpees'.$

5. Which exercises of which avatars will be performed after *squatJump* is performed? The query can be expressed by the following conjunction:

$$holds(trains(Avatar_2, Exercise, Len_2), TI_2) \land holds(trains(Avatar_1,$$

$$squatJump, Len_1), TI_1) \land after(TI_2, TI_1).$$

It uses the *after* predicate, which compares time intervals (cf. Definition 6.13). It does not matter which avatars perform the exercises. The query result consists of the following four answers:

```
1   % answer 1
2   Avatar₂ = Avatar₁, Avatar₁ = joe,
3   Exercise = pushUps,
4   Len₂ = 1,
5   TI₂ =' ti − joe − pushUps',
6   Len₁ = 2,
7   TI₁ =' ti − joe − squatJump'.
8
9   % answer 2
10  Avatar₂ = Avatar₁, Avatar₁ = joe,
11  Exercise = sideLunges,
12  Len₂ = 3,
13  TI₂ =' ti − joe − sideLunges',
14  Len₁ = 2,
15  TI₁ =' ti − joe − squatJump'.
16
17  % answer 3
18  Avatar₂ = alice,
19  Exercise = burpees,
20  Len₂ = 4,
21  TI₂ =' ti − alice − burpees',
22  Avatar₁ = joe,
23  Len₁ = 2,
24  TI₁ =' ti − joe − squatJump'.
25
26  % answer 4
27  Avatar₂ = katy,
28  Exercise = bearCrawl,
29  Len₂ = 1.5,
```

30   $T I_2 =' ti - katy - bearCrawl'$,
31   $Avatar_1 = joe$,
32   $Len_1 = 2$,
33   $T I_1 =' ti - joe - squat Jump'$.

6. Which exercise will Joe perform before he will perform *sideLunges*. The query can be expressed by the following conjunction:

$$holds(trains(joe, Exercise_1, Len_1), T I_1) \wedge holds(trains(joe, sideLunges,$$

$$Len_2), T I_2) \wedge before(T I_1, T I_2).$$

It uses the *before* predicate, which compares time intervals (cf. Definition 6.13). The query result consists of the following two answers:

```
1   % answer 1
2   Exercise₁ = squat Jump,
3   Len₁ = 2,
4   TI₁ =' ti - joe - squat Jump',
5   Len₂ = 3,
6   TI₂ =' ti - joe - sideLunges'.
7
8   % answer 2
9   Exercise₁ = pushUps,
10  Len₁ = 1,
11  TI₁ =' ti - joe - pushUps',
12  Len₂ = 3,
13  TI₂ =' ti - joe - sideLunges'.
```

7. Find two exercises such that the first exercise starts the second exercise in terms of the time intervals of the exercises? The query can be expressed by the following conjunction:

$$holds(trains(Avatar_1, Exercise_1, Len_1), T I_1) \wedge holds(trains(Avatar_2,$$

$$Exercise_2, Len_2), T I_2) \wedge starts(T I_1, T I_2).$$

It uses the *starts* predicate, which compares time intervals (cf. Definition 6.14). The query result is the following:

```
1   Avatar₁ = joe,
2   Exercise₁ = sideLunges,
3   Len₁ = 3,
4   TI₁ =' ti - joe - sideLunges',
5   Avatar₂ = alice,
6   Exercise₂ = burpees,
7   Len₂ = 4,
8   TI₂ =' ti - alice - burpees'.
```

9.2   Executing Explorable Environments

Explorable XR environments are executed by the *workflow execution algorithm*. The algorithm is performed by a separate thread in an infinite loop while the environment is running. The algorithm is continually evaluating the transitions of the workflow specification and executing those that are satisfied at the current time point. Executing transitions relies on invoking methods that are represented by events. In the following description of the algorithm, statements on events and states in transition bodies are called *term templates*—*event templates* for events and *state templates* for states, respectively. Event templates are statements based on the *time* predicate, whereas *state templates* are statements based on the *holdsAt* predicate. Templates are used to evaluate whether particular transitions can be executed at a particular time point. For this purpose, we also introduce the *matches* predicate.

Definition 9.1   The *matches* predicate is a predicate that is true for a given *term* and a *term template* if and only if any of the following is true:

1. The *term* is an atom $atom_1$ and one of the following is true:

   a. The *term template* is an atom $atom_2$, such that $atom_2 = atom_1$.
   b. The *term template* is a variable.

2. The *term* is a variable and the *term template* is a variable.
3. The *term* is a compound term of the form $functor_1(a_1, \ldots, a_n)$, the *term template* is a compound term of the form $functor_2(b_1, \ldots, b_m)$, and all the following are true:

   a. The functor of the *term* is equal to the functor of the *term template*: $functor_1 = functor_2$.
   b. The number of arguments of the *term* is equal to the number of arguments of the *term template*: $n = m$.
   c. Every argument of the *term* matches the corresponding argument of the *term template*: $\forall i = 1..n: matches(a_i, b_i)$.

The *workflow execution algorithm* performs the following steps:

1. Create a subset of the *workflow specification* (called *ruleset*). A horn clause from the *workflow specification* belongs to the *ruleset* if and only if it includes statements on fluents neither in the body nor in the head.
2. Run a reasoning algorithm for the *ruleset* and add all the inferred facts to the *workflow specification*.
3. For every fact from the *workflow specification* whose body includes a statement that matches the term $time(Event, TP)$, where $Event$ and TP are variables:

   a. Create a new *event item* equal to the statement.
   b. Add the *event item* to the *event item set*.

4. For every $eventItem = time(event, tp)$ in the *event item set*, such that tp is the current *time point*:

   a. Create a subset of the *workflow specification* (called *workflowSpecificationSubset*). A transition from the *workflow specification* belongs to *workflowSpecificationSubset* if and only if one of the following is true:

      i. Its body includes an *event template* that is matched by the *eventItem*.

$$\forall transition \in workflowSpecification:$$
$$transition \in workflowSpecificationSubset$$
$$\Leftarrow \exists body, eventTemplate: hasBody(transition, body)$$
$$\wedge includes(body, eventTemplate)$$
$$\wedge matches(eventItem, eventTemplate)$$

$$(9.1)$$

      ii. Its body includes a *state template* that is matched by one of:

         A. term $holdsAt(begin(event), TP)$,
         B. term $holdsAt(finish(event), TP)$,
         C. term $holdsAt(occurred(event, tp), TP)$,

      where TP is a time point.

$$\forall transition \in workflowSpecification:$$
$$transition \in workflowSpecificationSubset$$
$$\Leftarrow \exists body, stateTemplate: hasBody(transition, body)$$
$$\wedge includes(body, stateTemplate)$$
$$\wedge (matches(holdsAt(begin(event), TP), stateTemplate)$$
$$\vee matches(holdsAt(finish(event), TP), stateTemplate)$$
$$\vee matches(holdsAt(occurred(event, tp), TP),$$
$$stateTemplate))$$

$$(9.2)$$

   b. Create a subset of *workflowSpecificationSubset* (called *satisfiedSpecificationSet*). A transition from *workflowSpecificationSubset* belongs to *satisfiedSpecificationSet* if and only if one of the following is true:

      i. It meets the condition specified in point 4(a)i.
      ii. All state templates included in its body are matched by some terms of the form 4(a)iiA, 4(a)iiB, or 4(a)iiC specified on $event_2$ and tp_2, where $event_2$ is an event from the *event item set* and tp_2 is the time point when $event_2$ occurs.

$$\forall transition \in workflowSpecificationSubset:$$

$$transition \in satisfiedSpecificationSet$$

$$\Leftarrow \exists body: hasBody(transition, body)$$

$$\wedge \forall stateTemplate: includes(body, stateTemplate):$$

$$\exists eventItem_2 = (event_2, tp_2) \in eventItemSet:$$

$$(matches(holdsAt(begin(event_2), TP),$$

$$stateTemplate)$$

$$\vee matches(holdsAt(finish(event_2), TP),$$

$$stateTemplate)$$

$$\vee matches(holdsAt(occurred(event_2, tp_2), TP),$$

$$stateTemplate))$$

$$(9.3)$$

c. For every *transition* that belongs to *satisfiedSpecificationSet*:

i. If the head of the *transition* determines (cf. Sect. 7.3.2) the *invocation* of *mehod₁* of *class₁*, create a separate thread to invoke *method₂* of *class₂*, which overrides *method₁*.

ii. Else, if the head of the *transition* determines an event, add the statement included in the head to the event item set.

iii. Else, if the head of the *transition* determines the occurrence of a *state*, execute the instructions in Step 1(i)i of the composition algorithm for:

    A. $event_1 = begin(state)$,

    B. $event_2 = finish(state)$, if the time point of $event_2$ is specified in the transition body.

9.3 Generating Behavior Logs

A behavior log represents activities, including autonomous actions and interactions of users and objects during a particular session of using an explorable XR environment. Generating behavior logs is performed by the *log generation algorithm* while the environment is running. The algorithm is implemented by the *log library*, which is described in more detail in Sect. 10.6. Its functions are invoked by the code injected to class methods at Stage 4 of the development pipeline. For these methods, activities and features have been specified in an activity knowledge base at Stage 2. The log generation algorithm registers activities and features occurring in the environment. In the description of the algorithm, we refer to the entities specified in the *activity ontology* (cf. Sect. 7.1 and Definition 7.8–7.17).

The algorithm performs the following steps, which are initialized by every execution of a *method* that implements an activity or a feature:

1. For every activity and feature implemented by the *method*, determine the *subject*, the *predicate*, and the *object* or the *literal value* based on the activity *join point* that indicates the *method* using the *hasMethod* property.
   Comment: *Subjects and objects of activities and features may be method parameters, local method variables, global class variables, or literal values.*
2. For every feature implemented by the *method*, insert the statement *(subject, predicate, object)* to the triplestore.
   Comment: *As opposed to activities, processing features covers neither creation of time slices, time points, nor time intervals.*
3. For all join points that indicate the *method*, but have no *time points* assigned, create a common time point equal to the current date and time.
4. For every *join point* that indicates the *method*:

   a. If the *join point* is an *activity end join point* of an interval activity or the activity *predicate* is an OWL functional property, update the open time interval (with no *end* property set) associated with a *time slice* of the *subject* for which the *predicate* is specified, if such a time interval exists, by setting its *end* property to the *time point* created in Step 3.
      Comment: *An interval in which a subject has a particular predicate value may be closed explicitly by using a join point related to this subject and the predicate. However, if the predicate is a functional property, which may have at most one value for a particular subject, the same effect is caused by setting a new value for the predicate assigned to the subject.*
   b. If the *join point* belongs to an instant activity, assign the *time point* created in Step 3 to the *join point* using the *hasPoint* property.
      Comment: *The time point indicates the current moment when the activity occurs.*
   c. If the *join point* is an *activity start join point* of an interval activity, create a *time interval* and set its *start* property to the *time point* created in Step 3.
      Comment: *The time point indicates the current moment in time, which starts the time interval of the activity.*
   d. Create a *time slice* of the *subject* that is an individual of all the classes to which the *subject* belongs.
   e. Assign the *time point* used in Step 4b or the *time interval* created in Step 4c to the *subject time slice* using the *hasTimePoint* or *hasTimeInterval* property.
      Comment: *The time slice is a temporal representation of the subject with the predicate assigned for the given time point or time interval.*
   f. If the *predicate* is an OWL datatype property, set the *predicate* for the *subject time slice* to the *literal value* determined in Step 1.
   g. If the *predicate* is an OWL object property:

      i. Create a *time slice* of the *object* that is an individual of all the classes to which the *object* belongs.

   ii. Set the *predicate* for the *subject time slice* to the *object time slice*.

  iii. Assign the *time point* used in Step 4b or the *time interval* created in Step 4c to the *object time slice* using the *hasTimePoint* or *hasTimeInterval* property.

Comment: *If the predicate indicates an object, a temporal representation must be specified for the object as it was specified for the subject in points 4d–4e.*

9.4 Backward Exploration

Backward exploration enables reasoning on and queries about lasting activities as well as activities that occurred while an explorable XR environment was running. Therefore, backward exploration requires that the whole development pipeline is finished, and the environment is used with the execution algorithm and the log generation algorithm. Since backward exploration utilizes logs with registered activities, it does not require simulation of environment behavior, as opposed to forward exploration. Moreover, as temporal statements in behavior logs include visual descriptors, backward exploration permits visualization of occurred activities. Queries used for backward exploration are called *exploration queries*. The result of an exploration query is defined likewise for a simulation query (cf. Definition 3.24). Behavior logs are based on RDF. Therefore, backward exploration can employ the SPARQL language.

To illustrate a backward exploration, we use an *explorable immersive service guide for home appliances*. Its development process has been discussed in detail as an example accompanying the successive stages of the development pipeline in Chap. 8. Hence, in this section, we only present a visual semantic behavior log generated during a session of using the guide with possible queries to the log.

Behavior Log

A behavior log was generated while a serviceman was training in service of an induction hob in the immersive guide. The log is a set of temporal statements (cf. Definition 6.10) describing interactions of the serviceman with different elements of the hob. A fragment of the log is presented in Listing 9.7. The interactions are implemented by different class methods.

The log consists of four temporal statements that represent consecutive interactions and states following them. The statements are built according to the scheme depicted in Fig. 6.1. They refer to time-independent entities such as a user (serviceman) and three interactive objects: the hob with its elements—the oldCoil and the newCoil (lines 9–16). The identifiers of entities in the listing are distinguished by timestamps to keep their uniqueness. First, the user disassembles the oldCoil on the hob (20–33). It is an activity. Hence, both the user and the oldCoil are represented by time slices that belong to the User and Coil classes, respectively. As the interaction is an *instant activity*, the time slices indicate a time point. Furthermore, the time slices are linked by a visual descriptor, which includes an image captured at the time point of the activity. The disassembly activity also finishes the state when the oldCoil was a part of

the hob, which is expressed by the includes property in temporal statement 2
(37–54). The statement incorporates a visual descriptor with a movie, which
includes all frames from the environment that were captured within the time interval.
Next, the user assembles the newCoil, which also happens at a time point and
has an image as the visual descriptor (58–71). This activity, in turn, starts a new state
when the hob includes the newCoil (75–91). It is visualized by a movie.

Listing 9.7 Behavior log generated by immersive service guide

```
 1  @prefix do: <http://semantic3d.org/e-xr/service-guide/
       ontology#> .
 2  @prefix fo: <http://semantic3d.org/e-xr/fluent-ontology#> .
 3  @prefix log: <http://semantic3d.org/e-xr/service-guide/log#>.
 4  @prefix owl: <http://www.w3.org/2002/07/owl#> .
 5  @prefix rdf: <http://www.w3.org/1999/02/22-rdf-syntax-ns#> .
 6  @prefix xsd: <http://www.w3.org/2001/XMLSchema#> .
 7  @base <http://semantic3d.org/e-xr/service-guide/log> .
 8
 9  log:user-20200325T113226 rdf:type owl:NamedIndividual ,
10    do:User .
11
12  log:hob-20200325T113226 rdf:type owl:NamedIndividual ,
        do:InductionHob .
13
14  log:oldCoil-20200325T113226 rdf:type owl:NamedIndividual ,
        do:Coil .
15
16  log:newCoil-20200325T113226 rdf:type owl:NamedIndividual ,
        do:Coil .
17
18  # ------------- Temporal statement 1 -------------
19
20  log:user-20200325T113226-2-2144095554 rdf:type
        owl:NamedIndividual , fo:TimeSlice , do:User ;
21    fo:isTimeSliceOf log:user-20200325T113226 ;
22    fo:hasTimePoint "2020-03-25T11:32:27Z"^^xsd:dateTime .
23
24  log:oldCoil-20200325T113226-2-2144095554 rdf:type
        owl:NamedIndividual, fo:TimeSlice, do:Coil ;
25    fo:isTimeSliceOf log:oldCoil-20200325T113226 ;
26    fo:hasTimePoint "2020-03-25T11:32:27Z"^^xsd:dateTime .
27
28  log:user-20200325T113226-2-2144095554 do:disassembles
        log:oldCoil-20200325T113226-2-2144095554 .
29
30  log:disassembleOldCoilImageDescriptor rdf:type
        owl:NamedIndividual , fo:VisualDescriptor ;
31    fo:isVisualDescriptorOf log:user-20200325T113226
        -2-2144095554,
32      log:oldCoil-20200325T113226-2-2144095554 ;
33    fo:visualRepresentation <http://semantic3d.org/e-xr/
        service-guide/disassembleOldCoilImage> .
```

```
34
35    # ------------- Temporal statement 2 -------------
36
37    log:hob-20200325T113226-1-1424321809 rdf:type
          owl:NamedIndividual, fo:TimeSlice , do:InductionHob ;
38      fo:isTimeSliceOf log:hob-20200325T113226 ;
39      fo:hasTimeInterval log:timeinterval-20200325T113226
            -1-1424321809 .
40
41    log:oldCoil-20200325T113226-1-1424321809 rdf:type
          owl:NamedIndividual , fo:TimeSlice , do:Coil ;
42      fo:isTimeSliceOf log:oldCoil-20200325T113226 ;
43      fo:hasTimeInterval log:timeinterval-20200325T113226
            -1-1424321809 .
44
45    log:timeinterval-20200325T113226-1-1424321809 rdf:type
          owl:NamedIndividual , fo:TimeInterval ;
46      fo:start "2020-03-25T11:30:12Z"^^xsd:dateTime ;
47      fo:end "2020-03-25T11:32:27Z"^^xsd:dateTime .
48
49    log:hob-20200325T113226-1-1424321809 do:includes log:oldCoil
            -20200325T113226-1-1424321809 .
50
51    log:includesOldCoilMovieDescriptor rdf:type
          owl:NamedIndividual, fo:VisualDescriptor ;
52      fo:isVisualDescriptorOf log:hob-20200325T113226
            -1-1424321809,
53        log:oldCoil-20200325T113226-1-1424321809 ;
54      fo:visualRepresentation <http://semantic3d.org/e-xr/
            service-guide/includeOldCoilMovie> .
55
56    # ------------- Temporal statement 3 -------------
57
58    log:user-20200325T113226-3-2088027206 rdf:type
          owl:NamedIndividual , fo:TimeSlice , do:User ;
59      fo:isTimeSliceOf log:user-20200325T113226 ;
60      fo:hasTimePoint "2020-03-25T11:34:45Z"^^xsd:dateTime .
61
62    log:newCoil-20200325T113226-3-2088027206 rdf:type
          owl:NamedIndividual , do:Coil , fo:TimeSlice ;
63      fo:isTimeSliceOf log:newCoil-20200325T113226 ;
64      fo:hasTimePoint "2020-03-25T11:34:45Z"^^xsd:dateTime .
65
66    log:user-20200325T113226-3-2088027206 do:assembles
          log:newCoil-20200325T113226-3-2088027206 .
67
68    log:assembleNewCoilImage1Descriptor rdf:type
          owl:NamedIndividual , fo:VisualDescriptor ;
69      fo:isVisualDescriptorOf log:user-20200325T113226
            -3-2088027206,
70        log:newCoil-20200325T113226-3-2088027206 ;
71      fo:visualRepresentation <http://semantic3d.org/e-xr/
            service-guide/assembleNewCoilImage> .
72
```

```
73   # ------------- Temporal statement 4 -------------
74
75   log:hob-20200325T113226-3-379689319 rdf:type
         owl:NamedIndividual , fo:TimeSlice , do:InductionHob ;
76     fo:isTimeSliceOf log:hob-20200325T113226 ;
77     fo:hasTimeInterval log:timeinterval-20200325T113226
         -3-379689319 .
78
79   log:newCoil-20200325T113226-3-379689319 rdf:type
         owl:NamedIndividual , do:Coil , fo:TimeSlice ;
80     fo:isTimeSliceOf log:newCoil-20200325T113226 ;
81     fo:hasTimeInterval log:timeinterval-20200325T113226
         -3-379689319 .
82
83   log:timeinterval-20200325T113226-3-379689319 rdf:type
         owl:NamedIndividual , fo:TimeInterval ;
84     fo:start "2020-03-25T11:34:45Z"^^xsd:dateTime .
85
86   log:hob-20200325T113226-3-379689319 do:includes log:newCoil
         -20200325T113226-3-379689319 .
87
88   log:includesNewCoilMovieDescriptor rdf:type
         owl:NamedIndividual, fo:VisualDescriptor .
89     fo:isVisualDescriptorOf log:hob-20200325T113226
         -3-379689319 ,
90       log:newCoil-20200325T113226-3-379689319 ;
91     fo:visualRepresentation <http://semantic3d.org/e-xr/
         service-guide/includeNewCoilMovie> .
```

Exploration Queries to Behavior Log

Exploring users' and objects' behavior in the immersive service guide is possible with queries to the generated behavior logs. In particular, such exploration can provide information about how to accomplish different service activities, the sequence of activities, and what equipment is necessary. The answers to such queries can be used to teach beginner technicians. Examples of possible cases of exploration are the following:

1. Select information about a user who assembled a coil, with the time point (tp) and visual representation of the activity. The query is the following:

```
1   PREFIX fo: <http://semantic3d.org/e-xr/fluent-ontology#>
2   PREFIX do: <http://semantic3d.org/e-xr/service-guide/
3     ontology#>
4   PREFIX log: <http://semantic3d.org/e-xr/service-guide/
5     log#>
6
7   SELECT ?user ?element ?tp ?visualRepr WHERE {
8     ?user do:assembles ?element .
9     ?element rdf:type do:Coil .
10    ?user fo:hasTimePoint ?tp .
11    ?visualDesc fo:isVisualDescriptorOf ?user .
12    ?visualDesc fo:visualRepresentation ?visualRepr . }
```

The query result consists of one tuple (answer), which includes permitted values of the variables used in the query:

```
1   user = log:user-20200325T113226-3-2088027206,
2   element = log:newCoil-20200325T113226-3-2088027206,
3   tp = "2020-03-25T11:34:45Z"^^xsd:dateTime,
4   visualRepr = <http://semantic3d.org/e-xr/service-guide/
        assembleNewCoilImage>.
```

The time point is absolute, as it was registered in the behavior log. However, the relative time point can be calculated by subtracting the absolute time point of starting the guide from the requested time point. The visual representation is a single image (Fig. 9.1) because the activity was instant.

Fig. 9.1 Visualization of assembling a coil in explorable service guide

2. Show the visual representation of activities executed while the newCoil was included in the hob, with the beginning (tiStart) and the end (tiEnd, optionally) of the time interval. The query is the following:

```
1   PREFIX fo: <http://semantic3d.org/e-xr/fluent-ontology#>
2   PREFIX do: <http://semantic3d.org/e-xr/service-guide/
3     ontology#>
4   PREFIX log: <http://semantic3d.org/e-xr/service-guide/
5     log#>
6
7   SELECT ?tiStart ?tiEnd ?visualRepr WHERE {
8     ?hob fo:isTimeSliceOf log:hob-20200325T113226 .
9     ?coil fo:isTimeSliceOf log:newCoil-20200325T113226 .
10    ?hob do:includes ?coil .
11    ?coil fo:hasTimeInterval ?ti .
12    ?ti fo:start ?tiStart .
13    ?visualDesc fo:isVisualDescriptorOf ?coil .
14    ?visualDesc fo:visualRepresentation ?visualRepr .
15    OPTIONAL { ?ti fo:end ?tiEnd . } }
```

The query result consists of the following answer:

```
1   tiStart = "2020-03-25T11:34:45Z"^^xsd:dateTime,
2   visualRepr = <http://semantic3d.org/e-xr/service-guide/
        includeNewCoilMovie>.
```

The visual representation is a movie because it was created for an interval activity. Two frames of the movie presenting user's actions during the activity interval are depicted in Fig. 9.2. The time interval is not closed. Therefore, only its start time point has been selected.

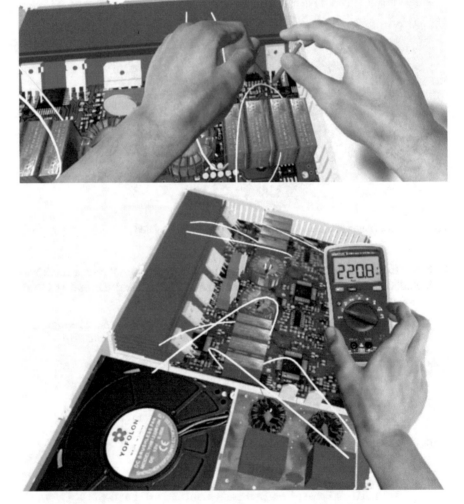

Fig. 9.2 Visualization of user's activities on a hob in explorable service guide

Chapter 10
E-XR Development Tools for Explorable Environments

In this chapter, we present *E-XR development tools for explorable XR environments* called *E-XR toolkit*. The toolkit enables creation of explorable environments through the successive stages of the development pipeline using different elements of the behavior model and the link model. Moreover, it extends the created XR environments with functions that generate behavior logs while the environments are running. The toolkit is an extension to the Eclipse and MS Visual Studio IDEs, which are widely used development tools. The E-XR toolkit consists of the following modules: the *ontology browser*, *activity editors*, *mapping editor*, *environment composer*, *activity compiler*, and *log library*, which are described in the following subsections. The particular modules of the toolkit assigned to the appropriate steps of the pipeline are depicted in Fig. 8.1.

In the toolkit, knowledge bases and behavior logs are encoded using the Semantic Web standards: RDF, RDFS, and OWL. The standards, which are based on description logics, provide sufficient expressivity to describe past and current behavior of running XR environments. The transition sets are encoded in the Prolog logic programming language, which is sufficiently expressive to describe events, states, time entities, and fluents, and to enable reasoning on such entities. It also permits negation, which is necessary to "close the world" and assert that selected activities did/do/will not occur.

10.1 Ontology Browser

The *ontology browser* is the module used at Stage 1 of the pipeline. It enables browsing domain ontologies with their classes and properties. The ontology browser is available in the Tools main menu of Visual Studio (Fig. 10.1). The browser can read arbitrary ontologies, whose classes, datatype properties, and object properties are presented in three neighboring list views (Fig. 10.2). The left list view presents

© The Author(s), under exclusive license to Springer Nature Switzerland AG 2020
J. Flotyński, *Knowledge-Based Explorable Extended Reality Environments*,
https://doi.org/10.1007/978-3-030-59965-2_10

all classes specified in the ontology. The central and right list views present all datatype and object properties specified in the ontology, or properties whose domain is the class selected in the left list view. Domain classes and properties are used by other modules of the E-XR toolkit responsible for creating and presenting activities and features.

Fig. 10.1 *Ontology browser* of *E-XR toolkit* in MS Visual Studio

Fig. 10.2 Lists of domain classes and properties in *ontology browser* of *E-XR toolkit*

10.2   Activity Editors

10.2.1   Visual Activity Editor

The *visual activity editor* is the first of two developed tools that enable completion of Steps 2–3 and 2–4—creation of activities and features. The editor employs the Open-Link Virtuoso triplestore (Open-Link 2020) to store activity knowledge bases. It communicates with the triplestore and processes knowledge bases using the dotNetRDF library (dotNetRDF 2020). The GUI of the editor has been implemented using the XAML GUI description language, and it is presented in Fig. 10.3.

The creation of activities in the visual editor requires to specify a start join point and, depending on the activity type, an end join point (Figs. 10.3 and 10.4). For every join point, a subject and an object should be given. A predicate specified in the editor is common to both join points. Features are created in a similar way.

Fig. 10.3 *Visual activity editor* of *E-XR toolkit*

Behavior Loggers

OnExit AspectModeling.Class.Assemble (this , http://semantic3d.org/aspects/household-ontology#assembles , applianceElement)
OnExit AspectModeling.Class.Assemble (appliance , http://semantic3d.org/aspects/household-ontology#includes , applianceElement)

Fig. 10.4 Creating activities in the *visual activity editor*

10.2.2   Textual Activity Editor

The *textual activity editor* is an alternative to the *visual activity editor*, enabling the creation of activities and features in the form of attributes applied to class methods. In contrast to the visual editor, it is integrated with the code editor, which can be more suitable for programmers than the GUI. The textual editor offers two functions: attribute presentation and attribute completion.

Attribute Presentation

Attributes are instances of the `SemanticLog` class, which inherits from the `System.Attribute` class in .NET (Listing 10.1). The `SemanticLog` class has four fields corresponding to elements of an attribute: subject, predicate, object, and timestamp. The last field is optional—it accepts attributes with and without timestamps. The `SemanticLog` class is added to the code project of an XR environment at Steps 2–3 of the pipeline (cf. Sect. 8.2.3). It enables the Visual Studio IDE to validate the syntax of the created attributes.

Listing 10.1 The `SemanticLog` class, which implements attributes for activities and features

```
1   [AttributeUsage(AttributeTargets.Method, AllowMultiple =
        true)]
2   class SemanticLog: Attribute {
3     private string subject;
4     private string predicate;
5     private string obj;
6     private string timestamp;
7
8     public string Subject { get => subject; set => subject =
          value; }
9     public string Predicate { get => predicate; set =>
          predicate = value; }
10    public string Object { get => obj; set => obj = value; }
11    public string Timestamp { get => timestamp; set =>
          timestamp = value; }
12
13    public SemanticLog(string subject, string predicate,
          string obj) {
14      Subject = subject;
15      Predicate = predicate;
16      Object = obj;
17    }
18
19    public SemanticLog(string subject, string predicate,
          string obj, string timestamp) {
20      Subject = subject;
21      Predicate = predicate;
22      Object = obj;
23      Timestamp = timestamp; } }
```

While attributes are programmed, the attribute presentation function paints their subjects, predicates, objects, and timestamps using distinct colors. An example of coloring attributes is presented in Fig. 10.5. The same subjects and objects have the same colors across different attributes, e.g., `user`, to denote that they refer to the same variables in the code. Besides, datatype properties (e.g., `name`) are distinguished from object properties (e.g., `isIn` and `seatsOn`).

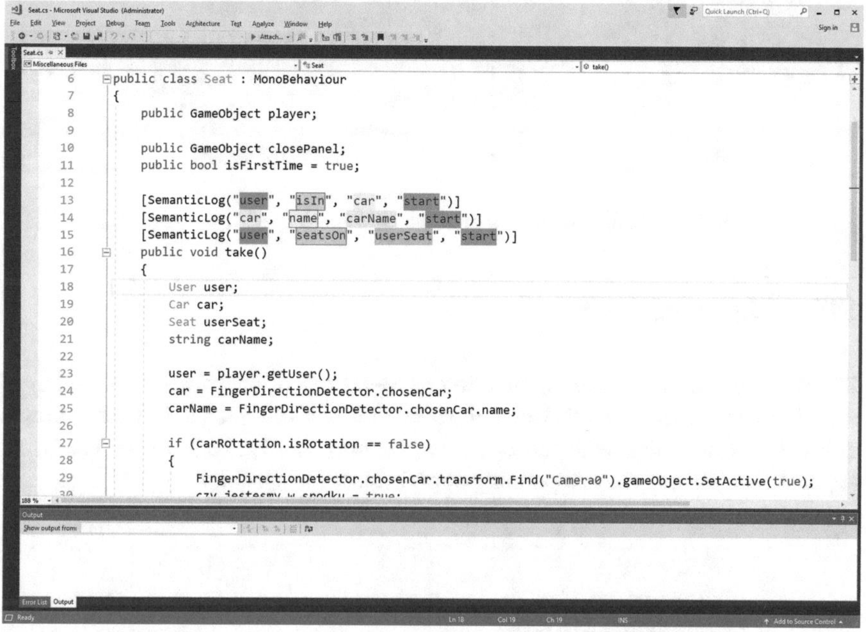
Seat.cs - Microsoft Visual Studio (Administrator)
public class Seat : MonoBehaviour
{
public GameObject player;
public GameObject closePanel;
public bool isFirstTime = true;
[SemanticLog("user", "isIn", "car", "start")]
[SemanticLog("car", "name", "carName", "start")]
[SemanticLog("user", "seatsOn", "userSeat", "start")]
public void take()
{
User user;
Car car;
Seat userSeat;
string carName;
user = player.getUser();
car = FingerDirectionDetector.chosenCar;
carName = FingerDirectionDetector.chosenCar.name;
if (carRottation.isRotation == false)
{
FingerDirectionDetector.chosenCar.transform.Find("Camera0").gameObject.SetActive(true);
Output
Error List
Ready

Fig. 10.5 Presentation of attributes in *textual activity editor* of *E-XR toolkit*

Attribute Completion

While programming, the textual activity editor provides suggestions, according to which attributes can be completed. Suggestions are contextual and depend on what has just been written in the text area. In Fig. 10.6a–d, suggested are, respectively, the entire attribute template, subject (from the list of method parameters and variables), predicate (from the list of properties in the ontology), and timestamp (dates and keywords).

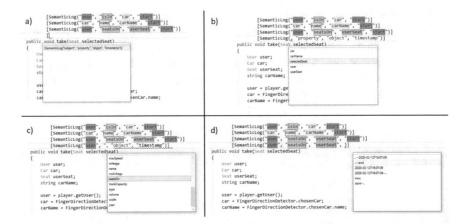

Fig. 10.6 Completion of attributes in *textual activity editor*

10.3 Mapping Editor

The *mapping editor* enables completion of Steps 2–5 of the pipeline—creation of mapping knowledge bases and mapping transition sets (cf. Sect. 8.2.5). An example of creating a mapping with the editor is presented in Fig. 10.7. In the editor, an application class and a corresponding domain class are specified.

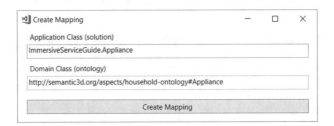

Fig. 10.7 Mapping application classes of XR environment to domain classes of domain ontology in *mapping editor* of *E-XR toolkit*

10.4 Environment Composer

The *environment composer* enables query-based composition of explorable XR environments at Stage 3 of the development pipeline (Flotyński, Walczak, & Krzyszkowski 2020).

10.4.1 Architecture

The architecture of the environment composer, interaction between users and the tool as well as the dataflow are depicted in Fig. 10.8. The composer consists of two main modules: the *visual query builder* and the *query processor*. The query builder is a Java-based desktop application that allows users to build queries and send them to the query processor. The query builder is based on Eclipse with the Oxygen plugin. Oxygen is a well-established tool for creating XML documents, which we use to permit users to visually build queries encoded in XML. XML queries are converted to Prolog by the *query translator*. Queries specify requirements that should be met by the XR environment being composed. Further, Prolog queries are encapsulated into HTTP requests and received by the environment composer using a *RESTful Web Service* installed on the Apache HTTP Server. A query is conveyed to the *reasoning engine*, which is based on the C#Prolog library (Pool 2017). The engine performs reasoning on the union of the query and an environment specification (cf. Definition 8.1) created on the basis of documents prepared in previous steps of the pipeline.

The result of the reasoning is a workflow specification (cf. Definition 8.4), which specifies the composition of activities that meets the user's requirements and determines the final customized explorable environment. The workflow specification is processed by the *scene manager*, which implements the workflow execution algorithm (cf. Sect. 9.2). Next, the generated environment is delivered to the user through the Apache HTTP server. We use WebGL-based implementations generated in Unity. Also, the workflow specification is published to the user to enable simulation and forward exploration of the environment.

10.4.2 Visual Query Design

One of our primary goals is to allow for on-demand generation of customized XR environments by average users and domain experts who are not IT specialists. Hence, composition queries (cf. Definition 8.2) should be built using domain-specific concepts in an intuitive and user-friendly way. It is enabled by the XML standard and available tools for creating XML documents due to their characteristics:

1. XML documents may be visually designed, which is intelligible to non-IT specialists.
2. XML enables encoding of any content using any set of entities, including domain-specific entities.
3. The structure of XML documents may be formally described using XML Schema.
4. XML documents may be efficiently transformed into other documents using XSL.

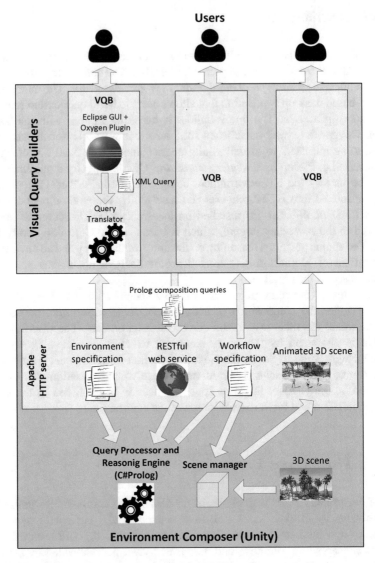

Fig. 10.8 Architecture of *environment composer* of *E-XR toolkit*

Because of the advantages mentioned above, XML is preferred over Prolog for
designing queries by users. Primarily, the visual query builder produces queries
that are XML documents. The GUI of the builder is presented in Fig. 10.9. In the
presented example, XML queries comply with the *XML Schema for the explorable*

XR fitness guide. The schema is depicted in Fig. 10.10. It specifies XML elements and attributes that enable:

1. Description of exercises and muscles: effects, difficulty, stimulation, and parts of the body;
2. Assignment of sequences of exercises to avatars;
3. Specification of variables to be determined by the reasoning engine while processing queries.

While the XML Schema for the fitness guide is specific to the selected application domain and use cases, the query builder can use XML Schema documents specific to various application domains. XML queries are further converted into semantically equivalent Prolog queries using the Java XML DOM library and sent to the query processor. The XML to Prolog transformation is performed on the client side to preserve the independence of the query processor from different types of clients and formats used for query preparation. In our approach, the preparation of queries in the Prolog format, which is acceptable by the query processor, is the job of query builders. Query builders are autonomous to offer different UIs and formats for primarily encoding of queries by users.

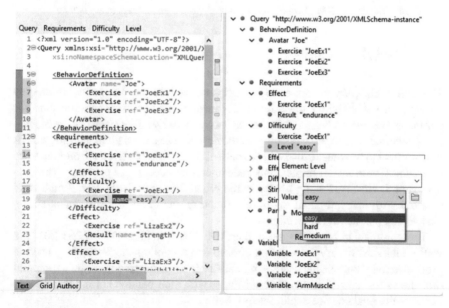

Fig. 10.9 *Visual query builder* of *environment composer* (on the right) with generated XML query (in the middle) and a prompt about permitted values of an attribute (small window)

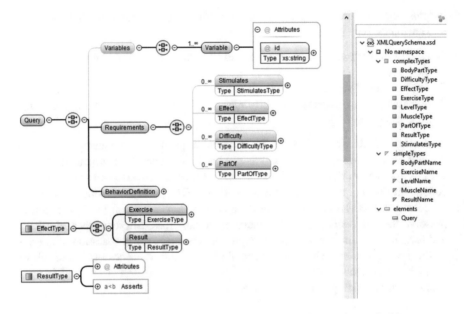

Fig. 10.10 Fragment of XML Schema for XR fitness guide used in *visual query builder*

10.5   Activity Compiler

The *activity compiler* processes specifications of activities and features, which may
have the form of activity knowledge bases (created with the visual activity editor) or
attributes over methods (created with the textual activity editor). It works at Stage 4
of the pipeline. The input parameters of the compiler are: the path of a prototype XR
environment to be transformed and the path of the explorable XR environment to be
generated. The compiler implements code injection according to the aspect-oriented
approach. It attaches the log library to the project, extends the bodies of annotated
methods with invocations of log library functions, and injects additional auxiliary
classes that prepare the invocations.

The compiler is based on the dotNetRDF library and ANTLR (Parr 2014), a
well-established library for creating parsers and compilers. dotNetRDF is used to
process activity knowledge bases, while ANTLR has been used to create a grammar
that allows for recognizing method attributes with their parameters and variables to
generate the final code of explorable environments.

10.6   Log Library

The *log library* is the module of the E-XR toolkit responsible for generating visual
semantic behavior logs while an explorable environment is running. The library
implements the log generation algorithm (cf. Sect. 9.3). Functions provided by the

library create temporal semantic statements (cf. Definition 6.10) based on activities as well as RDF statements based on features assigned to methods in the environment implementation.

10.6.1 Generating Temporal Statements

The library has been implemented as a dynamic-link library (DLL) in Visual Studio, and it is compatible with C# projects. Temporal statements and RDF statements are created using Semiodesk Trinity (Semiodesk GmbH 2015), an open project for ontology engineering in C# applications. The generated logs are stored in Semiodesk TinyVirtuoso (Open-Link 2020), which is a triplestore with an HTTP-based interface. The library is attached to the XR environment at Stage 4 of the pipeline (cf. Sect. 8.4) by the *E-XR activity compiler*. In the examples of explorable environments presented in this book, we use the library for projects developed in the Unity game engine.

10.6.2 Generating Visual Descriptors

The log library functions also capture the screen while the explorable environment is running and generate visual descriptors (cf. Sect. 6.1.3) of temporal statements. Images, which are screenshots, are captured using the `ScreenCapture.Capture Screenshot` method in Unity (Unity 3D 2020). Screen capturing is implemented in a common thread with 3D rendering and logging behavior. Thus, the captured images strictly reflect actions and interactions occurring in the 3D scenes. Further, we generate movies from the images using FFmpeg (FFmpeg 2020). Visual descriptors are linked to time points and time intervals of temporal statements as depicted in Fig. 6.1.

Chapter 11
Applications of E-XR

In this chapter, we present two examples of explorable XR environments, which have been developed in the virtual reality laboratory at the Poznań University of Economics and Business in Poland. The first environment is the *explorable immersive car showroom*. It has been intended for marketing and merchandising purposes to explore customers' interests and preferences in car configuration. The second environment is the *explorable immersive service guide for home appliances*. Its goal is to train technicians in servicing household equipment.

11.1 Explorable Immersive Car Showroom

The explorable immersive car showroom has been developed for rapid creation and evaluation of marketing and merchandising concepts (Poznań University of Economics and Business 2018; Nowak & Flotyński 2018; Flotyński, Nowak, & Walczak 2018; Flotyński & Nowak 2019). The development and modification of virtual products are typically less time consuming and permit faster feedback from potential customers than the development and modification of real products. In marketing and merchandising, explorable XR environments can provide valuable information about customers' behavior and preferences, e.g., in virtual stores and showrooms. So far, real stores, showrooms, and products have been mostly used in such research (Borusiak et al. 2017).

The immersive showroom permits virtual visits and configuration of cars. On the one hand, it can be attractive to potential customers of real car showrooms. On the other hand, it gives car producers and distributors an opportunity to improve their products based on quick feedback from customers. In addition, recent studies show that innovative methods are more successful in marketing strategies than traditional visual media (Fransen, Verlegh, Kirmani, & Smit 2015). XR can be seen as one of such innovative approaches.

© The Author(s), under exclusive license to Springer Nature Switzerland AG 2020   201
J. Flotyński, *Knowledge-Based Explorable Extended Reality Environments*,
https://doi.org/10.1007/978-3-030-59965-2_11

In the following subsections, we present the architecture, functionality, and development of the explorable immersive car showroom as well as the exploration of an example behavior log generated by the environment.

11.1.1   Architecture

The explorable immersive car showroom has been implemented as a Unity-based application, which uses the Oculus Rift HMD (Facebook Technologies 2018) and the Leap Motion hand tracking device (Ultraleap 2020). The architecture of the system is outlined in Fig. 11.1. The Unity web engine (Unity Technologies 2020a) supports various XR devices, such as HMDs and motion tracking systems. Oculus Rift enables immersive presentation of 3D content, while Leap Motion allows for interaction with 3D cars using hand gestures, which are a natural and intuitive user interface.

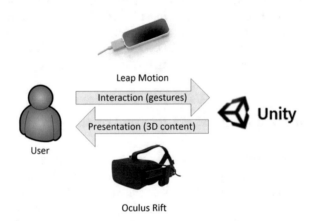

Fig. 11.1 Architecture of explorable immersive car showroom

11.1.2   Functionality

In the showroom, customers can accomplish the following activities implemented by distinct class methods, using different hand gestures.

1. *Select a car*, which is executed by indicating the car using the forefinger of the right hand (Fig. 11.2). The user is immediately moved to the car and can watch it from outside (Fig. 11.3). In the showroom, several different cars are accessible.
2. *Change the car's color*, which is executed for the currently watched car by selecting a color from a palette in the main menu using the forefinger of the

right hand (Fig. 11.4). The selected color is immediately applied to the body of
the car.

3. *Watch a car from around*, which is executed by selecting a direction of rotation
around the car from the main menu using the forefinger of the right hand
(Fig. 11.5). In this way, the user can view the car from all sides.

4. *Take a seat in the car*, which is executed by selecting a seat inside the car from the
main menu (Fig. 11.6). Once got in, the user can watch the car inside (Fig. 11.7).

Fig. 11.2 Selecting a car in explorable car showroom. ©Jakub Flotyński 2020, all rights reserved

11.1.3 Development of Explorable Car Showroom

In the successive stages of the showroom development pipeline, we have:

1. Elaborated a domain ontology using the Protégé ontology editor and the E-XR
ontology browser (cf. Sect. 10.1) at Stage 1.
2. Prepared XR components, mapped application classes to domain classes using
the E-XR mapping editor, and annotated the class methods mentioned in the
previous subsection using the E-XR textual activity editor (cf. Sect. 10.2.2) at
Stage 2.
3. Composed the XR components into the explorable showroom using the E-XR
environment composer (cf. Sect. 10.4) at Stage 3.

Fig. 11.3 Watching a car from outside in explorable car showroom. ©Jakub Flotyński 2020, all rights reserved

Fig. 11.4 Changing the color of a car in explorable car showroom. ©Jakub Flotyński 2020, all rights reserved

4. Compiled the activities and features using the activity compiler (cf. Sect. 10.5) and compiled the environment to its final executable form using the Visual Studio C# compiler at Stage 4.

Fig. 11.5 Watching a car from around in explorable car showroom. ©Jakub Flotyński 2020, all rights reserved

Fig. 11.6 Getting in a car in explorable car showroom. ©Jakub Flotyński 2020, all rights reserved

11.1.4 *Example of Behavior Log*

A behavior log has been generated while a customer was visiting the explorable immersive car showroom. A fragment of the log is shown in Listing 11.1. The log describes behavior demonstrated by the customer in the environment. The log

Fig. 11.7 Watching a car inside in explorable car showroom. ©Jakub Flotyński 2020, all rights reserved

consists of temporal statements that represent actions and interactions between the customer and cars in the showroom, which are implemented by the annotated methods listed in the previous sections.

Listing 11.1 Example of behavior log generated by explorable immersive car showroom

```
1   @prefix do: <http://semantic3d.org/e-xr/car-showroom/domain-
        ontology#> .
2   @prefix fo: <http://semantic3d.org/e-xr/fluent-ontology#> .
3   @prefix log: <http://semantic3d.org/e-xr/car-showroom/log#> .
4   @prefix owl: <http://www.w3.org/2002/07/owl#> .
5   @prefix rdf: <http://www.w3.org/1999/02/22-rdf-syntax-ns#> .
6   @prefix xsd: <http://www.w3.org/2001/XMLSchema#> .
7   @base <http://semantic3d.org/e-xr/car-showroom/log> .
8
9   log:customer-20200207T144053
10    rdf:type owl:NamedIndividual , do:Customer ;
11    foaf:name "John␣Kowalski" .
12
13  log:car-20200207T144053
14    rdf:type owl:NamedIndividual , do:Car ;
15    do:name "Volvo" .
16
17  log:customer-20200207T144053-1-1775502135
18    rdf:type owl:NamedIndividual , fo:TimeSlice , do:Customer;
19    fo:isTimeSliceOf log:customer-20200207T144053 ;
20    do:watches log:car-20200207T144053-1-1775502135 .
21
```

```
22  log:car-20200207T144053-1-1775502135
23    rdf:type owl:NamedIndividual , fo:TimeSlice , do:Car ;
24    fo:isTimeSliceOf log:car-20200207T144053 .

26  log:timeinterval-20200207T144053-1-1775502135
27    fo:isTimeIntervalOf log:car-20200207T144053-1-1775502135 ,
          log:customer-20200207T144053-1-1775502135 ;
28    fo:start "2020-02-07T13:41:06Z"^^xsd:dateTime ;
29    fo:end "2020-02-07T13:41:18Z"^^xsd:dateTime .

31  log:customer-20200207T144053-6-338709773
32    rdf:type owl:NamedIndividual , fo:TimeSlice , do:Customer;
33    fo:isTimeSliceOf log:customer-20200207T144053 ;
34    do:paints log:car-20200207T144053-6-338709773 .

36  log:car-20200207T144053-6-338709773
37    rdf:type owl:NamedIndividual , fo:TimeSlice , do:Car ;
38    fo:isTimeSliceOf log:car-20200207T144053 ;
39    do:color "RGBA(0.392,_0.000,_0.000,_1.000)" .

41  log:timeinterval-20200207T144053-6-338709773
42    rdf:type owl:NamedIndividual , fo:TimeInterval ;
43    fo:isTimeIntervalOf log:car-20200207T144053-6-338709773 ,
          log:customer-20200207T144053-6-338709773 ;
44    fo:start "2020-02-07T13:41:36Z"^^xsd:dateTime ;
45    fo:end "2020-02-07T13:41:51Z"^^xsd:dateTime .
```

Every object in the log is represented by an OWL named individual. The objects are described in a general way understandable to average users. The underlying 3D representation of the objects is irrelevant to the log as its target users are not necessarily familiar with computer graphics. The names of the individuals are distinct due to generated postfixes. The first part of a postfix is the date and time when the environment was started. The other two parts (after dashes) are hash codes.

The customer (lines 9–11) and the car (13–15) are basic individuals for time slices, with time-independent properties, such as name. The customer interacts with the car by watching it, which is expressed by time slices linked by the watches property (17–24). It is lasting from 2020-02-07T13:41:06Z to 2020-02-07T13:41:18Z, as specified by the time interval linked to both time slices (26–29). Later, the customer changed the color of the car for another time interval (31–45).

11.1.5   Reasoning and Querying on Behavior Logs

Exploring customers' behavior in the explorable car showroom is possible with reasoning on and queries to the generated behavior logs. Queries may be encoded in SPARQL (W3C 2013), the main query language for RDF-based ontologies and knowledge bases. Such exploration can provide information about customers' interests and preferences, which can be further used for marketing and merchandising, especially to prepare personalized offers. Examples of exploration cover the following use cases.

How much time did the customer spend to watch a particular car outside?

The SPARQL query and its result are presented in Fig. 11.8. This information can be used to investigate which cars are attractive to customers. In the example, the customer is watching a Lexus car. `Customer` and `car` time slices linked to common intervals are searched. Next, the length of the intervals is calculated. The found time intervals and the overall time are presented.

Which places does the customer prefer inside cars?

The SPARQL query and its result are presented in Fig. 11.9. This information can be used to discover whether the customer is mostly a driver or a passenger. The query looks for seats taken by the customer with no regard to the particular cars.

11.2 Explorable Immersive Service Guide for Home Appliances

The explorable immersive service guide for home appliances supports training technicians in servicing induction hobs. The guide has been developed in collaboration with Amica S.A., which is one of the main producers of household equipment in Poland (Walczak, Flotyński, Strugała, Rumiński, et al. 2019; Flotyński, Englert, et al. 2019; Flotyński, Strugała, et al. 2019). The development of immersive service and user's guides is one of the most promising application domains of XR. Such guides outperform more traditional textual, audio, and video guides in many respects. First, 3D content presented in XR guides can be interactive and react to users' activities with complex behavior. Such content can be visualized in different ways encompassing animations as well as different levels of products' detail and perspectives. Second, 3D products within scenes can be typically modified independently of each other, which simplifies and reduces the costs of guide updates. Finally, presentation of and interaction with XR user's guides can be more user friendly and attractive than in the case of other types of guides— by employing realistic graphics, immersive displays, and gesture-based interfaces, which are typically perceived as natural.

Query 1:

```
PREFIX fo: <http://semantic3d.org/annotation/fluent-ontology.owl#>
select ?customer ?car ?start ?end ?watching_time where {
  ?timeInterval fo:isTimeIntervalOf ?customer.
  ?timeInterval fo:isTimeIntervalOf ?car.
  ?customer <do:watches> ?car.
  ?car <do:name> "Lexus".
  ?timeInterval fo:start ?start.
  ?timeInterval fo:end ?end.
  BIND ((?end-?start) as ?watching_time)}
ORDER BY ?end
```

Response 1:

customer	car	start	end	watching_time
log:user-20200207T144053-5--2100734389	log:chosenCar-20200207T144053-5--2100734389	2020-02-07T13:41:07Z	2020-02-07T13:45:02Z	235
log:user-20200207T154249-6-681612438	log:chosenCar-20200207T154249-6-681612438	2020-02-07T14:43:13Z	2020-02-07T14:44:02Z	49

a)

Query 2:

```
PREFIX fo: <http://semantic3d.org/annotation/fluent-ontology.owl#>

select sum(?watching_time) where {
  ?timeInterval fo:isTimeIntervalOf ?customer.
  ?timeInterval fo:isTimeIntervalOf ?car.
  ?customer <do:watches> ?car.
  ?car <do:name> "Lexus".
  ?timeInterval fo:start ?start.
  ?timeInterval fo:end ?end.
  BIND ((?end-?start) as ?watching_time)}
```

Response 2: 284

b)

Fig. 11.8 How much time did customer spend to watch car outside? Particular intervals found (**a**) and the overall time (**b**)

In the following subsections, we present the architecture and functionality of the explorable immersive service guide. The development of the environment at the successive stages of the pipeline has been presented in Chap. 8. Examples of behavior logs and behavior exploration of the guide have been presented in Sects. 9.3 and 9.4.

Query:

```
PREFIX fo: <http://semantic3d.org/annotation/fluent-ontology.owl#>

select (count(?seat) as ?num) ?seat where {
  ?timeInterval fo:isTimeIntervalOf ?customer.
  ?timeInterval fo:isTimeIntervalOf ?car.
  ?customer <do:isIn> ?car.
  ?customer <do:seatsOn> ?seat.}
GROUP BY ?seat
ORDER BY DESC(?num)
```

Response:

num	seat
12	"leftFrontSeat"
7	"rightFrontSeat"
5	"leftBackSeat"
2	"rightBackSeat"

Fig. 11.9 Which places inside cars are preferred by a customer?

11.2.1 Architecture

The guide is a Unity-based application, whose architecture is outlined in Fig. 11.10. The presentation of 3D models of products to users is enabled by the HTC Vive HMD. The HMD enables immersive visualization of 3D content at a level of detail sufficient for step-by-step training in repairing defects and testing home appliances. Immersive visualization enhances the users' experience in comparison to the more traditional 2D presentation. Interaction of users with 3D products is permitted by the Leap Motion device, which tracks users' hand gestures. Different hand gestures trigger different activities on hobs, e.g., disassembling, assembling, and testing elements of hobs. Animated serviceman's hands are presented within the XR scene using realistic 3D models. It is an intuitive, user-friendly form of interaction. The used hardware forms an affordable platform, which is attainable to small distributors of household appliances and individual users.

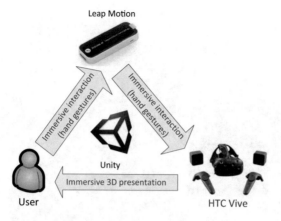

Fig. 11.10 Architecture of explorable immersive service guide for home appliances

11.2.2   Functionality

The guide implements several immersive scenarios of repairing the most common defects and testing induction hobs. The guide allows service members to look at different elements of hobs represented with high accuracy, zoom them in and out, and watch animations and movies that present activities to be performed. The guide covers the following immersive interactive 3D scenarios.

1. *Testing the power connection* (Fig. 9.2). This scenario is devoted to one of the most common failures. In an animation, the appropriate terminals are indicated, and their correct connection is shown. Finally, the voltage on the connection is measured using a virtual multimeter.
2. *Testing transistors and display* (Fig. 11.11). This scenario demonstrates how to verify transistors and display, which are vital to the correct work of the appliance. Once verified, the elements may be disassembled if they are broken, or the work of the hob may be tested in other scenarios.

Fig. 11.11 Testing display of an induction hob in explorable service guide

Fig. 11.12 Disassembling and assembling coils of an induction hob in explorable service guide

Fig. 11.13 Disassembling heating plates of an induction hob in explorable service guide

3. *Disassembling and assembling coils, heating plates, and fan* (Figs. 9.1, 11.12, 11.13, and 11.14). These scenarios are executed when coils, heating plates, or the fan is broken and needs to be exchanged. The scenarios allow service technicians to repair the hob, which can be verified in another scenario.

Fig. 11.14 Disassembling fan of an induction hob in explorable service guide

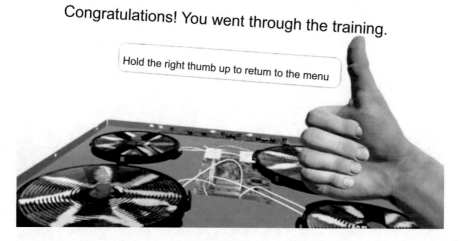

Fig. 11.15 Testing work of an induction hob in explorable service guide

4. *Testing the overall work of the hob* (Fig. 11.15). This scenario allows users to test powering on the hob and cooking with it. Possible problems that may occur during operation on the hob may be presented with solutions, or the correct work of the appliance is announced.

Chapter 12
Evaluation of E-XR

We have evaluated the E-XR approach in terms of users' effort in composing explorable environments, performance of the implemented development tools as well as size and complexity of data structures used in the development pipeline. The evaluation results are presented in Sects. 12.1–12.4. Next, we discuss conclusions drawn from the evaluation results and present a wider background for the E-XR concept in Sect. 12.5. The evaluation and discussion are based on the preliminary analysis of the approach presented in Flotyński, Walczak, & Krzyszkowski (2020).

12.1 Configuration of Testing System

The system used to complete the tests of the E-XR approach consists of the following workstations connected by the 10 Gigabit Ethernet.

1. *Workstation 1* was equipped with CPU Intel Core i7-5820K CPU 3.30GHz with 6 cores and 12 threads; 16 GB RAM 2400 MHz; GPU NVIDIA GeForce GTX 960; HD Western Digital WD2003FZEX with 64 MB cache and rotational speed 7200 as well as the Windows 10 operating system.
2. *Virtual workstation 2* was equipped with 2 CPU AMD EPYC 7551 32-Core 2.0 GHz with 32 cores and 64 threads; 8 GB RAM DDR; HD 160 GB as well as the Windows Server 2012 operating system.

J. Flotyński, *Knowledge-Based Explorable Extended Reality Environments*,
https://doi.org/10.1007/978-3-030-59965-2_12

12.2   Users' Effort in Environment Composition

Users' effort in composing explorable environments has been analyzed for E-XR in comparison to other selected tools for XR development. In contrast to E-XR, the available approaches have the following shortfalls:

1. They do not enable on-demand composition of XR in distributed environments. Instead, they enable visual modeling or programming of XR with locally used tools.
2. They do not enable composition of XR environments based on domain knowledge. Instead, they require the use of technical concepts specific to computer graphics and animation.

Hence, the possible comparison of E-XR approach to other solutions in terms of users' effort is limited to the process of creating XR environments and scenes in the manner permitted by a particular tool, regardless of remote or local access to the scenes being created, and the specificity level of XR representation. We have compared the E-XR environment composer (cf. Sect. 10.4) to Unity by measuring the effort as the sum of the number of mouse clicks and keystrokes.

We created several XR environments with animated avatars, each of which performs a sequence of exercises. In E-XR, we used the visual query builder of the environment composer. In Unity, we used the visual animation editor. For both tools, we counted clicks and keystrokes necessary to build the environments. The formulas below are based on the number of avatars in the created environments and the number of exercises every avatar performs. In E-XR, the creation of a query composing an explorable environment requires:

1. 9 initial clicks and keystrokes,
2. 9 clicks and keystrokes to add an avatar to the environment scene,
3. 6 and 17 clicks and keystrokes to add a variable and a requirement, respectively,
4. 9 clicks and keystrokes to assign an exercise described by a variable and a requirement to the avatar.

The overall formula for X avatars, each performing Y exercises, is the following:

$$E - XR_{clicks+keystrokes} = 9 + 9X + (6 + 17 + 9)Y = 9(1 + X) + 32Y.$$

In Unity, the composition of an environment with a single avatar requires 13 initial clicks and keystrokes plus 4 clicks and keystrokes for every exercise assigned to the avatar. Thus, the overall formula for X avatars, each performing Y exercises, is the following:

$$Unity_{clicks+keystrokes} = (13 + 4Y)X.$$

Figure 12.1 presents *gain* calculated as the ratio of Unity to E-XR clicks and keystrokes. The gain was calculated for 3D scenes comprising 1–100 avatars, each performing 2–100 exercises. The gain slightly grows with the increase in the number of avatars in the composed environment, and it rapidly grows with the increase in the number of exercises assigned to a single avatar. The E-XR environment composer outperforms Unity in most cases of the generated environments except the environments with up to 7 avatars. The highest gain greater than 10 occurred for the environment comprised of 100 avatars, each performing a sequence of 100 exercises. In contrast, the lowest gain occurred for the environment with 1 avatar performing 100 exercises.

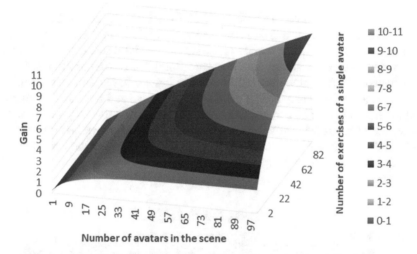

Fig. 12.1 Gain in the number of mouse clicks and keystrokes between the Unity game engine and the E-XR environment composer depending on the number of avatars in the environment scene and the number of exercises assigned to a single avatar. Values higher than 1 indicate scenes with lower modeling effort when created using E-XR

12.3 Performance of E-XR Tools

We have evaluated the performance of the implemented E-XR tools at different stages of the pipeline as well as in the use of explorable environments.

12.3.1 *Environment Composition*

The performance of composing explorable XR environments, which is the job of the E-XR environment composer, has been evaluated in terms of translating composition queries from XML to Prolog as well as in terms of reasoning on Prolog queries combined with environment specifications. For these tests, we used workstation 1.

Query Translation

In this test, we measured the time required for translating composition queries from XML to Prolog, which is performed by the query translator of the E-XR environment composer. The queries consisted of 100–1000 statements (Fig. 12.2). In environment specifications, statements are Horn clauses (in transition sets) and RDF statements (in ontologies and knowledge bases). In queries, statements are RDF statements. For every size, we randomly generated and translated 20 queries and calculated the average translation time. The translation time is proportional to the square of the number of statements in the query. The time varies from about 7 to 66 milliseconds, which is relatively short, taking into account the large numbers of conditions specified in the queries—each statement in a query expresses a single condition.

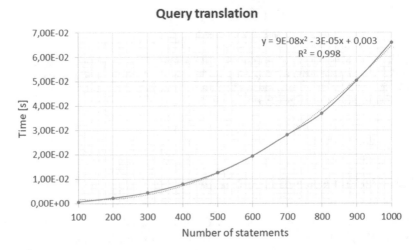

Fig. 12.2 Time required for query translation from XML to Prolog depending on the number of statements in the query

Query Processing

The performance of query processing was measured as the time required for reasoning on workflow specifications, each of which was the union of an environment
specification and a composition query describing conditions for the explorable XR
environment to be generated. We have completed two tests—modifying the size
of queries and modifying the size of environment specifications, measured in the
number of statements and the number of variables used in the statements.

Query Processing Time Depending on Query Size

In this test, we used an environment specification consisting of 1000 statements and
queries with different numbers of variables and statements. While the number of
variables in a query ranged from 1 to 7, the number of statements was between
20 and 100. For every combination, 20 different queries were randomly generated.
They were used to calculate the average processing time, which is presented as the
points in Figs. 12.3, 12.4, 12.5, 12.6, 12.7, 12.8, 12.9, 12.10, 12.11, 12.12, 12.13,
12.14, 12.15, and 12.16.
   Altering the number of variables. Figures 12.3, 12.4, 12.5, 12.6, 12.7, 12.8,
12.9, 12.10, and 12.11 depict the query processing time for queries including a
fixed number of statements, but a variable number of variables. As presented in
the graphs, adding a new variable to a query is followed by about a tenfold increase
in the processing time. The regression line and the coefficient of determination (R^2)
are shown in the graphs. R^2 is in the range 0.914–0.986, which denotes an excellent
determination. The resulting query processing time for different queries varies from
0.01 to tens of thousands of seconds.
   Altering the number of statements. A similar analysis was done for a variable
number of statements and a fixed number of variables in a query (Figs. 12.12,
12.13, 12.14, 12.15, and 12.16). The determined curves strongly oscillate around
the regression lines, which are poorly matched (R^2 in 0.020–0.694) and indicate
only a general trend. The growth in the query processing time slightly follows the
increase in the number of statements in most of the graphs. However, the relation is
much weaker than in the case of the fixed number of statements and the changing
number of variables in queries. In two cases (Figs. 12.14 and 12.15), time obtained
for larger queries is shorter than for smaller queries, which is accidental.

Query Processing Time Depending on Environment Specification Size

In this test, we used queries consisting of 10 statements with 5 variables and
environment specifications consisting of the variable number of statements ranging
from 200 to 1300 (Fig. 12.17). For every point in the graph, 20 environment
specifications were randomly generated. The increase in the number of statements
is followed by the exponential increase in the processing time. However, it is less

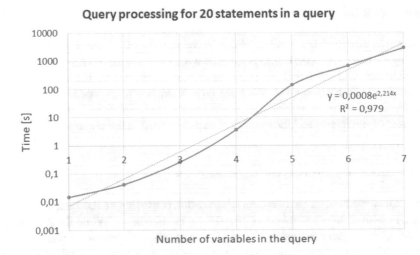

Fig. 12.3 Query processing time depending on the number of variables in the query. Determined for queries consisting of 20 statements

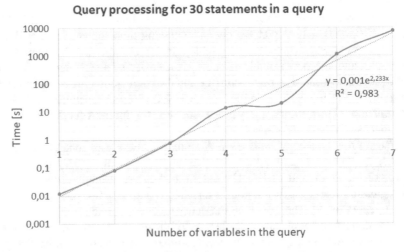

Fig. 12.4 Query processing time depending on the number of variables in the query. Determined for queries consisting of 30 statements

rapid than in the case of the increasing number of query variables (Figs. 12.3, 12.4, 12.5, 12.6, 12.7, 12.8, 12.9, 12.10, and 12.11). A threefold increase in the number of statements causes a tenfold increase in the query processing time. The query processing time for different environment specifications varies from 1 to 458 s.

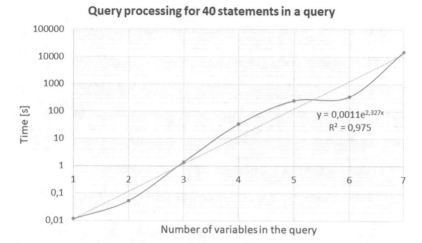

Fig. 12.5 Query processing time depending on the number of variables in the query. Determined for queries consisting of 40 statements

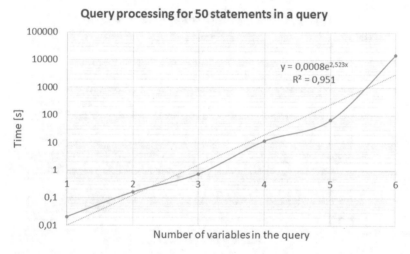

Fig. 12.6 Query processing time depending on the number of variables in the query. Determined for queries consisting of 50 statements

12.3.2 Activity Compilation

We have evaluated the performance of generating explorable XR environments using two possible types of representation of activities and features—knowledge bases as well as attributes. The representations were created using the E-XR activity editors (cf. Sect. 10.2). Activities and features were compiled using the E-XR activity compiler presented in Sect. 10.5. The tests employed workstation 1.

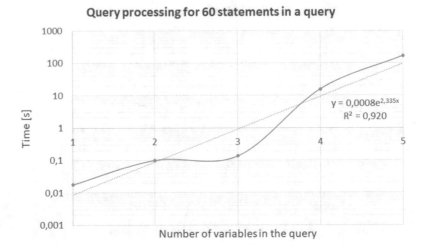

Fig. 12.7 Query processing time depending on the number of variables in the query. Determined for queries consisting of 60 statements

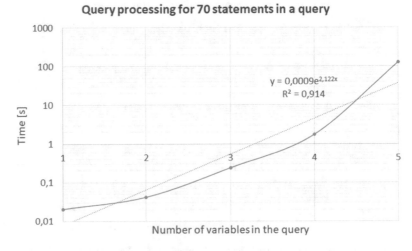

Fig. 12.8 Query processing time depending on the number of variables in the query. Determined for queries consisting of 70 statements

Compilation of Activity Knowledge Bases

We measured the time required for compiling XR environments to their explorable counterparts using activity knowledge bases. We generated activity knowledge bases including from 50 to 750 activities of a particular type. 5 activities were assigned to a single class method. Hence, the number of methods was in the range 10–150 for all types of activities except double method activities, which encompassed twice

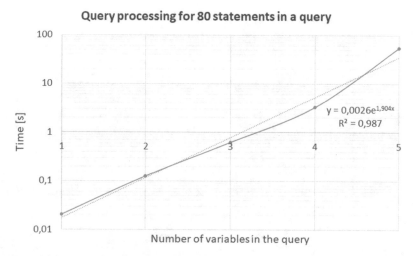

Fig. 12.9 Query processing time depending on the number of variables in the query. Determined for queries consisting of 80 statements

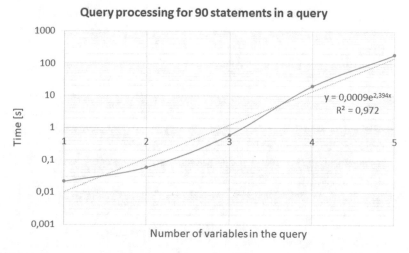

Fig. 12.10 Query processing time depending on the number of variables in the query. Determined for queries consisting of 90 statements

more methods. For every type and every number of activities, 20 different activity knowledge bases were generated and used to test activity compilation.

The compilation time is presented in the graph and table in Fig. 12.18. Every point in the curves represents the average time for 20 compilations. The compilation time varies in the range 10–20 ms (for 50 activities applied to 10 or 20 methods) to about 600–2000 ms (for 750 activities applied to 150 or 300 methods). The formulas calculated using interpolation as well as the coefficient of determination

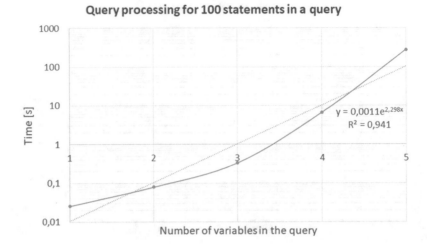

Fig. 12.11 Query processing time depending on the number of variables in the query. Determined for queries consisting of 100 statements

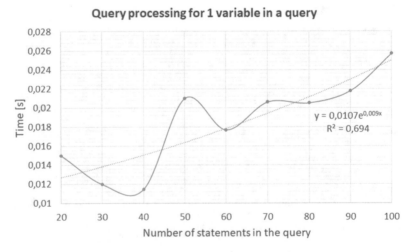

Fig. 12.12 Query processing time depending on the number of statements in the query. Determined for queries with 1 variable

(R^2) equal almost to 1 show that the compilation time is proportional to the square of the number of activities. The most time consuming is the compilation of double method activities as it injects code into two different methods. Also, the compilation of single invocation activities is relatively time consuming as it injects code at the beginning and end of methods. The compilation of instant activities, double invocation activities, and features is the most efficient as it affects only one method at its one point. The relation between the curves in the graph is confirmed by the calculated average time required for compiling a single activity or feature.

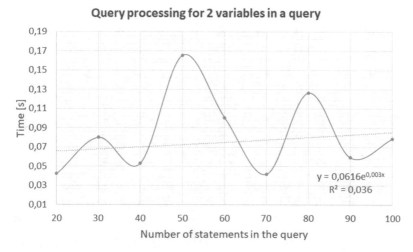

Fig. 12.13 Query processing time depending on the number of statements in the query. Determined for queries with 2 variables

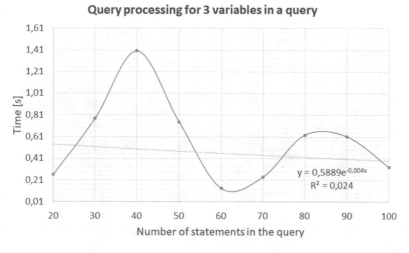

Fig. 12.14 Query processing time depending on the number of statements in the query. Determined for queries with 3 variables

Transformation of XR Environments

We also measured the time required for transforming XR environments into their explorable counterparts, which is the job of the E-XR activity compiler. We generated environments with the number of classes ranging from 10 to 100 (step 10), every class including from 10 to 100 methods (step 10). Each method was assigned from 1 to 5 attributes. The results of the transformation are presented in

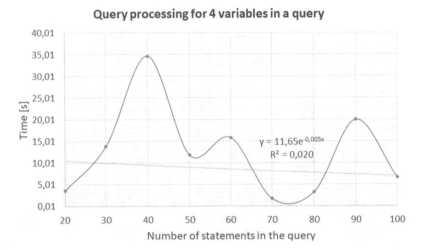

Fig. 12.15 Query processing time depending on the number of statements in the query. Determined for queries with 4 variables

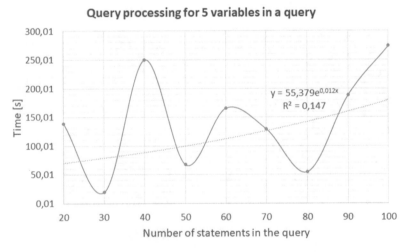

Fig. 12.16 Query processing time depending on the number of statements in the query. Determined for queries with 5 variables

Figs. 12.19, 12.20, 12.21, 12.22, and 12.23. For every number of classes and every number of methods, 20 explorable environments were generated. Hence, every point in the graphs is the average time for 20 transformations. Figure 12.24 presents the accumulated time for all the environments including methods with 5 attributes.

The results show that the transformation time grows linearly with the growth in the overall number of processed methods/attributes. It is confirmed by the high R^2 equal to 0.9803. However, the results show that the influence of the number of

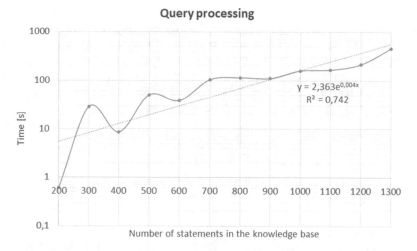

Fig. 12.17 Query processing time depending on the number of statements in environment specification. Determined for queries consisting of 10 statements with 5 variables

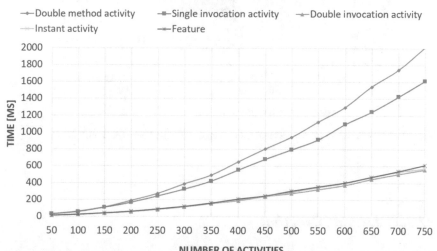

	Double method activity	Single invocation activity	Double invocation activity	Instant activity	Feature
Interpolation	$0,0031x^2 +$ $0,3814x - 7,4755$	$0,0022x^2 +$ $0,4801x - 12,16$	$0,0008x^2 +$ $0,162x - 3,6996$	$0,0008x^2 +$ $0,2008x - 7,7738$	$0,0009x^2 +$ $0,1635x - 2,0805$
R^2	0,9997	0,9996	0,9992	0,9984	0,9995
Avg. time for 1 activity [ms]	1,9406	1,6121	0,5638	0,5917	0,6111

Fig. 12.18 Performance of activity compilation

attributes on the transformation time is moderate. A fivefold increase in the number of attributes leads to a slight increase in the average transformation time equal to 6.14/5.62=1.09. It means that, in comparison to activity compilation, other actions during the transformation such as the creation of directories and copying files of the project are more time consuming. It is confirmed by Figs. 12.19, 12.20, 12.21, 12.22, and 12.23, where the increase in the number of classes affects the transformation time more than the increase in the number of methods in a class.

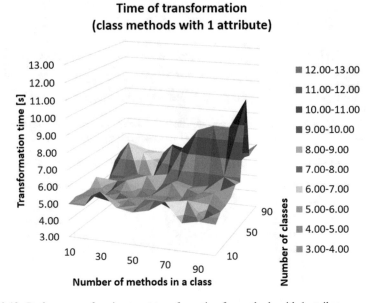

Fig. 12.19 Performance of environment transformation for methods with 1 attribute

12.3.3 Logging Behavior

We have evaluated the performance of the log library, which registers the behavior of users and objects while explorable XR environments are running (cf. Sect. 10.6). An experimental explorable environment was streaming the generated temporal statements to a triplestore. The logged behavior was an animation of a moving object that lasted for 10 min. The tests were performed for 2 system configurations that differ in terms of the triplestore location: on the localhost at workstation 1 (together with the XR environment), and on the remote host (workstation 2) in the same campus area network (CAN). With every update of the animated object, temporal statements about its position were generated and transmitted to the triplestore. For every configuration of the testing system, we repeated streaming 20 times.

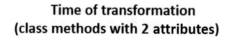

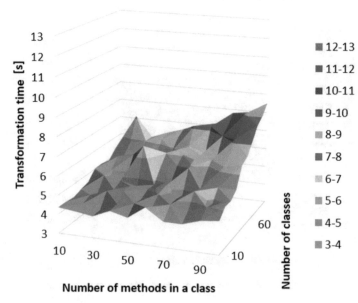

Fig. 12.20 Performance of environment transformation for methods with 2 attributes

The average results are summarized in Table 12.1. Whereas inserting statements to the triplestore at the localhost required 26 ms, the performance for the CAN was 2.55 times lower. It is caused by the average network delay equal to 41 ms. The standard deviation divided by the average (coefficient of variation) is twice larger for the CAN, which means the less stable transmission. It corresponds to the increasing ratio between the minimum and maximum values for both configurations. As rendering and logging were executed within the same thread, the upper limit of FPS was 38 for the localhost and 15 for the CAN.

12.3.4 FPS in Explorable Environments

We used workstation 2 to complete two sessions of using the immersive car showroom with a triplestore installed on the same station. The first session was completed using the explorable showroom, whereas the second session using the prototype (non-explorable) showroom. For every session, we were registering the average number of FPS continuously calculated for the last 10 frames. Each session lasted for 3 min. The results are shown in Fig. 12.25. While the average number of FPS for the session in the prototype environment is 9% higher than for the explorable environment, logging behavior increases the coefficient of variation

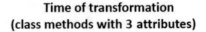

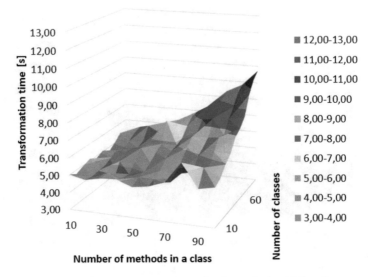

Fig. 12.21 Performance of environment transformation for methods with 3 attributes

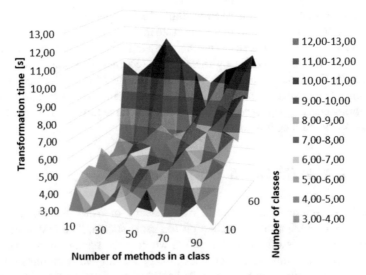

Fig. 12.22 Performance of activity compilation for methods with 4 attributes

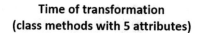

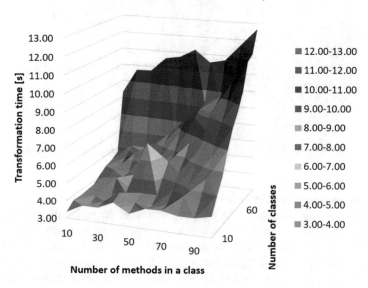

Fig. 12.23 Performance of environment transformation for methods with 5 attributes

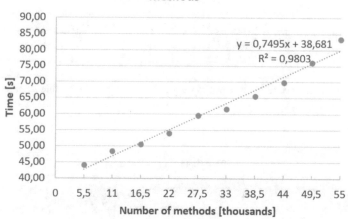

Fig. 12.24 Time of environment transformation for methods with 5 attributes depending on the overall number of methods in environment

that is twice higher than without logging (0.2–0.1). It can be seen as the vertical distribution of the points in the graphs. The sessions consisted of three parts in which three cars were being watched from outside and inside and painted. Painting the cars

Table 12.1 Performance of logging behavior on a localhost and over a campus area network with complexity and size of generated logs

	Criteria	Localhost	Campus area network (CAN)	CAN / Localhost
Time [ms]	Average	26,35	67,19	2,55
	Standard deviation	1,88	9,54	5,08
	Coefficient of variation	0,07	0,14	1,99
	Minimum	110,69	273,91	2,47
	Maximum	183,98	864,48	4,70
Number of	Temporal statements	21 000	8 005	0,38
	RDF statements	78 856	31 858	0,40
	Objects	13 146	5 313	0,40
Size	Temporal statement [B]	234,71	247,43	1,05
	Log [KB]	4 813,39	1 934,27	0,40

was being executed continuously by streams of mouse move events occurring over a palette of colors. Therefore, the painting generated streams with large numbers of temporal statements about colors sent to the triplestore. It mostly decreased the number of FPS, which is visible as the breakdowns in Fig. 12.25a in the intervals around 1:00, 1:42, and 2:40. In other periods of the session, 3D content was rendered sufficiently smoothly, with no visible difference in comparison to the session without logging.

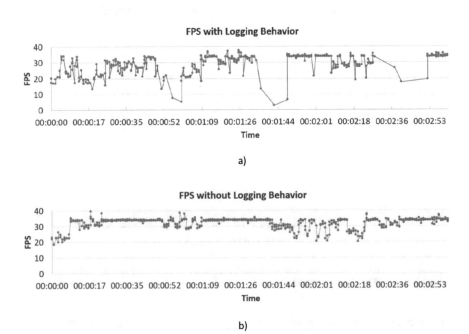

Fig. 12.25 FPS for sessions of using immersive car showroom: explorable environment—with logging behavior (**a**), and prototype (non-explorable) environment—without logging (**b**)

12.4 Complexity and Size of E-XR Data Structures

We have evaluated the complexity and size of data structures used at the consecutive stages of the development pipeline and generated while using explorable XR environments: representations of activities and features, mapping knowledge bases, environment code before and after activity compilation, and behavior logs generated by explorable environments.

12.4.1 Activity Representation

The complexity and size of activities and features have been analyzed with regard to the possible types of their representation: activity ontology and knowledge bases as well as attributes. The use of different types of entities in the activity ontology is summarized in Table 12.2. The ontology includes classes and properties presented in Figs. 7.1, 7.2, and 7.3. Qualified cardinality restrictions (typically *OWL exact cardinality*) are used to determine the structure of activities and features, e.g., an instant activity has exactly one join point. *OWL has value* restrictions are used to determine timestamps for start and end activity join points. The overall number of RDF statements in the activity ontology is 238, while its overall size is equal to 18.9 KB.

Table 12.2 Complexity of activity ontology

Concepts	Number
classes	27
datatype properties	7
object properties	12
qualified cardinality restrictions	17
has value restrictions	2
RDF statements	238

We have also evaluated the size of activity knowledge bases created with the E-XR visual activity editor. The knowledge bases comprised a single activity of a particular type or a single feature (Table 12.3). The largest is the size of a single invocation activity, which, however, is similar to the size of a double invocation activity and a double method activity. The reason is the same structure of such activities, which include two join points. It is reflected by the same number of RDF statements that form an activity or a feature. Instant activities and features are significantly smaller because of including only one join point. The difference between them is minor as instant activities include one additional RDF statement, which expresses the timestamp of a join point.

Table 12.3 Size of activities and features as well as code injected during activity compilation

Activities / Features			Size [bytes]	Number of RDF statements	Injected code		
					Class code [bytes]	Method code [bytes]	Overall code size [bytes]
Instant activity			1161	29	1859	425	2284
Activity	Interval activity	Single method activity	Single invocation activity	2120	52	1859	857	2716
		Double invocation activity	2119	52	1859	425	2284
	Double method activity		2115	52	3718	850	4568
Feature			1126	28	1859	296	2155

12.4.2   Code Injected to Explorable Environments

The injection of logging code into the environment follows compiling activities and features at Stage 4 of the pipeline. We have compared the size of activity and feature representations with the injected code. It has enabled us to investigate the gain in the developer's effort when using E-XR in comparison to implementing the logging functions from scratch.

Code Injected by Processing Activity Knowledge Bases

We have analyzed the relation between the size of a single activity and feature created with the E-XR visual activity editor and the size of the logging code injected into the classes and methods by the E-XR activity compiler (Table 12.3). Taking into account the overall injected code, which includes the code extending a class method and the code extending the class, the largest is the code injected while compiling double method activities. Such code spreads across two methods of some (possibly different) classes, which start and stop logging. A single invocation activity affects only one class, which reduces the class-specific code. However, the method-specific code is almost the same as in the case of a double method activity because the method is extended in two points. The code imposed by other activities (instant activities and double invocation activities) as well as features is much smaller and similar. It is because a single method of a class is extended while compiling such activities and features. Slightly smaller code of features is caused by the lack of instructions that compute timestamps. Although the overall size of the injected code is larger than the size of a single activity, the majority (about 80%) is constituted by the code injected at the class level, which is commonly used by the code injected to different class methods. The method-specific code constitutes 13–32% of the overall code imposed by an activity or a feature.

We have also compared the overall size of activity knowledge bases with the size of the described classes of XR environments before and after activity compilation. We used activity knowledge bases including from 50 to 750 activities of different

types. The results are presented in Fig. 12.26, 12.27, 12.28, 12.29, and 12.30. The
classes before activity compilation were the same in all the cases. The largest is the
size of activity knowledge bases that consist of interval activities: single invocation,
double invocation, and double method activities, which have two join points. Their
size is about twice larger than the size of instant activities and features, which
have one join point. Activity knowledge bases are about 8–16 times larger than
the generated classes, which are 4–8 times larger than the classes before the activity
compilation.

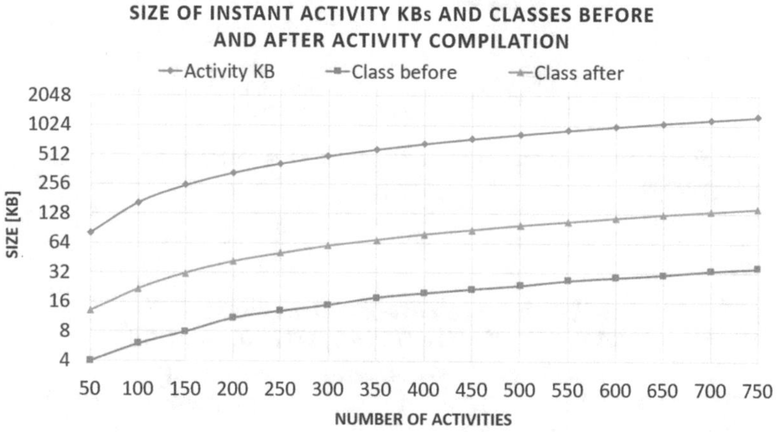

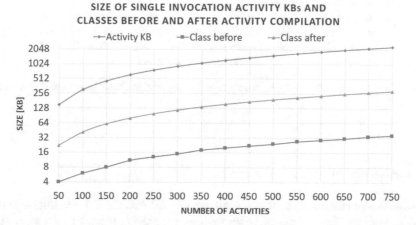

Fig. 12.26 Size of instant activities as well as application classes before and after activity
compilation

Fig. 12.27 Size of single invocation activities as well as application classes before and after
activity compilation

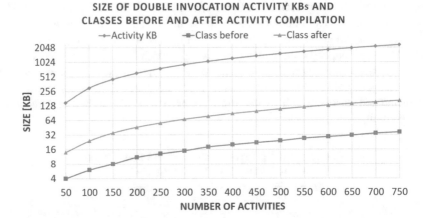

Fig. 12.28 Size of double invocation activities as well as application classes before and after activity compilation

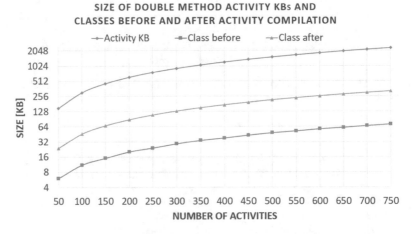

Fig. 12.29 Size of double method activities as well as application classes before and after activity compilation

Code Injected by Processing Attributes

We have also compared the size of attributes created with the E-XR textual activity editor with the size of imperative instructions for logging behavior injected to the attributed classes and methods by the E-XR activity compiler. For the comparison, we used environments mentioned in Sect. 12.3.2 with 100 classes, each one

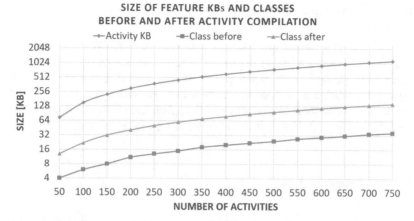

Fig. 12.30 Size of features as well as application classes before and after activity compilation

including 100 methods. All the methods were assigned a number of attributes ranging from 1 to 5. The results are presented in Fig. 12.31. The gain ratio is proportional to the number of attributes assigned to a method. It varies from 3.5 for methods with a single attribute to 7 for methods with 5 attributes.

Using at least one attribute for a method in a class is followed by extending the class with additional auxiliary methods of the size equal to 911 bytes. The size of the annotation template (without parameters) is equal to 29 bytes (`[SemanticLog("", "", "", "")]`), while the size of the generated instructions is equal to 729 bytes, which gives the gain ratio equal to 25.

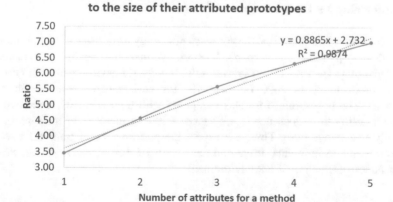

Fig. 12.31 Ratio of the size of generated methods/classes to the size of their prototypes with attributes

12.4.3   Mapping Knowledge Bases

The E-XR mapping editor generates mappings in the RDF Turtle format (World Wide Web Consortium 2014). In the explorable service guide, the size of the mapping knowledge base is equal to 696 B. The part that is common to every mapping knowledge base specifies classes and properties and has size 318 B. The rest are the individual mappings of 9 application classes to domain classes (presented in Fig. 8.2). Hence, the average size of a single mapping is 42 B.

12.4.4   Behavior Logs

The size of the behavior logs generated by streaming temporal statements (cf. Sect. 12.3.3) is summarized in Table 12.1. The log generated on the localhost has the size equal to 4813 KB. It is more than twice larger than the log for the CAN, which strictly corresponds to the time required for inserting a single temporal statement to the triplestore for both configurations. This proportion spreads on the numbers of temporal statements in the logs and, consequently, the numbers of RDF statements and objects in the logs. The logged temporal statements were of similar size in both cases.

12.5   Discussion of E-XR Approach

12.5.1   Evaluation Results

Transforming XR Environments

The obtained results show that the approach efficiently transforms XR environments into their explorable counterparts. The transformation time, on a moderately efficient computer, varies from several milliseconds, for environments with dozens of methods, to about 2000 milliseconds, for environments with hundreds of methods. The polynomial formulas computed with high accuracy show that the transformation time does not rapidly grow with the increase in the size of the activity knowledge base. Thus, we expect the performance of transformation to be acceptable to individual users and developers of web services—to enable on-demand transformation of XR environments.

Composing XR Environments

Comparison to Other Tools

In terms of users' effort in composing XR environments, E-XR offers higher performance than Unity, which is a widely used representative of XR development tools. The gain increases with the growing complexity of 3D scenes, which include more avatars that perform more exercises. Only for 3D scenes with a few avatars, Unity outperforms E-XR. The advantage of E-XR over Unity for larger scenes is caused by modeling environments at a high level of abstraction (related to an application or domain) using semantic concepts and hiding technical details from content authors.

Division of Environment Specifications and Queries

The performance tests show that E-XR is efficient enough to solve practical problems that demand environment specifications with hundreds of statements and queries with tens of statements. The most important limitation is the number of variables in queries. It significantly influences processing time in comparison to the number of statements in queries and environment specifications. However, the burden of multiple variables in a query could be reduced to some extent. Both queries and environment specifications can be divided into smaller sub-queries and sub-specifications, which could be further separately processed. Such division could be done with regard to the semantics, taking into account statements used in different parts of queries and selecting appropriate parts of environment specifications to be verified against the sub-queries. For instance, in the explorable fitness guide, some sub-queries can be devoted to stimulated body parts, while others to the difficulty of exercises. Sub-specifications of environments would reduce the number of statements, while sub-queries would reduce the number of statements and possibly the number of variables in the statements. Once obtained, the results of sub-queries would be joined. Such division could decrease the overall processing time. However, the exact outcomes would depend on particular applications and use cases. In some applications, fragments of environment specifications could be distinguished in advance on the basis of disjoint sets of possible values of variables used in statements based on different predicates. For instance, statements describing the effects of exercises are disjoint with statements describing relations between body parts and muscles. In other applications, subsets would need to be dynamically built, taking into account a particular query. Moreover, the results of frequently issued queries could be cached and provided without redetermining them upon every request.

Parallel Processing

Also, reasoning on sub-queries and subsets could be done in parallel. Such a solution would be sufficient for the analyzed examples to provide customized environments in a reasonable time using synchronous client–server communication on the Web. Composing environments with more complex 3D scenes requiring queries with over a dozen variables, which needs more processing time, would demand asynchronous communication with notifications about the generated 3D content. For instance, once an environment is generated, an e-mail with its URL is sent to the user. It would prevent XR environments in web browsers from timeouts when waiting for the response.

Translating Queries and Generating Environments

In comparison to the query processing time, the time required for query translation from XML to Prolog and the time required for generating environments are negligible. There is no limitation in the entire process of composing customized XR environments.

Mapping

The size of mapping knowledge bases is small in comparison to the other knowledge bases and transition sets used in the approach. It should not matter to any practical applications. Likewise, the size of the activity ontology is moderate. Hence, we do not consider it any problem to practical usage.

Logging Behavior

The performance of logging behavior strongly depends on the relative location of the explorable environment and its triplestore. It is highest in the case of the environment and triplestore installed on the same host, which enables logging animations while maintaining acceptable FPS. The logging time is much higher when temporal statements are transmitted over a network, which significantly decreases FPS. In such cases, the approach is appropriate for logging occasional events rather than animations. Hence, non-functional requirement 2 is partially satisfied (cf. Sect. 5.2.2). The problem can be solved in different ways. First, logging behavior can be performed by a different thread than the one responsible for rendering the 3D content. In such a case, temporal statements can wait in a FIFO queue to be saved in the triplestore, without stopping the rendering thread. Second, the transmission can gather multiple temporal statements into larger packages to reduce the average delay. Third, other triplestores should be tested in terms of efficient network communication.

The behavior logs generated in the analyzed use cases are of acceptable size taking into account possible practical applications of E-XR, such as training, marketing, and merchandising, even in the case of streaming temporal statements to a triplestore. However, the structure of activity knowledge bases generated by Virtuoso is verbose compared to classes generated by activity compilation. Encoding activity knowledge bases in a more concise form would help create repositories of activity knowledge bases. A solution can be to organize and collect Turtle triples for common subjects and common predicates, which can significantly reduce their final size. Also, RDF/JSON (World Wide Web Consortium 2013) and JSON for linked data (JSON-LD) (World Wide Web Consortium 2020a) can be tested as possible formats for activity knowledge bases.

12.5.2   Alternative Implementation of E-XR Tools

Extending explorable XR environments with new functions does not require a lot of programmers' effort due to the use of the aspect-oriented approach. It meets non-functional requirement 3 (cf. Sect. 5.2.2). However, a few alternative solutions related to the system implementation can be discussed.

Activities and Features Representing Parts of Methods

In addition to the guidelines of programming behavior of XR components presented in Sect. 8.2.2, we have also considered linking activities and features with individual instructions or arbitrary groups of instructions in the project code, in addition to linking them with entire methods. It would help deal with the mentioned inconveniences. However, the approach would get more requiring to comprehend by users with limited skills in programming and more complicated to create user-friendly editors. As opposed to individual instructions, methods, which are currently the target for activities and features, can be effectively recognized in the code and presented to users. Such a presentation can respect the domain-specific semantics of the methods expressed by their names, parameters, and local variables. Moreover, it does not require digging into methods' implementations, which are hardly understandable to non-IT-specialists.

Using Aspect-Oriented Libraries

The current implementation of the E-XR activity compiler is based on classes from the `System.Text.RegularExpressions` namespace in .NET. As an alternative, we have considered using aspect-oriented libraries (e.g., PostSharp (SharpCrafters 2020)). The use of such libraries could facilitate the structure and code of the activity compiler. Moreover, it would enable a relatively simple distinction of throwing exceptions by methods of activities and features. However, according to our best knowledge, currently, no aspect-oriented libraries integrate with Unity, which we use in our projects.

Using Declarative 3D Formats

Some 3D formats, e.g., Extensible 3D (X3D) (Web3D Consortium 2020b), enable programming of 3D content using scripts, e.g., ECMAScript. Such scripts access declaratively specified elements of 3D scenes, e.g., based on XML. Such declarative 3D formats could be used to create reusable XR components that would be further composed, as components purely based on imperative programming are.

12.5.3   Requirements of Technical Knowledge and Skills in Using E-XR

We intend to facilitate the creation of explorable XR environments by average users and domain experts, who typically have limited programming and 3D modeling skills. The main requirement for using E-XR is the knowledge of the basic assumptions of the object-oriented approach: classes, methods, and variables as well as the RDF data model based on triples. Such knowledge is sufficient to use the E-XR development tools, in which the concepts are utilized in a user-friendly visual way. The other requirement is the knowledge of the selected domain ontology. The selection of class methods, variables, and parameters for predicates, subjects, and objects of activities and features can be supported by dataflow and activity diagrams (e.g., in UML). Thereby, the approach can also be used by project managers and users familiar with software design tools. Technical support from programmers is necessary if the prototype XR environment must be refactored before the transformation, as explained in Sect. 8.2.2.

12.5.4   Logical System Properties

The proposed approach is based on logical systems that are fragments of first-order logic: description logics and Horn logic. Therefore, the applicable reasoning algorithms, which are resolution as well as forward and backward chaining, are sound and complete (cf. Sect. 3.1.2). In this regard, non-functional requirement 4 is satisfied (cf. Sect. 5.2.2).

To enable complex queries, we have permitted the use of the *unsaid* predicate (cf. Definition 8.3), which enables negation in transitions. However, it makes the system non-monotonic as a new statement added to a workflow specification may be contradictory to other statements included in the specification (cf. Definition 3.12). Hence, if monotonicity is a crucial property to be maintained while creating explorable XR environments, the *unsaid* predicate should be deprecated.

As the transition sets used in E-XR consist of Horn clauses, reasoning on them falls into the P class, which satisfies non-functional requirement 4. However, the ontologies, which are components of the E-XR behavior and link models, require the OWL 2 DL profile (cf. Sect. 3.3.5). It categorizes such reasoning tasks as instance checking, concept satisfiability, concept subsumption, and knowledge base consistency into the N2EXPTIME class (cf. Sects. 3.1.3 and 3.3.4), and conjunctive query answering into the class whose decidability remains open. In this regard, the approach could be improved. In particular, the use of OWL 2 EL and QL profiles (W3C 2012b) would limit the reasoning time for some of the problems to the P and NLSPACE classes, respectively, and make all possible instances of the problems tractable in practical applications. Union ($\mathcal{U}$) and qualified cardinality restrictions ($\mathcal{Q}$) must be prohibited to achieve this goal. These constructors are used to restrict possible structures of individuals in ABox, including domains and ranges of properties as well as the number of objects linked via the properties. Therefore, knowledge base consistency checking would be confined if we remove the constructors. However, the other reasoning tasks would not suffer from this limitation.

12.5.5 Knowledge Exploration with Probabilistic Approaches

The knowledge-based representation of XR behavior in E-XR is based on logical systems. However, an interesting aspect would be the extension of E-XR with methods from other fields of artificial intelligence—machine learning and probabilistic systems—to represent and explore users' and objects' behavior and features in probabilistic domains. Machine learning can enable discovery, semantic representation, and exploration of behavior and features of non-explorable environments. A set of behavior logs covering activities of multiple users and objects in a non-explorable XR environment can contain valuable knowledge about users' interests, preferences, and needs as well as users' and objects' characteristics and relationships. In this regard, machine learning methods, e.g., neural networks and support vector machines, may extend the analysis of behavior logs with data mining tasks, such as semantic users' and objects' classification, clustering, summarization, association, anomaly detection, and prediction.

In addition, machine learning can permit inductive reasoning to create generalized probabilistic models of users' and objects' behavior based on particular examples described in behavior logs of a training set. In particular, it is possible to discover probabilistic workflow specifications (cf. Definition 8.4) from behavior logs, comprising transitions that rule the environment.

Probabilistic knowledge representation, e.g., first-order probabilistic models (Nilsson 1986; Braz, Amir, & Roth 2008) and fuzzy logic (Zadeh 1965; Novák,

Perfilieva, & Mockor 2012), can be used to represent uncertain users' and objects' characteristics and workflow specifications induced by machine learning methods. Further, knowledge exploration based on queries and probabilistic reasoning, e.g., using Bayesian networks (Neapolitan 2003) and the Dempster–Shafer theory (Dempster 2008; Shafer 1976), can be used to conclude from probabilistic knowledge representations. Specifically, methods of probabilistic temporal reasoning may be applied, e.g., dynamic Bayesian networks (Neapolitan 2003) and hidden Markov models (Ibrahim, Tawfik, & Ngom 2007).

Chapter 13
Conclusions

In recent years, we can observe significant research effort in the area of XR, including human–system interfaces as well as development methods and tools. Human–system interfaces, which encompass HMDs and large displays, motion and eye tracking systems, controllers, touchscreens, and haptic devices, have enabled immersive presentation of XR environments and rich interaction between users and objects in such environments. Information about users' and objects' behavior in XR environments can be collected and analyzed to acquire new knowledge ranging from primary users' and objects' characteristics to complex descriptions of their activities in the virtual worlds. For instance, the captured motion, touch, and haptic information can help recognize the users' gender, age, and determination. Eye tracking can help identify the main points of interest and users' preferences. Recorded sequences of users' actions can provide patterns on completing specific tasks.

Nonetheless, the available methods and tools, including programming languages and libraries, 3D content formats, visual 3D and animation modeling tools, and game engines, have a significant limitation. They do not enable creation of XR environments in which information collected from human–system interfaces is combined with the domain-oriented environment specification and can be used to acquire knowledge about users' and objects' behavior. So far, such an analysis has been possible exclusively in solutions on the intersection of mathematics and artificial intelligence devised for knowledge representation, without application to XR. The most well-known approaches in this domain cover first-order logic, description logics, and the Semantic Web.

The main contribution of this book is the E-XR approach, which enables creation of explorable XR environments. In such environments, users' and objects' behavior, including their interactions and autonomous actions, can be explored with queries and automated reasoning with regard to knowledge in the particular domain for which the environments have been developed. It permits monitoring, analyzing,

J. Flotyński, *Knowledge-Based Explorable Extended Reality Environments*,
https://doi.org/10.1007/978-3-030-59965-2_13

comprehending, examining, and controlling XR environments, and users' skills, experience, interests, and preferences, and XR objects' features. Explorable XR environments are an emerging field on the intersection of multiple disciplines in computer science: computer graphics and interactive environments, knowledge representation, logic programming, Semantic Web, service-oriented architectures, data engineering, and data modeling as well as procedural and object-oriented programming. The rapid development and dissemination of new solutions in these disciplines have allowed them to be counted among the most successful technologies influencing people's life. These disciplines gain the lively interest of researchers, practitioners, students, and users, which is reflected by the market situation. The intersection of these disciplines is still a very new field, poorly covered by the available literature, development tools, and implemented systems.

Explorable XR environments are based on knowledge representation technologies: logic programming and the Semantic Web, which implement first-order logic and description logics. These technologies have enabled desirable expressivity while controlling such essential properties as computational complexity, decidability, soundness, and completeness. E-XR consists of four interrelated elements:

1. The visual knowledge-based behavior model, which enables representation of past, current, and potential future behavior of users and objects in XR environments.
2. The semantic link model, which links the knowledge-based behavior model to procedural or object-oriented implementation prepared using prevalent tools for XR development.
3. The development pipeline of explorable environments, which uses both models in a step-by-step process to involve different users equipped with different tools in the creation of knowledge-based explorable XR environments.
4. The exploration methods, which enable knowledge acquisition from explorable XR environments created using the pipeline. The exploration is based on reasoning and queries.

E-XR has been implemented and evaluated. The analysis of the approach and evaluation results have proven that E-XR enables:

1. Knowledge-based representation of XR behavior oriented to domain semantics rather than technical elements of 3D graphics and animation.
2. Declarative specification of users' and objects' behavior in the XR development process focused on the goals to be achieved.
3. On-demand composition of XR behavior according to users' requirements.
4. Representation of past, current, and potential future XR behavior, including users' and objects' interactions and autonomous actions.
5. Knowledge-based exploration of XR behavior based on queries and automated reasoning.
6. Development of new as well as transformation of existing XR environments into the knowledge-based explorable form.

7. Compatibility with common tools and languages, particularly procedural and object-oriented languages, libraries, and game engines.
8. Low delay in logging XR behavior while using XR environments.
9. Maintaining use cases and performance of the original XR environments by ensuring sufficient efficiency of the new functions related to knowledge-based exploration.
10. Efficient reasoning and query processing with respect to the crucial properties of logical systems.

Thereby, E-XR goes beyond the functionality of the available methods and tools for XR development. It satisfies the functional and non-functional requirements specified in Sect. 5.2. We have proven the book's thesis: *The E-XR approach enables efficient creation and use of explorable XR environments based on domain knowledge.* Hence, the goal of the book has been achieved. The potential of explorable XR environments can open new opportunities in the domains in which valuable knowledge can be acquired from the behavior of users and objects in XR. Such domains encompass education, training, medicine, design, tourism, marketing, merchandising, engineering, and entertainment.

In addition to the E-XR approach, the main research achievements of this book are the following:

1. The *discussion* of the available approaches to XR development as well as human–system interfaces. On the one hand, we have analyzed how interactive 3D content, which is a key element of XR environments, can be created using programming languages and libraries, 3D formats, 3D and animation modeling tools as well as visual tools such as game engines. On the other hand, the presented outline of XR systems has indicated the leading technologies in the domain and possibilities of collecting information about users' behavior in XR, which can potentially be subject to knowledge-based exploration.
2. The *classification* of the available approaches to ontology-based creation of extended reality. The classification is based on various criteria and covers a large number of approaches. The classification and review of the available approaches have enabled a comprehensive discussion of the current state of the art in the area of XR systems based on the Semantic Web. It has also permitted the specification of the requirements for the E-XR approach, which fills the gap in the available approaches.
3. The *discussion* of knowledge representation technologies derived from mathematical methods applied in artificial intelligence. The analysis goes beyond the available publications as it addresses the technologies in the context of building XR environments with possibilities of semantic queries and reasoning. The knowledge representation technologies have been discussed with regard to the critical properties of logical systems and their influence on creating XR.

Possible directions of future research and development activities include several aspects.

1. Alternative implementations of network communication can be tested to enable logging animations, which stream temporal statements to triplestores. We plan to evaluate other existing libraries and triplestores and consider own implementation of critical components.
2. The aspect-oriented implementation of explorable XR environments can be extended in case of the availability of aspect-oriented libraries compatible with game engines, in particular Unity.
3. We plan to extend the concept of explorable environments to configurable environments, whose state can be modified by semantic queries at any point in time regarding the current and potential future users' and objects' behavior. Such environments could be launched from the altered states. It would be especially flexible and useful for domain-oriented simulation, training, and education.

References

Acien, A., Morales, A., Fiérrez, J., Vera-Rodríguez, R., & Hernandez-Ortega, J. (2019). Active detection of age groups based on touch interaction. *IET Biom.*, *8*, 101–108.

Adobe Systems. (2015). *JavaScript for Acrobat 3D Annotations API Reference.* URL https://www.adobe.com/content/dam/acom/en/devnet/acrobat/pdfs/AcrobatDC_js_3d_api_reference.pdf

AIM@SHAPE. (2017). URL http://cordis.europa.eu/ist/kct/aimatshape_synopsis.htm

Albertoni, R., Papaleo, L., Pitikakis, M., Robbiano, F., Spagnuolo, M., & Vasilakis, G. (2005). Ontology-based searching framework for digital shapes. In *On the move to meaningful internet systems 2005: Otm 2005 workshops* (pp. 896–905).

Albrecht, S., Wiemann, T., Günther, M., & Hertzberg, J. (2011). Matching CAD object models in semantic mapping. In *Proceedings ICRA 2011 workshop: Semantic perception, mapping and exploration, SPME.*

Allen, J. F. & Ferguson, G. (1997). Actions and events in interval temporal logic. In O. Stock (Ed.), *Spatial and temporal reasoning* (pp. 205–245). Dordrecht: Springer Netherlands. URL https://doi.org/10.1007/978-0-585-28322-7_7

Allied Market Research. (2019). *Mobile Application Market.* URL https://www.alliedmarketresearch.com/mobile-application-market/

Alpcan, T., Bauckhage, C., & Kotsovinos, E. (2007). Towards 3D internet: Why, what, and how? In *Cyberworlds, 2007. CW'07. International conference on* (pp. 95–99).

Al-Showarah, S., Al-Jawad, N., & Sellahewa, H. (2015). User-age classification using touch gestures on smartphones.

Aminifar, A., Sopic, D., Atienza Alonso, D., & Zanetti, R. (2019). A wearable system for real-time detection of epileptic seizures. URL http://infoscience.epfl.ch/record/272991

ARCO. (accessed March 24, 2015). Virtual museum system [Software-Handbuch]. URL http://www.wirtualne-muzea.pl/en/

Arndt, R., Troncy, R., Staab, S., & Hardman, L. (2009). Comm: A core ontology for multimedia annotation. In *Handbook on ontologies* (pp. 403–421). Springer.

Arndt, R., Troncy, R., Staab, S., Hardman, L., & Vacura, M. (2007). Comm: Designing a well-founded multimedia ontology for the web. In *Proceedings of the 6th international the semantic web and 2nd Asian semantic web conference on Asian semantic web conference* (pp. 30–43). Berlin, Heidelberg: Springer-Verlag.

Artale, A. & Franconi, E. (2001, March). A survey of temporal extensions of description logics. *Annals of Mathematics and Artificial Intelligence*, *30* (1–4), 171–210. URL https://doi.org/10.1023/A:1016636131405

Artale, A., Kontchakov, R., Ryzhikov, V., & Zakharyaschev, M. (2011). Tailoring temporal description logics for reasoning over temporal conceptual models. In C. Tinelli & V. Sofronie-

Stokkermans (Eds.), *Frontiers of combining systems* (pp. 1–11). Berlin, Heidelberg: Springer Berlin Heidelberg.

Artale, A. & Lutz, C. (2004). A correspondence between temporal description logics. *Journal of Applied Non-Classical Logic, 14* (1–2), 209–233.

Artec Europe. (2020). *Artec Eva.* URL https://www.artec3d.com/portable-3d-scanners/artec-eva

Ashley Watters. (2020). *10 Emerging Trends in Information Technology for 2020.* URL https://www.comptia.org/blog/10-emerging-trends-in-information-technology-for-2020/

Attene, M., Robbiano, F., Spagnuolo, M., & Falcidieno, B. (2007). Semantic Annotation of 3D Surface Meshes Based on Feature Characterization. In *Proceedings of the semantic and digital media technologies 2nd international conference on semantic multimedia* (pp. 126–139). Berlin, Heidelberg: Springer-Verlag.

Attene, M., Robbiano, F., Spagnuolo, M., & Falcidieno, B. (2009, October). Characterization of 3D shape parts for semantic annotation. *Comput. Aided Des., 41* (10), 756–763. URL http://dx.doi.org/10.1016/j.cad.2009.01.003

AutoCAD Civil 3D. (2020). URL http://www.autodesk.com/products/autocad-civil-3d/

Autodesk. (2020a). *3ds Max.* URL https://www.autodesk.pl/products/3ds-max/overview

Autodesk. (2020b). *Motion Builder.* URL https://www.autodesk.com/products/motionbuilder/overview

Away3D. (2020). *AwayJS.* URL https://github.com/awayjs

Aylett, R. & Cavazza, M. (2001). Intelligent virtual environments: a state-of-the-art report. In *Eurographics 2001, star reports volume* (pp. 87–109).

Baader, F., Calvanese, D., McGuinness, D. L., Nardi, D., & Patel-Schneider, P. F. (2010). *The description logic handbook: Theory, implementation and applications* (2nd ed.). USA: Cambridge University Press.

Baral, C. & Gelfond, M. (1994). Logic programming and knowledge representation. *The Journal of Logic Programming, 19*, 73–148.

Baset, S. & Stoffel, K. (2018). Object-oriented modeling with ontologies around: A survey of existing approaches. *International Journal of Software Engineering and Knowledge Engineering, 28* (11n12), 1775–1794.

Batsakis, S., Petrakis, E., Tachmazidis, I., & Antoniou, G. (2009). Temporal representation and reasoning in OWL 2. *Semantic Web*, 1–20. URL http://www.semantic-web-journal.net/system/files/swj855.pdf

Bebop Sensors. (2020). *Haptic Gloves for Enterprise Virtual Reality Training.* URL https://bebopsensors.com/

Ben Ellefi, M., Drap, P., Papini, O., Merad, D., Royer, J., Nawaf, M., et al. (2019). Ontology-based web tools for retrieving photogrammetric cultural heritage models. *Underwater 3D Recording & Modeling. ISPRS, Limassol, Cyprus.*

Bernard Marr. (2019). *The 7 Biggest Technology Trends In 2020. Everyone Must Get Ready For Now.* URL https://www.forbes.com/sites/bernardmarr/2019/09/30/the-7-biggest-technology-trends-in-2020-everyone-must-get-ready-for-now/

Berners-Lee, T., Hendler, J., & Lassila, O. (2001, May). The semantic web. *Scientific American, 284* (5), 34–43. URL http://www.sciam.com/article.cfm?articleID=00048144-10D2-1C70-84A9809EC588EF21

Bevan, C. & Fraser, D. S. (2016). Different strokes for different folks? revealing the physical characteristics of smartphone users from their swipe gestures. *International Journal of Human-Computer Studies, 88*, 51–61.

Bilasco, I. M., Villanova-Oliver, M., Gensel, J., & Martin, H. (2007). Semantic-based rules for 3D scene adaptation. In *Proceedings of the twelfth international conference on 3D web technology* (p. 97–100). New York, NY, USA: Association for Computing Machinery. URL https://doi.org/10.1145/1229390.1229406

Bille, W. (2006-2007). *Conceptual modeling of complex objects for virtual environments.* (Unpublished doctoral dissertation). Vrije Universiteit Brussel.

Bille, W., De Troyer, O., Kleinermann, F., Pellens, B., & Romero, R. (2004). Using ontologies to build virtual worlds for the web. In P. T. Isaías, N. Karmakar, L. Rodrigues, & P. Barbosa (Eds.), *Icwi* (p. 683–690). IADIS.

Bille, W., De Troyer, O., Pellens, B., & Kleinermann, F. (2005). Conceptual modeling of articulated bodies in virtual environments. In H. Thwaites (Ed.), *Proceedings of the 11th international conference on virtual systems and multimedia (VSMM)* (p. 17–26). Ghent, Belgium: Archaeolingua.

Bille, W., Pellens, B., Kleinermann, F., & De Troyer, O. (2004). Intelligent modelling of virtual worlds using domain ontologies. In *Proceedings of the workshop of intelligent computing (WIC), held in conjunction with the Micai 2004 conference* (p. 272–279). Mexico City, Mexico.

Bitmanagement. (2020). *BS Contact*. URL http://www.bitmanagement.com/en/products/interactive-3d-clients/bs-contact

Blender Foundation. (2020). *Blender*. URL http://www.blender.org

Borusiak, B., Pierański, B., & Strykowski, S. (2017). Perception of in-store assortment exposure. *Studia Ekonomiczne*, 108–119.

Bramer, M. (2014). *Logic programming with prolog* (2nd ed.). Springer Publishing Company, Incorporated.

Braz, R. d. S., Amir, E., & Roth, D. (2008). A survey of first-order probabilistic models. In D. E. Holmes & L. C. Jain (Eds.), *Innovations in Bayesian networks: Theory and applications* (pp. 289–317). Berlin, Heidelberg: Springer Berlin Heidelberg. URL https://doi.org/10.1007/978-3-540-85066-3_12

Buche, C., Bossard, C., Querrec, R., & Chevaillier, P. (2010). Pegase: A generic and adaptable intelligent system for virtual reality learning environments. *International Journal of Virtual Reality, 9* (2), 73–85.

Buche, C., Querrec, R., Loor, P. D., & Chevaillier, P. (2003). Mascaret: Pedagogical multi-agents system for virtual environment for training. In *Cw* (p. 423–431). IEEE Computer Society.

Bulling, A., Roggen, D., & Tröster, G. (2009 April). Wearable EOG goggles: Seamless sensing and context-awareness in everyday environments. *J. Ambient Intell. Smart Environ., 1* (2), 157–171.

Cambridge University. (2020). *Cambridge Dictionary*. URL https://dictionary.cambridge.org/dictionary/english/knowledge

Cao, X. & Klusch, M. (2013). Advanced Semantic Deep Search for 3D Scenes. In *Semantic computing (ICSC), 2013 IEEE seventh international conference on* (pp. 236–243).

Catalano, C. E., Mortara, M., Spagnuolo, M., & Falcidieno, B. (2011). Semantics and 3D media: Current issues and perspectives. *Computers & Graphics, 35* (4), 869–877.

Cavazza, M. & Palmer, I. (2000). High-level interpretation in virtual environments. *Applied Artificial Intelligence, 14* (1), 125–144.

Chen, C., Thomas, L., Cole, J., & Chennawasin, C. (1999). Representing the semantics of virtual spaces. *IEEE MultiMedia, 6* (2), 54–63.

Chevaillier, P., Trinh, T., Barange, M., Loor, P. D., Devillers, F., Soler, J., et al. (2012). Semantic modeling of virtual environments using Mascaret. In *Searis* (p. 1–8). IEEE.

Chu, Y. & Li, T. (2008). Using pluggable procedures and ontology to realize semantic virtual environments 2.0. In *Proceedings of the 7th ACM Siggraph international conference on virtual-reality continuum and its applications in industry* (pp. 27:1–27:6). New York, NY, USA: ACM.

Chu, Y. & Li, T. (2012). Realizing semantic virtual environments with ontology and pluggable procedures. *Applications of Virtual Reality*.

Clocksin, W. F. & Mellish, C. S. (1984). *Programming in prolog (2nd ed.)*. Berlin, Heidelberg: Springer-Verlag.

Cohen, M. H., Giangola, J. P., & Balogh, J. (2004). *Voice user interface design*. USA: Addison Wesley Longman Publishing Co., Inc.

Coninx, K., De Troyer, O., Raymaekers, C., & Kleinermann, F. (2006). VR-demo: a tool-supported approach facilitating flexible development of virtual environments using conceptual modelling. In *Proceedings of virtual concept*. Springer-Verlag.

Cortona3D. (2018). *Cortona3D Viewer*. URL http://www.cortona3d.com/en/cortona3d-viewer

Crane, H. D. (1994). The Purkinje image eyetracker, image stabilization, and related forms of stimulus manipulation. *Visual science and engineering: Models and applications*, 15–89.

Cunningham, D. (2012). *A logical introduction to proof*. Springer Science & Business Media.

Dantsin, E., Eiter, T., Gottlob, G., & Voronkov, A. (2001, September). Complexity and expressive power of logic programming. *ACM Comput. Surv., 33* (3), 374–425. URL https://doi.org/10.1145/502807.502810

Daras, P., Axenopoulos, A., Darlagiannis, V., Tzovaras, D., Bourdon, X. L., Joyeux, L., et al. (2011). Introducing a unified framework for content object description. *IJMIS, 2* (3/4), 351–375.

Dassault Systémes. (2020). *3dvia*. URL http://www.3dvia.com/

De Floriani, L., Hui, A., Papaleo, L., Huang, M., & Hendler, J. (2007). A semantic web environment for digital shapes understanding. In *Semantic multimedia* (pp. 226–239). Springer.

De Floriani, L. & Spagnuolo, M. (2007). *Shape analysis and structuring*. Springer.

Dempster, A. P. (2008). Upper and lower probabilities induced by a multivalued mapping. In R. R. Yager & L. Liu (Eds.), *Classic works of the Dempster-Shafer theory of belief functions* (pp. 57–72). Berlin, Heidelberg: Springer Berlin Heidelberg. URL https://doi.org/10.1007/978-3-540-44792-4_3

De Troyer, O., Bille, W., Romero, R., & Stuer, P. (2003). On generating virtual worlds from domain ontologies. In *Proceedings of the 9th international conference on multi-media modeling* (p. 279–294). Taipei, Taiwan.

De Troyer, O., Kleinermann, F., Mansouri, H., Pellens, B., Bille, W., & Fomenko, V. (2007). Developing semantic VR-shops for e-commerce. *Virtual Reality, 11* (2–3), 89–106.

De Troyer, O., Kleinermann, F., Pellens, B., & Bille, W. (2007). Conceptual modeling for virtual reality. In J. Grundy, S. Hartmann, A. H. F. Laender, L. Maciaszek, & J. F. Roddick (Eds.), *Tutorials, posters, panels and industrial contributions at the 26th int. conference on conceptual modeling - ER 2007* (Vol. 83, p. 3–18). Auckland, New Zealand.

Dittrich, K. R., Gatziu, S., & Geppert, A. (1995). The active database management system manifesto: A rulebase of ADBMS features. In T. K. Sellis (Ed.), *Rules in database systems* (Vol. 985, p. 3–20). Springer.

Dix, A., Finlay, J. E., Abowd, G. D., & Beale, R. (2003). *Human-computer interaction (3rd edition)*. USA: Prentice-Hall, Inc.

dotNetRDF. (2020). *dotNetRDF - an Open Source .NET Library for RDF*. URL https://www.dotnetrdf.org/

Drap, P., Papini, O., Sourisseau, J.-C., & Gambin, T. (2017). Ontology-based photogrammetric survey in underwater archaeology. In *European semantic web conference* (pp. 3–6).

Duchowski, A. T. (2003). Eye tracking techniques. In *Eye tracking methodology: Theory and practice* (pp. 55–65). London: Springer London.

ECMA International. (2007). *Universal 3D File Format*. URL http://www.ecma-international.org/publications/files/ECMA-ST/ECMA-3634thEdition.pdf

ECMA International. (2020). *ECMAScript 2020 Language Specification*. URL https://www.ecma-international.org/publications/files/ECMA-ST/ECMA-262.pdf

Epic Games. (2020). *Unreal Engine*. URL https://www.unrealengine.com/

eTeks. (2020). *Sweet Home 3D*. URL http://www.sweethome3d.com/

Facebook Technologies. (2018). *Oculus Rift*. URL https://support.oculus.com

Facebook Technologies. (2020). *Oculus Rift*. URL https://www.oculus.com/

Falcidieno, B. & Spagnuolo, M. (1998). A shape abstraction paradigm for modeling geometry and semantics. In *Computer graphics international* (p. 646-). IEEE Computer Society.

Falcidieno, B., Spagnuolo, M., Alliez, P., Quak, E., Vavalis, E., & Houstis, C. (2004). Towards the Semantics of Digital Shapes: The AIM@SHAPE Approach. In *Ewimt*.

Feiner, S., Macintyre, B., & Seligmann, D. (1993, July). Knowledge-based augmented reality. *Commun. ACM, 36* (7), 53–62.

FFmpeg. (2020). *A complete, cross-platform solution to record, convert and stream audio and video*. URL https://www.ffmpeg.org/

Fischbach, M., Wiebusch, D., Giebler-Schubert, A., Latoschik, M. E., Rehfeld, S., & Tramberend, H. (2011). SiXton's curse - Simulator X demonstration. In M. Hirose, B. Lok, A. Majumder, & D. Schmalstieg (Eds.), *Virtual reality conference (VR), 2011 IEEE* (p. 255–256). URL http://dx.doi.org/10.1109/VR.2011.5759495

Flotyński, J. (2013). Harvesting of Semantic Metadata from Distributed 3D Web Content. In *Proceedings of the 6th international conference on human system interaction (HSI), June 06–08, 2013, Sopot (Poland)*. IEEE.

Flotyński, J. (2014). Semantic modelling of interactive 3D content with domain-specific ontologies. *Procedia Computer Science, 35*, 531–540. (18th International Conference on Knowledge-Based and Intelligent Information & Engineering Systems)

Flotyński, J., Brutzman, D., Hamza-Lup, F. G., Malamos, A., Polys, N., Sikos, L. F., et al. (2019). The semantic Web3D: Towards comprehensive representation of 3D content on the semantic web. In *International conference on 3D immersion (IC3D), December 11–12, 2019, Brussels, Belgium*.

Flotyński, J., Dalkowski, J., & Walczak, K. (2012) September 2–5. Building multi-platform 3D virtual museum exhibitions with Flex-VR. In *The 18th international conference on virtual systems and multimedia* (p. 391–398). Milan, Italy.

Flotyński, J., Englert, A., Nowak, A., & Walczak, K. (2019). An architecture for distributed explorable HMD-based virtual reality environments. In L. Borzemski, J. Świątek, & Z. Wilimowska (Eds.), *Information systems architecture and technology: Proceedings of 40th anniversary international conference on information systems architecture and technology – ISAT 2019; advances in intelligent systems and computing* (Vol. 1050, p. 38–47). Springer.

Flotyński, J., Krzyszkowski, M., & Walczak, K. (2017). Semantic Composition of 3D Content Behavior for Explorable Virtual Reality Applications. In *Proceedings of EUROVR 2017, lecture notes in computer science* (p. 3–23). Springer.

Flotyński, J., Krzyszkowski, M., & Walczak, K. (2018). Query-based composition of 3D contents animations for VR/AR web applications. In *Web3D '18; proceedings of the 23rd international ACM conference on 3D web technology Poznań, Poland — June 20–22, 2018*, (p. Article No 15). ACM Digital Library.

Flotyński, J., Malamos, A. G., Brutzman, D., Hamza-Lup, F. G., Polys, N. F., Sikos, L. F., et al. (2020). Recent advances in Web3D semantic modeling. In *Recent advances in 3D imaging, modeling, and reconstruction* (p. 23–49). IGI Global.

Flotyński, J. & Nowak, A. (2019). Annotation-based development of explorable immersive VR/AR environments. In *International conference on 3D immersion (IC3D), December 11–12, 2019, Brussels, Belgium*. IEEE.

Flotyński, J., Nowak, A., & Walczak, K. (2018). Explorable Representation of Interaction in VR/AR Environments. In *Proceedings of AVR 2018, lecture notes in computer science* (p. 589–609). Springer International Publishing.

Flotyński, J. & Sobociński, P. (2018a). Logging Interactions in Explorable Immersive VR/AR Applications. In *2018 International Conference on 3D Immersion (IC3D), Brussels, 5–6 Dec. 2018* (p. 1–8). IEEE.

Flotyński, J. & Sobociński, P. (2018b). Semantic 4-dimensional modeling of VR content in a heterogeneous collaborative environment. In *Proceedings of the 23rd international ACM conference on 3D web technology* (pp. 11:1–11:10). New York, NY, USA: ACM. URL http://doi.acm.org/10.1145/3208806.3208830

Flotyński, J., Strugała, D., Walczak, K., Englert, A., Maik, M., Nowak, A., et al. (2019). An Immersive Service Guide for Home Appliances. In *2018 IEEE 8th international conference on consumer electronics - Berlin (ICCE-Berlin)* (p. 370–375). IEEE Xplore. URL https://ieeexplore.ieee.org/document/8966215

Flotyński, J. & Walczak, K. (2013a). Attribute-based Semantic Descriptions of Interactive 3D Web Content. In L. Kiełtyka (Ed.), *Information technologies in organizations - management and applications of multimedia* (p. 111–138). Wydawnictwa Towarzystwa Naukowego Organizacji i Kierownictwa - Dom Organizatora.

Flotyński, J. & Walczak, K. (2013b). Conceptual Semantic Representation of 3D Content. *Lecture Notes in Business Information Processing: 16th International Conference on Business Information Systems, Poznań, Poland, 19–20 June, 2013, 160,* 244–257.

Flotyński, J. & Walczak, K. (2013c). Describing Semantics of 3D Web Content with RDFa. In *The first international conference on building and exploring web based environments, Sevilla (Spain), January 27–February 1, 2013* (p. 63–68). ThinkMind.

Flotyński, J. & Walczak, K. (2013d). Microformat and Microdata Schemas for Interactive 3D Web Content. In M. Ganzha, L. Maciaszek, & M. Paprzycki (Eds.), *Proceedings of the 2013 federated conference on computer science and information systems Kraków, Poland, 8–11 September, 2013* (Vol. 1, p. 549–556). Polskie Towarzystwo Informatyczne.

Flotyński, J. & Walczak, K. (2013a) December 11–13. Semantic modelling of interactive 3D content. In *Proceedings of the 5th joint virtual reality conference.* Paris, France.

Flotyński, J. & Walczak, K. (2013b) September 8–11. Semantic Multi-layered Design of Interactive 3D Presentations. In *Proceedings of the federated conference on computer science and information systems* (p. 541–548). Kraków, Poland: IEEE.

Flotyński, J. & Walczak, K. (2014a) August. Conceptual knowledge-based modeling of interactive 3D content. *The Visual Computer,* 1–20.

Flotyński, J. & Walczak, K. (2014b) April 7–9. Multi-platform Semantic Representation of Interactive 3D Content. In *Proceedings of the 5th doctoral conference on computing, electrical and industrial systems.* April 7–9, Lisbon, Portugal.

Flotyński, J. & Walczak, K. (2014). Semantic Representation of Multi-platform 3D Content. *Computer Science and Inf. Systems, 11, No 4, October 2014,* 1555–1580.

Flotyński, J. & Walczak, K. (2015). Ontology-based Creation of 3D Content in a Service-Oriented Environment. In *Lecture notes in business information processing, 18th international conference on business information systems.* Springer Verlag.

Flotyński, J. & Walczak, K. (2016). Customization of 3D content with semantic meta-scenes. *Graphical Models, 88,* 23–39.

Flotyński, J. & Walczak, K. (2017a). Knowledge-based representation of 3D content behavior in a service-oriented virtual environment. In *Proceedings of the 22nd international conference on Web3D technology, Brisbane (Australia), June 5–7, 2017,* (p. Article No 14). ACM, New York.

Flotyński, J. & Walczak, K. (2017b). Ontology-Based Representation and Modelling of Synthetic 3D Content: A State-of-the-Art Review. *Computer Graphics Forum, 35,* 329–353.

Flotyński, J., Walczak, K., & Krzyszkowski, M. (2020). Composing customized web 3D animations with semantic queries. *Graphical Models, 107, January 2020,* Article Number: 101052.

Fransen, M. L., Verlegh, P. W., Kirmani, A., & Smit, E. G. (2015). A typology of consumer strategies for resisting advertising, and a review of mechanisms for countering them. *International Journal of Advertising, 34* (1), 6–16.

Fraunhofer IGD. (2020a). *Instant Reality.* URL http://www.instantreality.org/

Fraunhofer IGD. (2020b). *X3DOM.* URL http://www.x3dom.org/

Gaildrat, V. (2007). Declarative modelling of virtual environments, overview of issues and applications. In *International conference on computer graphics and artificial intelligence (3IA), Athens, Greece* (Vol. 10, pp. 5–15).

García-Rojas, A., Vexo, F., Thalmann, D., Raouzaiou, A., Karpouzis, K., & Kollias, S. (2006). Emotional body expression parameters in virtual human ontology. In Proceedings of 1st International Workshop on Shapes and Semantics, Matsushima, Japan, June 2006, pp. 63–70.

Gayathri, R. & Uma, V. (2018). Ontology based knowledge representation technique, domain modeling languages and planners for robotic path planning: A survey. *ICT Express, 4* (2), 69–74. URL http://www.sciencedirect.com/science/article/pii/S2405959518300985 (SI on Artificial Intelligence and Machine Learning)

Genesereth, M. R. & Nilsson, N. J. (1987). Logical foundations of artificial intelligence. *Intelligence. Morgan Kaufmann.*

Ghost Productions. (2020). *Ghost Productions: Medical Animation & Virtual Reality.* URL http://www.ghostproductions.com/

Google. (2020a). *Daydream.* URL https://arvr.google.com/daydream/

Google. (2020b). *Google Cardboard.* URL https://arvr.google.com/cardboard/

Google. (2020c). *Google Glass.* URL https://www.google.com/glass/start/

Gosele, M., Stuerzlinger, W., et al. (1999). Semantic constraints for scene manipulation. In *Proceedings Spring conference in computer graphics' 99 (Budmerice, Slovak Republic).*

Grosof, B. N., Horrocks, I., Volz, R., & Decker, S. (2003). Description logic programs: Combining logic programs with description logic. In *Proceedings of the 12th international conference on world wide web* (p. 48–57). New York, NY, USA: Association for Computing Machinery. URL https://doi.org/10.1145/775152.775160

Gruber, T. R. (1995). Toward principles for the design of ontologies used for knowledge sharing? *International journal of human-computer studies, 43* (5), 907–928.

Grussenmeyer, P., Koehl, M., & Nourel, M. (1999). *3D geometric and semantic modelling in historic sites.* Olinda, Brazil.

Gutierrez, C., Hurtado, C., & Vaisman, A. (2005). Temporal RDF. In A. Gómez-Pérez & J. Euzenat (Eds.), *The semantic web: Research and applications* (pp. 93–107). Berlin, Heidelberg: Springer Berlin Heidelberg.

Gutiérrez, M. (2005). Semantic virtual environments, EPFL.

Gutiérrez, M., García-Rojas, A., Thalmann, D., Vexo, F., Moccozet, L., Magnenat-Thalmann, N., et al. (2007) (2007, February). An ontology of virtual humans: Incorporating semantics into human shapes. *Vis. Comput., 23* (3), 207–218.

Gutiérrez, M., Thalmann, D., & Vexo, F. (2005). Semantic virtual environments with adaptive multimodal interfaces. In Y.-P. P. Chen (Ed.), *Mmm* (p. 277–283). IEEE Computer Society.

Harris, R. A. (2004). *Voice interaction design: Crafting the new conversational speech systems.* San Francisco, CA, USA: Morgan Kaufmann Publishers Inc.

HTC Corporation. (2020). *HTC Vive.* URL https://www.vive.com/

Ibrahim, Z. M., Tawfik, A. Y., & Ngom, A. (2007). A qualitative hidden markov model for spatio-temporal reasoning. In K. Mellouli (Ed.), *Symbolic and quantitative approaches to reasoning with uncertainty* (pp. 707–718). Berlin, Heidelberg: Springer Berlin Heidelberg.

IDC. (2019). *Worldwide Spending on Augmented and Virtual Reality Expected to Reach $18.8 Billion in 2020.* URL https://www.idc.com/getdoc.jsp?containerId=prUS45679219

Informa. (2020). *Artificial Intelligence Market Forecasts.* URL https://tractica.omdia.com/research/artificial-intelligence-market-forecasts/

J. P. Gownder, C. Voce, M. Mai, D. Lynch. (2016). *Breakout Vendors: Virtual And Augmented Reality.* URL https://www.forrester.com/report/Breakout+Vendors+Virtual+And+Augmented+Reality/-/E-RES134187

Kalogerakis, E., Christodoulakis, S., & Moumoutzis, N. (2006) March 25–29. Coupling ontologies with graphics content for knowledge driven visualization. In *Vr '06 proceedings of the IEEE conference on virtual reality* (p. 43–50). Alexandria, Virginia, USA.

Kapahnke, P., Liedtke, P., Nesbigall, S., Warwas, S., & Klusch, M. (2010). ISReal: An Open Platform for Semantic-Based 3D Simulations in the 3D Internet. In *International semantic web conference (2)* (p. 161–176).

Khronos Group. (2020a). *OpenGL.* URL https://www.opengl.org/

Khronos Group. (2020b). *WebGL.* URL https://get.webgl.org/

Kiczales, G., Lamping, J., Mendhekar, A., Maeda, C., Lopes, C., Loingtier, J.-M., et al. (1997). Aspect-oriented programming. In *ECOOP'97 — object-oriented programming* (pp. 220–242). URL http://dx.doi.org/10.1007/BFb0053381

Klein, M. & Fensel, D. (2001). Ontology versioning on the semantic web. In *Proceedings of the first international conference on semantic web working* (pp. 75–91). Aachen, Germany: CEUR-WS.org. URL http://dl.acm.org/citation.cfm?id=2956602.2956610

Kleinermann, F., De Troyer, O., Mansouri, H., Romero, R., Pellens, B., & Bille, W. (2005). Designing semantic virtual reality applications. In *Proceedings of the 2nd intuition international workshop, Senlis* (pp. 5–10).

Kowalski, R. (1979, July). Algorithm = logic + control. *Commun. ACM, 22* (7), 424–436. URL https://doi.org/10.1145/359131.359136

Kowalski, R. & Sergot, M. (1989). A logic-based calculus of events. In *Foundations of knowledge base management* (pp. 23–55). Springer.

Kowalski, R. A. & Sadri, F. (1994). The situation calculus and event calculus compared. In *Proceedings of the 1994 international symposium on logic programming, ILPS '94, Melbourne* (pp. 539–553). Cambridge, MA: MIT Press.

Krötzsch, M., Simancik, F., & Horrocks, I. (2012). A description logic primer. *CoRR, abs/1201.4089.* URL http://arxiv.org/abs/1201.4089

Langshaw, M. (2014). *Magnavox Odyssey retrospective: How console gaming was born.* URL https://www.digitalspy.com/videogames/retro-gaming/a616235/magnavox-odyssey-retrospective-how-console-gaming-was-born/

Latoschik, M. E. & Blach, R. (2008). Semantic modelling for virtual worlds – a novel paradigm for realtime interactive systems? In *Proceedings of the ACM VRST 2008* (p. 17–20).

Latoschik, M. E. & Tramberend, H. (2011). Simulator X: A Scalable and Concurrent Software Platform for Intelligent Realtime Interactive Systems. In *Proceedings of the IEEE VR 2011.*

Leap Motion. (2020). *Leap Motion's Unity SDK 4.4.0.* URL https://leapmotion.github.io/UnityModules/class_leap_1_1_unity_1_1_detector.html

Le Roux, O., Gaildrat, V., & Caube, R. (2004). Constraint satisfaction techniques for the generation phase in declarative modeling. In *Geometric modeling: techniques, applications, systems and tools* (pp. 193–215). Springer.

Liu, W. (2006). Knowledge exploitation, knowledge exploration, and competency trap. *Knowledge and Process Management, 13* (3), 144–161. URL https://onlinelibrary.wiley.com/doi/abs/10.1002/kpm.254

Liu, W., Xu, W., Wang, D., Liu, Z., & Zhang, X. (2012). A temporal description logic for reasoning about action in event. *Information Technology Journal, 11* (9), 1211.

Luck, M. & Aylett, R. (2000). Applying artificial intelligence to virtual reality: Intelligent virtual environments. *Applied Artificial Intelligence, 14* (1), 3–32.

Lugrin, J.-L. (2009). *Alternative reality and causality in virtual environments.* (Doctoral dissertation). University of Teesside, Middlesbrough, United Kingdom.

Lugrin, J.-L. & Cavazza, M. (2007). Making sense of virtual environments: Action representation, grounding and common sense. In *Proc. of the 12th int. conf. on intelligent user interfaces* (p. 225–234). New York, NY, USA: ACM.

Lukka, T. J., Stewart, J., et al. (2009). *FreeWRL.* URL http://freewrl.sourceforge.net/

Magic Leap. (2020). *Spatial Computing for Enterprise.* URL https://www.magicleap.com/

Mansouri, H. (2004–2005). *Using semantic descriptions for building and querying virtual environments.* (Doctoral dissertation). Vrije Universiteit Brussel.

MarketWatch. (2020). *Virtual and Augmented Reality Market Global Size, Industry Growth, Future Prospects, Opportunities and Forecast 2020–2025.* URL https://www.marketwatch.com/press-release/virtual-and-augmented-reality-market-global-size-industry-growth-future-prospects-opportunities-and-forecast-2020-2025-2020-04-17

Maxon. (2020). *Cinema 4D.* URL https://www.maxon.net/en-us/products/cinema-4d/

Merriam-Webster. (2020). *Activity.* URL https://www.merriam-webster.com/dictionary/activity

Microsoft. (2020). *Direct3D.* URL https://docs.microsoft.com/windows/win32/direct3d?redirectedfrom=MSDN

Microsoft. (2020). *Microsoft HoloLens.* URL https://www.microsoft.com/hololens/

Microsoft. (2020). *Windows Presentation Foundation.* URL https://docs.microsoft.com/dotnet/framework/wpf/graphics-multimedia/3-d-graphics-overview

Microsoft. (2020). *XBox.* URL https://www.xbox.com/

Milgram, P., Takemura, H., Utsumi, A., & Kishino, F. (1995). Augmented reality: A class of displays on the reality-virtuality continuum. In *Telemanipulator and telepresence technologies* (Vol. 2351, pp. 282–292).

Mkhinini, M. M., Labbani-Narsis, O., & Nicolle, C. (2020). Combining UML and ontology: An exploratory survey. *Computer Science Review, 35,* 100223. URL http://www.sciencedirect.com/science/article/pii/S1574013719300231

Mortara, M., Patané, G., & Spagnuolo, M. (2006, April). From geometric to semantic human body models. *Comput. Graph.*, *30* (2), 185–196.

Natasha Noy, P. H. C. W., Alan Rector. (2006). *Defining n-ary relations on the semantic web.* URL https://www.w3.org/TR/swbp-n-aryRelations/

Neapolitan, R. E. (2003). *Learning bayesian networks.* USA: Prentice-Hall, Inc.

Nilsson, N. J. (1986, February). Probabilistic logic. *Artif. Intell.*, *28* (1), 71–88.

Nintendo. (2020). *Nintendo—Official Site—Video Game Consoles, Games.* URL https://www.nintendo.com/

Novák, V., Perfilieva, I., & Mockor, J. (2012). *Mathematical principles of fuzzy logic* (Vol. 517). Springer Science & Business Media.

Nowak, A. & Flotyński, J. (2018). A Virtual Car Showroom. In *Proceedings of the 23rd International ACM Conference on 3D Web Technology.* New York, NY, USA: Association for Computing Machinery. URL https://doi.org/10.1145/3208806.3208832

NVIS. (2020). *nVisor ST50.* URL https://www.nvisinc.com/product/products.html

Open-Link. (2020). *Virtuoso Open-Source Edition.* URL http://vos.openlinksw.com/owiki/wiki/VOS

Oracle. (2020). *Java3D.* URL https://www.oracle.com/java/technologies/javase/java-3d.html

O'Regan, G. (2020). Computability and decidability. In *Mathematics in computing: An accessible guide to historical, foundational and application contexts* (pp. 209–220). Cham: Springer International Publishing. URL https://doi.org/10.1007/978-3-030-34209-8_13

Otto, K. (2005a). The semantics of multi-user virtual environments. In *Proceedings of the workshop towards semantic virtual environments.*

Otto, K. (2005b) May 10–14. Semantic virtual environments. In *Special interest tracks and posters of the 14th international conference on world wide web* (p. 1036–1037). Chiba, Japan.

Papadimitriou, C. H. (1994). *Computational complexity.* Addison-Wesley.

Papaleo, L., Albertoni, R., Marini, S., & Robbiano, F. (2005). An ontology-based approach to acquisition and reconstruction. In *Workshop towards semantic virtual environment, Villars, Switzerland.*

Papaleo, L., De Floriani, L., Hendler, J., & Hui, A. (2007). Towards a semantic web system for understanding real world representations. In *Proceedings of the tenth international conference on computer graphics and artificial intelligence.*

Parr, T. (2014). *ANTLR.* URL https://www.antlr.org/

Pearl, C. (2016). *Designing voice user interfaces: Principles of conversational experiences* (1st ed.). O'Reilly Media, Inc.

Pelkey, C. D. & Allbeck, J. M. (2014). Populating semantic virtual environments. *Computer Animation and Virtual Worlds, 25* (3–4), 405–412.

Pellens, B. (2006–2007). *A conceptual modelling approach for behaviour in virtual environments using a graphical notation and generative design patterns.* (Doctoral dissertation). Vrije Universiteit Brussel.

Pellens, B., De Troyer, O., Bille, W., Kleinermann, F., & Romero, R. (2005). An ontology-driven approach for modeling behavior in virtual environments. In R. Meersman, Z. Tari, & P. Herrero (Eds.), *Proceedings of on the move to meaningful internet systems 2005: Ontology mining and engineering and its use for virtual reality (WOMEUVR 2005) workshop* (p. 1215–1224). Agia Napa, Cyprus: Springer-Verlag.

Pellens, B., De Troyer, O., & Kleinermann, F. (2008) August 09–10. Codepa: a conceptual design pattern approach to model behavior for X3D worlds. In *Proceedings of the 13th international symposium on 3D web technology* (p. 91–99). Los Angeles.

Pellens, B., Kleinermann, F., & De Troyer, O. (2006). Intuitively specifying object dynamics in virtual environments using VR-wise. In *Proceedings of the ACM symposium on virtual reality software and technology* (pp. 334–337). New York, NY, USA: ACM.

Pellens, B., Kleinermann, F., & De Troyer, O. (2009). A Development Environment Using Behavior Patterns to Facilitate Building 3D/VR Applications. In *Proc. of the 6th Australasian conf. on int. entertainment* (pp. 8:1–8:8). ACM.

Perez-Gallardo, Y., Cuadrado, J. L. L., Crespo, Á. G., & Jesús, C. G. de. (2017). GEODIM: A Semantic Model-Based System for 3D Recognition of Industrial Scenes. In *Current trends on knowledge-based systems* (pp. 137–159). Springer.

Pittarello, F. & De Faveri, A. (2006). Semantic Description of 3D Environments: A Proposal Based on Web Standards. In *Proceedings of the eleventh international conference on 3D web technology* (pp. 85–95). New York, NY, USA: ACM.

Polhemus. (2020). *Patriot Wireless*. URL https://polhemus.com/motion-tracking/all-trackers/patriot-wireless

Pool, J. (2017). *C#Prolog - a Prolog interpreter written in managed C#*. URL https://sourceforge.net/projects/cs-prolog/

Pouriyeh, S. A., Allahyari, M., Liu, Q., Cheng, G., Arabnia, H. R., Qu, Y., et al. (2018). Graph-based ontology summarization: A survey. *CoRR, abs/1805.06051*. URL http://arxiv.org/abs/1805.06051

Poznań University of Economics and Business. (2018). *Immersive Car Showroom*. URL https://www.youtube.com/watch?v=qdM10ErmsXQ

PQ Labs. (2019). *G5 Multi-Touch Screen*. URL https://www.pqlabs.com/g5-spec.html

Randell, D. A., Cui, Z., & Cohn, A. G. (1992). A spatial logic based on regions and connection. In *Proceedings of the third international conference on principles of knowledge representation and reasoning* (p. 165–176). San Francisco, CA, USA: Morgan Kaufmann Publishers Inc.

Reiter, R. (1991). The frame problem in situation the calculus: A simple solution (sometimes) and a completeness result for goal regression. In *Artificial intelligence and mathematical theory of computation: Papers in honor of John Mccarthy* (p. 359–380). USA: Academic Press Professional, Inc.

Reiter, R. (2001). *Knowledge in action*. MIT Press.

Reitmayr, G. & Schmalstieg, D. (2005). Semantic world models for ubiquitous augmented reality. In *Proceedings of workshop towards semantic virtual environments' (SVE) 2005*.

Robbiano, F., Attene, M., Spagnuolo, M., & Falcidieno, B. (2007). Part-Based Annotation of Virtual 3D Shapes. *2013 International Conference on Cyberworlds, 0*, 427–436.

Rudolph, S. (2011). Foundations of description logics. In A. Polleres et al. (Eds.), *Reasoning web. semantic technologies for the web of data: 7th international summer school 2011, Galway, Ireland, August 23–27, 2011, tutorial lectures* (pp. 76–136). Berlin, Heidelberg: Springer Berlin Heidelberg. URL https://doi.org/10.1007/978-3-642-23032-5_2

Rumiński, D. (2015). An experimental study of spatial sound usefulness in searching and navigating through AR environments. *Virtual Reality, 19*, 223–233. URL http://dx.doi.org/10.1007/s10055-015-0274-4

Rumiński, D. & Walczak, K. (2014). Semantic contextual augmented reality environments. In *The 13th IEEE international symposium on mixed and augmented reality (ISMAR 2014), ISMAR 2014* (p. 401–404). IEEE.

Russell, S. & Norvig, P. (2009). *Artificial intelligence: A modern approach* (3rd ed.). USA: Prentice Hall Press.

Samsung. (2020). *Gear VR*. URL https://www.samsung.com/wearables/gear-vr-r324/

Semiodesk GmbH. (2015). *Semiodesk Trinity*. URL https://bitbucket.org/semiodesk/trinity/

Shafer, G. (1976). *A mathematical theory of evidence*. Princeton: Princeton University Press.

Shanahan, M. (1999). The event calculus explained. In *Artificial intelligence today* (pp. 409–430). Springer.

SharpCrafters. (2020). *PostSharp*. URL https://www.postsharp.net/

Sikos, L. F. (2017a). 3D Model Indexing in Videos for Content-based Retrieval via X3D-based Semantic Enrichment and Automated Reasoning. In *Proceedings of the 22nd international conference on 3D web technology* (pp. 19:1–19:7). New York, NY, USA: ACM. URL http://doi.acm.org/10.1145/3055624.3075943

Sikos, L. F. (2017b). *Description logics in multimedia reasoning* (1st ed.). Springer Publishing Company, Incorporated.

Sony Computer Entertainment, Khronos Group. (2008). *COLLADA – Digital Asset Schema Release 1.5.0*. URL https://www.khronos.org/files/collada_spec_1_5.pdf

Sony Interactive Entertainment. (2020). *PlayStation.* URL https://www.playstation.com/

Sotnykova, A., Vangenot, C., Cullot, N., Bennacer, N., & Aufaure, M.-A. (2005). Semantic mappings in description logics for spatio-temporal database schema integration. In S. Spaccapietra & E. Zimányi (Eds.), *Journal on data semantics III* (pp. 143–167). Berlin, Heidelberg: Springer Berlin Heidelberg.

Spagnuolo, M. & Falcidieno, B. (2008). *The role of ontologies for 3D media applications.* Springer.

Spagnuolo, M. & Falcidieno, B. (2009). 3D media and the semantic web. *IEEE Intelligent Systems, 24* (2), 90–96.

Spring Framework. (2020). *Aspect Oriented Programming with Spring.* URL https://docs.spring.io/spring/docs/2.0.x/reference/aop.html

Stair, R. & Reynolds, G. (2017). *Fundamentals of information systems (9th edition).* Boston, MA, USA: Course Technology Press.

Stanford University. (2020). *Protégé.* URL http://protege.stanford.edu/

SWI Prolog. (2020). *Robust, mature, free. Prolog for the real world.* URL https://www.swi-prolog.org/

Thielscher, M. (1998). Introduction to the fluent calculus. *Electronic Transactions on Artificial Intelligence, 2,* 179–192. URL http://www.ep.liu.se/ej/etai/1998/006/

Thorne, C. & Calvanese, D. (2010). Controlled english ontology-based data access. In N. E. Fuchs (Ed.), *Controlled natural language* (pp. 135–154). Berlin, Heidelberg: Springer Berlin Heidelberg.

Three.js. (2020). URL https://threejs.org/

Tracklab. (2020). *Organic Motion OpenStage 2.0.* URL https://tracklab.com.au/products/hardware/organic-motion-openstage-2-0/

Trellet, M., Ferey, N., Baaden, M., & Bourdot, P. (2016). Interactive visual analytics of molecular data in immersive environments via a semantic definition of the content and the context. In *Immersive analytics (IA), 2016 workshop on* (pp. 48–53).

Trellet, M., Férey, N., Flotyński, J., Baaden, M., & Bourdot, P. (2018). Semantics for an integrative and immersive pipeline combining visualization and analysis of molecular data. *Journal of Integrative Bioinformatics, 15 (2),* 1–19.

Trimble. (2020). *SketchUp.* URL http://www.sketchup.com

Tutenel, T., Bidarra, R., Smelik, R. M., & De Kraker, K. J. (2008). The role of semantics in games and simulations. *Computers in Entertainment (CIE), 6* (4), 57.

Ultraleap. (2020). *Leap Motion Documentation.* URL https://developer.leapmotion.com/documentation

Unity 3D. (2020). *ScreenCapture.CaptureScreenshot.* URL https://docs.unity3d.com/ScriptReference/ScreenCapture.CaptureScreenshot.html

Unity Technologies. (2020a). *Unity.* URL http://unity.com/

Unity Technologies. (2020b). *Unity Scripting API.* URL https://docs.unity3d.com/ScriptReference/

Valve Corporation. (2020). *Controllers.* URL https://www.valvesoftware.com/index/controllers

Vanacken, L., Raymaekers, C., & Coninx, K. (2007). Introducing semantic information during conceptual modelling of interaction for virtual environments. In *Proceedings of the 2007 workshop on multimodal interfaces in semantic interaction* (pp. 17–24). New York, NY, USA: ACM.

Vasilakis, G., García-Rojas, A., Papaleo, L., Catalano, C. E., Robbiano, F., Spagnuolo, M., et al. (2010). Knowledge-Based Representation of 3D Media. *International Journal of Software Engineering and Knowledge Engineering, 20* (5), 739–760.

Volfoni. (2020). *Active 3D glasses.* URL http://volfoni.com/en/active-3d-glasses-4/

W3C. (2004a). *SWRL: A Semantic Web Rule Language Combining OWL and RuleML.* URL http://www.w3.org/Submission/SWRL/

W3C. (2004b). *OWL Web Ontology Language Reference.* URL https://www.w3.org/TR/owl-ref/

W3C. (2012a). *Ontology for Media Resources 1.0.* URL http://www.w3.org/TR/mediaont-10/

W3C. (2012b). *OWL 2 Web Ontology Language Profiles (Second Edition).* URL http://www.w3.org/TR/owl2-profiles/

W3C. (2012). *OWL 2 Web Ontology Language Structural Specification and Functional-Style Syntax (Second Edition)*. URL https://www.w3.org/TR/owl2-syntax/

W3C. (2013). *RDFa 1.1 Primer - Second Edition*. URL http://www.w3.org/TR/xhtml-rdfa-primer/

W3C. (2013). *SPARQL 1.1 Query Language*. URL https://www.w3.org/TR/sparql11-query/

W3C. (2014a). *RDF 1.1 Concepts and Abstract Syntax*. URL https://www.w3.org/TR/rdf11-concepts/

W3C. (2014b). *RDF Schema 1.1*. URL https://www.w3.org/TR/rdf-schema/

W3C. (2020). *Building the Web of Data*. URL http://www.w3.org/2013/data/

Walczak, K. (2012a). Building configurable 3D web applications with Flex-VR. In W. Cellary & K. Walczak (Eds.), *Interactive 3D multimedia content* (pp. 103–136). Springer.

Walczak, K. (2012b). Dynamic database modeling of 3D multimedia content. In W. Cellary & K. Walczak (Eds.), *Interactive 3D multimedia content* (p. 55–102). Springer.

Walczak, K., Cellary, W., & White, M. (2006, March). Virtual museum exhibitions. *Computer*, *39* (3), 93–95.

Walczak, K., Chmielewski, J., Stawniak, M., & Strykowski, S. (2006). Extensible metadata framework for describing virtual reality and multimedia contents. In Hamza, MH (Ed.), *Proc. of the IASTED Int. Conf. on Databases and Applications* (p. 168–175). (IASTED Int. Conf. on Databases and Applications, Innsbruck, Austria, Feb 14–16, 2006)

Walczak, K. & Flotyński, J. (2014). On-Demand Generation of 3D Content Based on Semantic Meta-Scenes. In *Lecture Notes in Computer Science; Augmented and Virtual Reality; First International Conference, AVR 2014, Lecce, Italy, September 17–20, 2014* (p. 313–332). Springer International Publishing.

Walczak, K. & Flotyński, J. (2015). Semantic Query-based Generation of Customized 3D Scenes. In *Proceedings of the 20th international conference on 3D web technology* (pp. 123–131). New York, NY, USA: ACM. URL http://doi.acm.org/10.1145/2775292.2775311

Walczak, K. & Flotyński, J. (2019). Inference-based creation of synthetic 3D content with ontologies. *Multimedia Tools and Applications*, *78, 9*, 12607–12638. URL https://link.springer.com/article/10.1007/s11042-018-6788-5

Walczak, K., Flotyński, J., & Strugała, D. (2019). Semantic Contextual Personalization of Virtual Stores. In L. T. de Paolis & P. Bourdot (Eds.), *Augmented reality, virtual reality, and computer graphics. AVR 2019. Lecture notes in computer science* (Vol. 11613, p. 220–236). Springer.

Walczak, K., Flotyński, J., Strugała, D., Rumiński, D., Maik, M., Englert, A., et al. (2019). Virtual and augmented reality for configuring, promoting and servicing household appliances. In T. J., C. O., M. J., & P. I. (Eds.), *Advances in manufacturing II. Lecture notes in mechanical engineering* (p. 368–380). Springer, Cham.

Walczak, K., Rumiński, D., & Flotyński, J. (2014). Building contextual augmented reality environments with semantics. In *Proceedings of the 20th international conference on virtual systems & multimedia, Hong Kong, 9–12 September.*

Walker, G. (2012). A review of technologies for sensing contact location on the surface of a display. *Journal of The Society for Information Display*, *20*, 413–440.

Web3D Consortium. (1995). *VRML Virtual Reality Modeling Language*. URL https://www.w3.org/MarkUp/VRML/

Web3D Consortium. (2020a). *X3D Ontology for Semantic Web*. URL https://www.web3d.org/x3d/content/semantics/semantics.html

Web3D Consortium (2020b). *Getting Started with X3D*. URL http://www.web3d.org/getting-started-x3d

Welty, C. & Fikes, R. (2006). A Reusable Ontology for Fluents in OWL. In *Proceedings of the 2006 conference on formal ontology in information systems: Proceedings of the fourth international conference (FOIS 2006)* (pp. 226–236). Amsterdam, The Netherlands: IOS Press. URL http://dl.acm.org/citation.cfm?id=1566079.1566106

Whissel, C. M. (1989). Emotion: Theory, research and experience. In *The dictionary of affect in language* (Vol. 4). New York.

White, M., Mourkoussis, N., Darcy, J., Petridis, P., Liarokapis, F., Lister, P. F., et al. (2004). ARCO - an architecture for digitization, management and presentation of virtual exhibitions. In *Computer graphics international* (p. 622–625). IEEE Computer Society.

Wiebusch, D. & Latoschik, M. E. (2012). Enhanced Decoupling of Components in Intelligent Realtime Interactive Systems using Ontologies. In *Software engineering and architectures for realtime interactive systems (SEARIS), proceedings of the IEEE virtual reality 2012 workshop.*

Wojciechowski, R., Walczak, K., White, M., & Cellary, W. (2004). Building virtual and augmented reality museum exhibitions. In *Proceedings of the ninth international conference on 3d web technology* (pp. 135–144). New York, NY, USA: ACM.

World Wide Web Consortium. (2013). *RDF 1.1 JSON Alternate Serialization (RDF/JSON).* URL https://www.w3.org/TR/rdf-json/

World Wide Web Consortium. (2014). *RDF 1.1 Turtle.* URL http://www.w3.org/TR/turtle/

World Wide Web Consortium. (2020a). *JSON-LD 1.1 - A JSON-based Serialization for Linked Data.* URL https://www.w3.org/TR/json-ld/

World Wide Web Consortium. (2020b). *Time Ontology in OWL - W3C Candidate Recommendation 26 March 2020.* URL https://www.w3.org/TR/2020/CR-owl-time-20200326/

XML.org. (2020). *XML3D.* URL http://xml3d.org

Xu, K., Stewart, J., & Fiume, E. (2002). Constraint-based automatic placement for scene composition. In *Graphics interface* (Vol. 2).

Yost Labs. (2020). *3-Space Sensors.* URL https://yostlabs.com/3-space-sensors/

Zadeh, L. A. (1965). Fuzzy sets. *Information and Control, 8,* 338–353. URL http://www-bisc.cs.berkeley.edu/Zadeh-1965.pdf

Zaid, L. A., Kleinermann, F., & De Troyer, O. (2009). Applying semantic web technology to feature modeling. In *Proceedings of the 2009 ACM symposium on applied computing* (pp. 1252–1256). ACM.

Zinnikus, I., Cao, X., Klusch, M., Krauss, C., Nonnengart, A., Spieldenner, T., et al. (2013). A collaborative virtual workspace for factory configuration and evaluation. In *Collaborative computing: Networking, applications and worksharing (collaboratecom), 2013 9th international conference on* (pp. 353–362).

Index

Printed in the United States
by Baker & Taylor Publisher Services